The Second Republic: The Disintegration of Post-Munich Czechoslovakia (October 1938 - March 1939)

Theodore Procházka, Sr.

EAST EUROPEAN MONOGRAPHS, BOULDER
DISTRIBUTED BY COLUMBIA UNIVERSITY PRESS
NEW YORK

1981

EAST EUROPEAN MONOGRAPHS, NO. XC

Library of Congress Card Catalog Number 81-065161
ISBN 0-914710-84-2

Printed in the United States of America

CONTENTS

PREFACE

The origins of this book lay in my Sorbonne dissertation covering the history of Czechoslovakia from October 1938 to March 1939. At the time of its writing in the early fifties several primary sources were already at my disposal, such as the British and German diplomatic documents and the Nuremberg material. There were even some memoirs. All of this documentation, though incomplete, together with information gleaned from the daily press, furnished an adequate base for my monograph. From April 1938 through the whole period in question, I acted as the Berlin correspondent of the Czechoslovak Press Agency (Československá tisková kancelář), and in that capacity I met several personalities mentioned in this book.

During my journalistic work in the United States in subsequent years I followed closely the new literature and, as time permitted, pursued my archival research. Retirement offered an opportunity to tap more intensively the microfilmed German documents and recent scholarly periodicals. The Prague Spring brought forth numerous articles dealing with this period and even one of the rare monographs dedicated exclusively to the history of the Second Republic.

The material thus assembled is quite abundant, in some cases there is even a certain amount of over-documentation. For instance, the complicated Czechoslovak negotiations with Hungary can be followed in minute detail utilizing the diplomatic documents of several countries, especially the Hungarian documents published in several volumes in Budapest in 1962-1970. The same applies to the negotiations with Poland. The complex question of Podkarpatská Rus (Subcarpathian Ruthenia) forms a maze of several problems of its own and the array of documentation was not always easy to marshal and organize coherently into an intelligible whole. The same could be said about the twisted events leading up to the declaration of Slovak independence. Here, too, a mass of heterogeneous material had to be digested and assimilated, while at the same time trying to avoid the danger of overloading the narration with excessive detail.

In my original French dissertation I concentrated on the diplomatic aspect of the events. This was quite natural, for the main events occurred in this sphere, especially Prague's negotiations with Germany, Hungary, and Poland, and its frustrating endeavors to get the frontier guarantee promised at Munich. This book includes an expanded chapter on the domestic evolution of rump-Czechoslovakia. The Munich Agreement revived many old nationalisms and resuscitated so many dormant problems in Central Europe that it would have been proper to precede the present volume with a special, separate monograph crossing the disciplinary boundaries and dealing with the political geography, history, and social structure of the whole area. I have confined myself to only briefly indicating the problems as they occurred in my narration.

When naming the long list of those to whom I am indebted for their assistance, I must certainly recall first the kindness of the late Dean of the Faculty of Letters of the University of Paris, Pierre Renouvin. In the first difficult years after my arrival in France he offered his help and it was he who secured a grant for me from the Centre National de la Recherche Scientifique. Dean Renouvin directed my thesis; the other members of the jury before whom I defended my dissertation were Professor Maurice Baumont and the late Victor-L. Tapié. They also assisted with pertinent advice and suggestions.

During the war years I had made several contacts which were valuable to the theme of the present volume. Several long conversations with the former Foreign Minister of the Second Republic, Dr. František Chvalkovský, who narrated the events during President Hácha's visit to Berlin, provided good background data. Though he tried to justify his action, his account was not in contradiction to documents which came to light after the war. There were also several conversations with the former Czechoslovak minister to Berlin, Dr. Vojtěch Mastný, whom I knew from my previous contacts in Berlin. The former counsellor of the Czechoslovak legation in Berlin, Dr. Miroslav Schubert, has been an inexhaustible source of information and documentary material. Among other Czechoslovak diplomats whom I interviewed are the late General Secretary of the Foreign Ministry Arnošt Heidrich and the late minister to Warsaw, Dr. Juraj Slávik. With a former member of the governments of the Second Republic, Dr. Ladislav Feierabend, I was able to exchange views on innumerable occasions during our common employment with the Voice of America in Washington. Another member of these governments, Dr. Vladislav Klumpar, was, in the course of his visits to Washington, another source of solid information and kindly lent me the manuscript of his memoirs. Last, but not least I should like to thank Dr. Josef Anderle, professor of the University of North Carolina, who read over the first version of my manuscript making numerous helpful suggestions. Equally I am indebted to professors Victor S. Mamatey (U. of Georgia) and Stanley B. Winters (New Jersey Institute of Technology) for their valuable advice.

I am also grateful to the staff of the National Archives in Washington, D.C., and the Bibliothèque de Documentation Internationale Contemporaine in Paris for their help and cooperation. Many thanks go to Drs. Alois Böhmer, Paul B. Horecký and Vladimír Palic of the Library of Congress who helped in every aspect of my research.

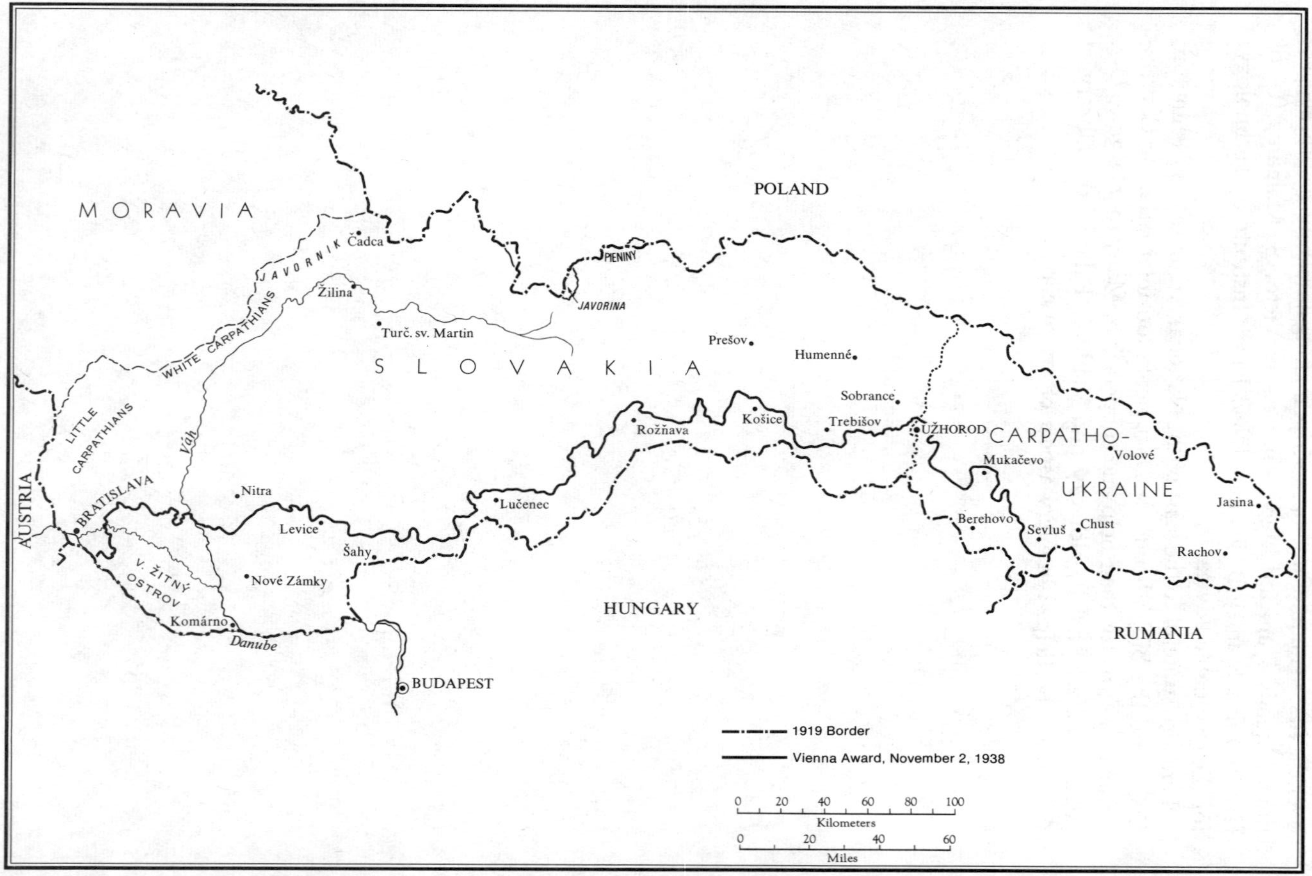
MORAVIA
POLAND
SLOVAKIA
CARPATHO-UKRAINE
HUNGARY
RUMANIA
AUSTRIA
JAVORNIK
WHITE CARPATHIANS
LITTLE CARPATHIANS
PIENINY
JAVORINA
Čadca
Žilina
Turč. sv. Martin
Prešov
Humenné
Sobrance
Košice
Trebišov
Rožňava
UŽHOROD
Volové
Mukačevo
Berehovo
Sevluš
Chust
Jasina
Rachov
Váh
Nitra
Levice
Lučenec
Šahy
Nové Zámky
BRATISLAVA
V. ŽITNÝ OSTROV
Komárno
Danube
BUDAPEST
1919 Border
Vienna Award, November 2, 1938
0 20 40 60 80 100
Kilometers
0 20 40 60
Miles

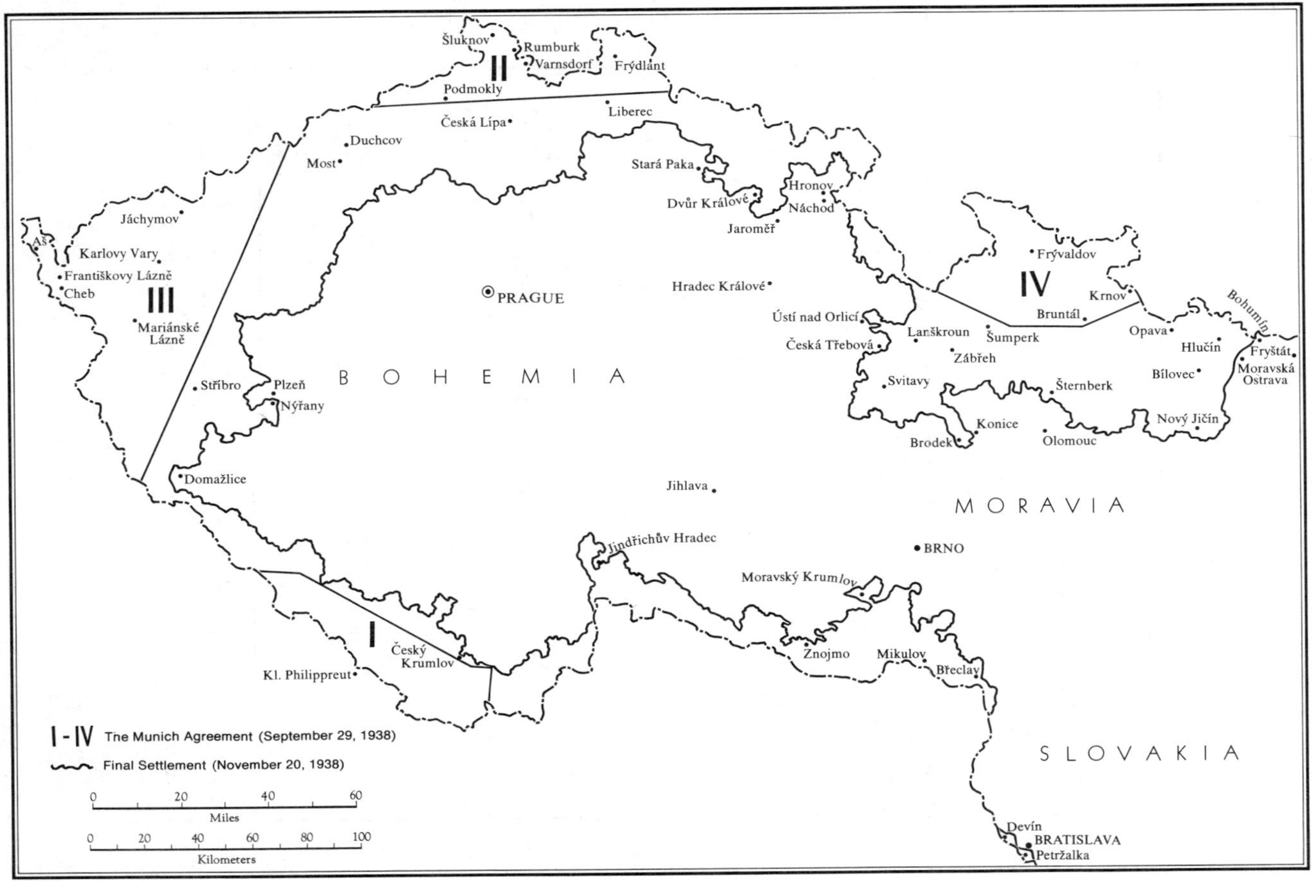
Šluknov
Rumburk
Varnsdorf
Frýdlant
II
Podmokly
Liberec
Česká Lípa
Duchcov
Most
Stará Paka
Hronov
Náchod
Dvůr Králové
Jaroměř
Jáchymov
Aš
Karlovy Vary
Františkovy Lázně
Cheb
III
Mariánské Lázně
PRAGUE
Hradec Králové
Frývaldov
IV
Krnov
Bruntál
Bohumín
Ústí nad Orlicí
Lanškroun
Šumperk
Opava
Hlučín
Fryštát
Moravská Ostrava
Česká Třebová
Zábřeh
Střibro
Plzeň
Nýřany
B O H E M I A
Svitavy
Šternberk
Bílovec
Konice
Nový Jičín
Brodek
Olomouc
Domažlice
Jihlava
M O R A V I A
Jindřichův Hradec
BRNO
Moravský Krumlov
I
Český Krumlov
Kl. Philippreut
Znojmo
Mikulov
Břeclav
S L O V A K I A
I - IV The Munich Agreement (September 29, 1938)
Final Settlement (November 20, 1938)
0
20
40
60
Miles
0
20
40
60
80
100
Kilometers
Devín
BRATISLAVA
Petržalka

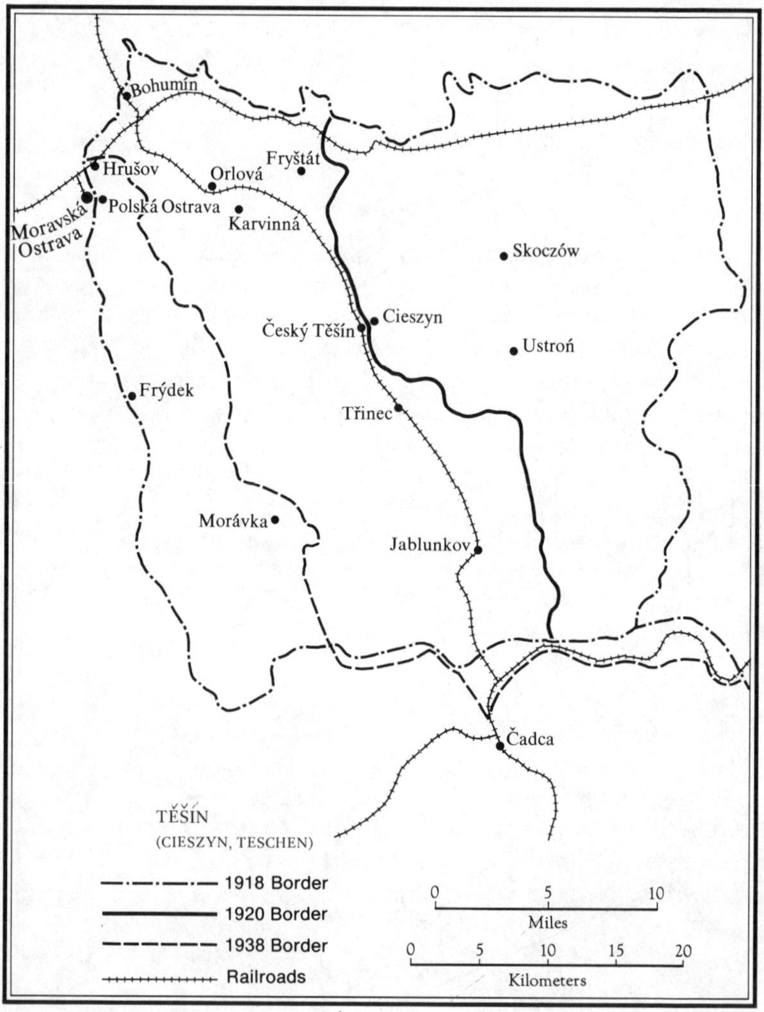
Bohumín
Hrušov
Fryštát
Orlová
Polská Ostrava
Moravská Ostrava
Karvinná
Skoczów
Cieszyn
Český Těšín
Ustroń
Frýdek
Třinec
Morávka
Jablunkov
Čadca
TĚŠÍN
(CIESZYN, TESCHEN)
1918 Border
1920 Border
1938 Border
Railroads
0 5 10
Miles
0 5 10 15 20
Kilometers

INTRODUCTION
MUNICH, ITS ANTECEDENTS AND ITS AFTERMATH IN PRAGUE

The rising wave of intransigent nationalism in Hitler's Germany reopened problems in Central Europe which the Versailles Treaty had attempted to solve. In the first place, the issue of German populations along the borders of the Reich reappeared. When the fate of Austria was settled by the Anschluss in March 1938, Czechoslovakia, with her three and one-half million German speaking inhabitants was the next square to be occupied on Hitler's chessboard. Accordingly, after the annexation of Austria, Germany's pressure on Czechoslovakia increased. German revisionism also revived the ambitions of Hungary and Poland, who were striving for the revision of their frontiers with Czechoslovakia. Not only the frontiers, but the very existence of the state was thus threatened.

Czechs and Germans

Since the beginning of their national history, the Czechs had continuous contacts with their German neighbor. In the 12th and especially in the 13th century a wave of eastward emigration from the overpopulated areas of Germany reached Bohemia and other regions of East-Central Europe. It was encouraged by the kings of Bohemia, the great noblemen and powerful church dignitaries who sought to increase their incomes by colonizing the feebly populated border regions and by founding new towns. In Bohemia and Moravia the new settlers formed the core of the later Sudeten German population. At the beginning they occupied a rather narrow band of land in the deep forests along the frontier. In the interior, they expanded the existing towns or founded several entirely new ones. About two centuries later, owing to a strong Czech nationalism born during the Hussite wars, the influence of the German settlers in towns diminished, though some of them preserved their Germanic character.

The loss of Czech independence in 1620 marked the beginning of an intensive germanization and from then on the linguistic frontier separating the Czechs from the Germans was shifting continuously toward the interior of the country. The enlightened absolutism of Maria Theresa and Joseph II brought a new wave of germanization. Inspired by the rationalistic ideas of the 18th century, both rulers tried to impose the German language on the administrative and educational system of the whole Habsburg Empire.[1]

At that point, however, a reaction was visible. A literary renascence of the Czech people, which began in the second half of the 18th century, was followed by a political revival. This process did not proceed without opposition, for the Germans viewed with mistrust the efforts of the Czech element and defended fiercely their vested positions. Thus Bohemia and Moravia became the theatre for an intense nationalistic struggle whose violence increased when the prestige of the German Reich began to attract the sympathies of those Austrian Germans who were disappointed by the inertia and weakness of the dual monarchy. In this feverish atmosphere, the first symptoms of future Nazism appeared toward the end of the 19th century.

The dissolution of the Austro-Hungarian monarchy in 1918 radically changed the political picture of Central Europe. The Czech people together with the Slovaks again became masters of their own political destiny and the Germans were relegated to a secondary plane. The Versailles Treaty respected the centuries-old frontier between Bohemia and Germany and left the borderland inhabited by the Germans in the new republic. In the eastern part of the state, on the border with Hungary, there was a zone inhabited by Magyars and the interior included some sparse German enclaves.

In Czechoslovakia the Germans stayed several years in parliamentary opposition. Only in 1926 did the German Agrarian party join the government, followed soon by the Christian Democrats. The German Social Democrats were the last to leave the opposition.

The arrival of Hitler had immediate repercussions in Czechoslovakia. The regrouping of the German ultranationalist camp was somewhat complicated. The Czechoslovak government banned the small German National Socialist Party on October 4, 1933. However, expecting the prohibition, the Party dissolved itself voluntarily the day before. At that moment it already had a successor. On October 1, a former gymnastics teacher, Konrad Henlein, founded a new movement on the same ideological basis, aimed at uniting all Germans in the state, The Sudeten German Home Front (*Sudetendeutsche Heimatfront*). Later the Front changed its name to the Sudeten German party and in the election of 1935 it polled 66% of the German votes.[2]

According to the political philosophy of the Third Reich, Bohemia and Moravia were a natural complement of the German *Raum* and their independence transitory and doomed to an early end. Here the Austrian background of Hitler played an important role. Even before the First World War, Hitler adopted opinions that were current in broad masses of the German-speaking population of Vienna that the Czechs were a second-rate race apt only to occupy inferior positions and dangerous for the Germanic character of the monarchy. Their Slavonic origin made them inacceptable to Hitler and even before his accession to power he attributed in his dreams about the future organization of the world no place to the state of the Czechs and Slovaks.[3]

In the first article of its program of February 24, 1920, the National Socialist Party demanded "the union of all Germans to form a Greater Germany on the basis of the right of self-determination.[4] Hitler did not deviate from this line. At the conference held in Berlin on November 5, 1937 he set forth his views on future objectives of German foreign policy: Germany needed urgently a greater living space, *Lebensraum*, and to this purpose Austria and Czechoslovakia were to be annexed to Germany.[5]

It would exceed the scope of this book to follow closely the events leading up to the Munich Agreement.[6] The main stages were: On September 15, Hitler told British Prime Minister Neville Chamberlain that he intended to annex the Sudeten German territory. On September 19, this demand was passed on in a Franco-British note to Prague. At the same time France and Great Britain promised an international guarantee of the new frontiers of Czechoslovakia. Prague surrendered on September 21. At Godesberg, on September 23, Hitler asked for a prompt cession of the Czechoslovak territory and proposed plebiscites in some other places (Jihlava, Brno). At the same time, he raised the question of the Polish and Hungarian minorities in Czechoslovakia. Prague refused these demands which were inacceptable even to France and Great Britain and mobilized. Only on September 28, when Chamberlain announced in the House of Commons that Hitler had invited him, Mussolini and French Premier, Edouard Daladier, to Munich did it become clear that the dispute would not develop into an armed conflict.

Hungarian Revisionism

The successful fight of Hitler's Germany against the embarrassing clauses of the peace treaties greatly encouraged the Hungarians, who were convinced that they were one of the chief victims of the peace settlement of 1920. Trianon indeed broke up the ancient entity symbolized by the mystic bond of Saint Stephen's Crown, and the areas inhabited by non-Magyar peoples were detached and occupied by neighboring states, namely, Czechoslovakia, Yugoslavia and Rumania, giving all of them rather numerous Magyar minorities.[7] In 1927 Hungary gained the support of Italy, herself dissatisfied with the share attributed to her by the peace treaties and endeavoring to spread her influence in Central Europe. In the same year the English press magnate, Lord Rothermere, started his campaign for the revision of the Trianon Treaty.

After Hitler's advent, with German ascendency steadily increasing, Hungarian policy turned not only to Rome, but also toward Berlin. However, there had always been in Hungarian minds a certain fear of the German influence and an instinctive distrust of Germany. These sentiments played their role even at this juncture, for it would have been quite unattractive for the militarily weak Hungary to be drawn into an armed action should Germany decide to attain her aims by force. Moreover, Hungary would have been at the mercy of an aggrandized Germany.[9] For these reasons she hesitated to join the German camp without reserve and this attitude marked all her moves in the course of the critical year 1938. The Hungarian reserve became evident most clearly shortly before Munich, in August 1938, during a visit of the Hungarian statesmen in Germany where they were invited to discuss the possibilities of German-Hungarian cooperation in the Sudeten German crisis. They hesitated to "seize opportunity by the forelock" as Ribbentrop invited them[10] and the results of the talks were rather unsatisfactory. The Hungarian Prime Minister Béla Imrédy was evidently relieved when in the end the disappointed Hitler declared to him that in this particular case he required nothing of Hungary.[11]

After Hitler's meeting with Prime Minister Chamberlain in Berchtesgaden, Herrmann Göring invited the Berlin minister of Hungary Döme Sztójay to his country residence to reproach him for Hungary's inactivity in the crisis. Bowing to these reproaches Hungary promised to activate her ethnic group in Czechoslovakia and to press her demands in Prague and London.[12] Hungary's attitude toward Czechoslovakia gradually stiffened and Budapest assumed a place in the German camp with greater ostentation. On September 16, the same day that Sztójay had to endure Göring's reproaches, Foreign Minister Kálmán Kánya called the British minister in Budapest and in the presence of Prime Minister Béla Imrédy declared that Hungary would struggle "by every possible means in her power" against any decision to simply transfer the Sudeten German areas to Germany or to organize a plebiscite without granting the same treatment to the Hungarian minority. Hungary was using similar strong terms when communicating with London in the days preceding the Munich conference.[13]

At the same time military measures were taken. Militarily Hungary was still unprepared and her armaments were poor with ammunition enough only for thirty-six hours' fighting. Thus, she mobilized on a very small scale calling up two classes.[14] The Hungarian press that so far had only been reprinting German dispatches about Czechoslovakia started a hostile anti-Czech campaign of its own.[15]

In spite of the German pressure Hungary was cautiously steering a middle course. Besides her military weakness there was still another factor contributing to her hesitancy, the fear of Yugoslavia and Rumania, the two members of the Little Entente, a defensive alliance formed especially against the Hungarian revisionism. Budapest was above all concerned about Yugoslavia. Germany, in her efforts to gain Hungary for a common action against the third member of the Little Entente, Czechoslovakia, attempted in vain to allay these fears.[16]

Hungary got a new lesson from Germany when on September 20, two days before his meeting with Chamberlain in Godesberg, Hitler invited the Hungarian representatives to Berchtesgaden. The scene repeated itself. With the Hungarians flinching from a firm decision, Germany was urging them to participate in an attack on Czechoslovakia, otherwise they would not be able to realize their national ambitions. They had to put up with reproaches of an angered Führer: If they did not avail themselves of this last opportunity, it wouldn't certainly be him, Hitler, who would defend their interests. Accordingly, Hitler urged them to demand without delay a plebiscite in the territory they claimed and to refuse to guarantee any future borders of Czechoslovakia unless their conditions were met.[17]

Hungary then quickened her pace. On September 22, her minister in London wrote a letter to British Foreign Secretary, Lord Halifax, declaring that the Hungarian government expected an urgent decision regarding its minority on lines analogous to those adopted by Prague with regard to the German problem.[18] A similar note was handed over the same day to Prague. Czechoslovakia answered on the 26th, agreeing with the settlement of the problem, but within the frame of the Czechoslovak state and on the basis of friendly negotiations.[19] Budapest then sent to Prague a second, more urgent note on the 28th. The note requested self-determination for all minorities living in Czechoslovakia and the cession of the areas inhabited by the Magyars. According to Czechoslovak Foreign Minister Kamil Krofta, Czechoslovakia could not for the time being negotiate on this basis.[20] Things remained at this stage until Munich.

Hungary aimed not only at the incorporation of the southern fringe of Slovakia and Subcarpathian Ruthenia inhabited by the Magyar population, but at the return of the whole eastern part of the Czechoslovak state, the "Hungarian solution," as termed by the Hungarian minister in Berlin. The Hungarian minister in Prague spoke about "a voluntary union" of Slovakia, including Subcarpathian Ruthenia, with Hungary. Outwardly this aim was camouflaged by the ambiguous term "self-determination."[21]

In these endeavors Hungary was supported—and at times even pressured—by Poland. A close cooperation with Warsaw, cemented by a "gentlemen's agreement" of September 8, 1938, to coordinate the policy of both countries with regard to Czechoslovakia, was an important aspect of Hungarian policy in the course of the Czechoslovak crisis. Foreign Minister Beck was strongly recommending a plebiscite in former Hungarian regions of Czechoslovakia and was attempting to win the Slovaks for a "Hungarian solution."[22] However, the hesitancy of Hungary was hampering the possibilities of a military cooperation and Poland confined herself only to political and diplomatic support of Hungarian demands.[23]

Both states attributed a special significance to the fate of Subcarpathian Ruthenia. They both strived for a common frontier, which, in their opinion, could have been realized only by the acquisition of this region by Hungary. For Budapest, this meant a politically rather uncomplicated question of revisionist aspirations, and the prospects of further breaking the chains of the Trianon Peace Treaty and of advancing the frontiers to the former border of Saint Stephen's Crown.

More complicated was the case of Poland. The political and national renascence of the Sub-Carpathian branch of the Ukrainian nation was bound to have repercussion among the large Ukrainian population of neighboring Eastern Galicia. It was in the interest of Warsaw to check this extension of Ukrainian nationalism emanating from the southern slopes of the Carpathians—and this could happen only through occupation by Hungary. Besides this purely domestic aspect, the fate of Subcarpathian Ruthenia had for Poland a significance also from the international point of view. If Hungary occupied the province, the last link would have been established connecting the chain of states forming a North-South axis in East-Central Europe, a "third Europe," as the Polish diplomats called it, stretching from Finland and Scandinavia to the Balkans via Hungary. In the complex maneuvering of Polish diplomacy between Germany and the Soviet Union, the axis was intended to become a bulwark protecting Poland against the two neighboring giants. This preoccupation runs through subsequent Hungarian and Polish action like a connecting thread until the common frontier materialized in March 1939, although it was under completely changed circumstances and devoid of any real political or strategic value.

Polish-Czechoslovak Relations

The Czechoslovak crisis also furnished Warsaw an occasion to force its demands on Prague. Since the restoration of their independence in 1918, the relations of the two neighboring states had never been particularly satisfactory. In the changing international situation, Poland tried to maintain a strict neutrality toward the Germany of Hitler, whereas Czechoslovakia stayed in the camp of the advocates of collective security. The diplomatic controversy between Warsaw and Paris had its impact on Polish-Czechoslovak relations, too. They were deteriorating at the same pace as Polish policy was detaching itself from France.[24]

The apple of discord was the area of Těšín (in Czech; Cieszyn in Polish, Teschen in German). It was one of the most industrialized areas of Central Europe and a territory through which passed the main railroad link between the western and eastern parts of Czechoslovakia. A typical borderland, it was the boundary between two Slavic languages. There the Silesian dialect of the Czech language merges gradually with the Polish so that the fixation of the frontiers could not be based solely on linguistic factors. The Polish language spread there only in the second half of the 19th century, when the Poles from Galicia sought employment in the Těšín mining industry. By a decision of the Conference of the Ambassadors of July 28, 1920, the former Duchy of Těšín and the town itself were divided. To the west, on the western bank of the river Olše, was Český Těšín with the important railroad station of the line Bohumín - Košice; on the right bank was the Polish Cieszyn, with the old castle of the Piasts. With this partition Czechoslovakia acquired a Polish minority of about 80,000 persons.

In 1938, in connection with the May crisis created by alleged movements of the German army, Polish foreign minister Józef Beck notified the French government that Poland demanded equal treatment for the Polish minority in Czechoslovakia. "A concession given by Prague to any minority and not extended to the Polish one would immediately provoke tension between Poland and Czechoslovakia," declared the Polish note of May 22.[25]

When Chamberlain's visit to Berchtesgaden on September 15 presaged an imminent solution of the Sudeten problem, Poland reasserted her claims. Late in the evening of September 15, Polish ambassador, Józef Lipski, telephoned on Beck's order, from Berlin to Ernst von Weizsäcker, State Secretary in the German foreign ministry, who was staying in Berchtesgaden. He informed him that if the "Czech question" were to be settled by a plebiscite, Poland would formally demand the same procedure for the Těšín area.[26] On September 16, Beck relayed the Polish demands to London and a similar demarche was made in Paris.[27]

When it became known that the western Allies were recommending the cession of the Sudeten territory, Warsaw repeated its demands. On September 19, the Polish ambassador in London, Count Edward Raczyński, delivered a message in the form of a verbal communication claiming the rectification of the frontier in the Těšín area.[28] At that moment Germany appeared on the scene, too. As in the case of Hungary, Hitler wanted to use Polish demands to increase his pressure on Chamberlain, whose visit he was awaiting on September 20. He invited the Polish ambassador to Berchtesgaden to urge him to proceed with energy.[29]

On September 21, Warsaw turned directly to Prague. It was a dramatic day in the Czechoslovak capital. Early in the morning, at two o'clock, the ministers of France and Great Britain visited the President of the Republic and pressed him to accept the Franco-British proposals from the preceding day. Feverish deliberations were started at four in the morning. In the afternoon, Minister of Foreign Affairs Krofta informed the two ministers that Czechoslovakia had ceded. The official communiqué announcing the decision was broadcast at 7:00 P.M. Emotion spread in Prague and spontaneous demonstrations protesting the surrender took place.

In this atmosphere the first Polish note arrived requesting an immediate decision analogous to that taken by the Czechoslovak government in the case of the Sudeten German problem.[30] At the same time, Warsaw denounced the minority clauses of the Polish-Czechoslovak treaty of 1925. On September 23 General Wladyslaw Bortnowski of the Polish army began forming a group to occupy the disputed area west of the river Olše and east of Ostrava and Frýdek. According to the instructions given by Marshal Edward Śmigly-Rydz it was to be ready by the 1st of October to fight or occupy Těšín, no matter how negotiations turned out between Warsaw and Prague.[31]

Prague answered the Polish note on September 25, declaring its readiness to start immediate negotiations to reach a détente between the two states.[32] At the same time Prague was attempting to establish a contact between the heads of states. On September 26, President Beneš sent a letter by airplane to President Ignacy Mościcki suggesting an "open and friendly" discussion of all controversial points and proposing a rectification of the frontier.[33]

Poland replied to these two moves on the 27th. Mościcki's answer was vague, expressing a wish for "a courageous decision" by Prague and indicating that the proposals of the Czechoslovak president would be submitted to the Polish government.[34] Another note which the Polish envoy handed to Krofta at the same time was much more concrete. Poland proposed an immediate agreement which would settle the gist of the problem in two stages. In the first place regions inhabited by an indisputable Polish majority (roughly the districts of Těšín and Fryštát) should be ceded immediately. Then, in the areas inhabited by a "major proportion" of Poles (according to the figures of 1919), the will of the population should be ascertained by a plebiscite. The note stressed the need for a prompt answer, particularly with regard to the first point (immediate cession), and stated that the Polish minister in Prague, Kazimierz Papée, had been given full powers to start preliminary talks immediately. In his subsequent conversation with the Polish envoy, President Beneš reaffirmed the Prague decision to cede territory in the Těšín area. In view of the situation he could not, however, lose immediately the Bohumín railroad crossing the Těšín territory, as it was the backbone of communications connecting the western and eastern parts of Czechoslovakia. Furthermore, this strategic aspect was not negligible at a moment when the danger of a war had not yet disappeared and such a cession would have created a precedent which could have been exploited by Hitler to seize immediately the territory requested in the Godesberg memorandum. Beneš could not grant to Poland what he was still refusing to Germany.[35]

Beck was adamant. On September 29 he urged Prague to "give a favorable answer with the shortest delay, during the day if possible." That day the Munich conference was opening, and Beck did not want to stay behind with his demands. On the other hand Prague wished to see which way the conference would turn before proceeding to an irrevocable move.[36]

Munich and Its Aftermath in Prague

In the meantime, the conference of four powers was in session in Munich. Hitler was defending the German demands. Mussolini was the mouthpiece of Hungarian and Polish interests.

The Munich Agreement, by which it was decided to sever from Czechoslovakia the areas inhabited by Germans (and to settle later the fate of other minorities), ruled that the evacuation of these areas was to take place between the 1st and the 10th of October. On the map attached to the Agreement were marked four zones to be occupied by German troops from the 1st to the 7th of October. The choice of the remaining territory to be ceded was to be made by an International Commission composed of representatives of Germany, Great Britain, France, Italy and Czechoslovakia. According to the Agreement, the Commission had to lay down in detail the conditions governing the evacuation of the four territories fixed by the Munich conference, to ascertain "the remaining territory of preponderantly German character" to be occupied by German troops by the 10th of October, then to determine the territories in which a plebiscite was to be held and to fix the date of the plebiscite, not later than the end of November. Finally, the Commission was to make the final determination of the frontiers and to recommend to the four Powers minor modifications in certain exceptional cases.

In the annex to the Agreement, France and Great Britain renewed their offer of an international guarantee of the new boundaries of the Czechoslovak state against unprovoked aggression. "When the question of the Polish and Hungarian minorities in Czechoslovakia has been settled, Germany and Italy for their part will give a guarantee to Czechoslovakia."

As to the problem of the Polish and Hungarian minorities, annex 2 stated that if not settled within three months by agreement between the respective governments, they should form the subject of another meeting of the heads of governments of the four powers present in Munich.[37]

In Prague, at five o'clock in the morning of September 30, the German Chargé d'affaires, Andor Hencke, on order from Berlin, announced his visit to Minister Krofta. He was received at 6:20 A.M. He transmitted the text of the Munich Agreement and added that the map would be handed over by the British legation. At the same time, he invited Czechoslovakia to send a representative and a military expert to the meeting of the International Commission which was to meet the same day at 5:00 P.M. in Berlin.[38]

There seems to have been some uncertainty about the way to ensure the acceptance of the Munich Agreement by Czechoslovakia. Prague was not officially represented in Munich and was allowed to send only observers there. Chamberlain and Daladier communicated the decision of the conference to them in the early hours of September 30 (at 1:30 A.M.). On this occasion the Secretary General of the Quai d'Orsay, Alexis Léger, declared that no reply was expected from them and that the Munich powers regarded the Agreement as accepted.[39] This line was, however, soon abandoned and Prague was pressed for a clearly worded declaration. Two hours after Léger's statement Daladier, still in Munich, instructed the French minister in Prague to make "a highly urgent" demarche to assure the acceptance.[40] Chamberlain sent the same instruction to the British envoy: "There is no time for argument; it must be a plain acceptance."[41]

At 8:00 A.M. Vojtěch Mastný, the Czechoslovak minister in Berlin, who in Munich had the ungrateful role of passive observer, landed in Prague. He was bringing the text of the Agreement and the maps and was received by the President at 9:00A.M. At 9:30 A.M. a meeting of the leaders of the political parties was held at the President's chancellery at the Hradčany castle. The cabinet met at the office of the Prime Minister. Afterwards there was a combined meeting of the cabinet and the political leaders in the presence of the representatives of the army.[42] At the cabinet meeting foreign minister Krofta stated that the report he was going to submit would be the most painful duty of his life. He read the text of the Munich Agreement to his colleagues and declared: "In theory it is possible to reject it. It would be followed by a German invasion, by a war in which nobody would join us, and by a Polish aggression. It is doubtful whether in such a situation the Soviets would wish to help us and whether their help would be effective. Or it is possible to accept the Munich Agreement and by negotiations in the Commission (i.e. the International Commission which was about to meet in Berlin) perhaps to ward off the worst and to have frontiers guaranteed." According to Krofta an immediate decision was imperative. There was no time to convene Parliament. The question was to accept or to reject the Agreement. The military experts were of the opinion that in the situation created by the Munich Agreement Czechoslovakia was unable to defend herself alone. As General Ludvík Krejčí, the chief of staff, later wrote the Czechoslovak army was at the moment of Munich in a kettle resembling that in which the German general Friedrich Paulus found himself at Stalingrad.[43] The meeting decided to accept the Agreement. The session ended at 11:30 A.M. and the deliberations then continued at the castle of Hradčany in the presence of President Beneš. They took only fifteen minutes. The President was for the acceptance: "If we didn't accept, we would fight an honorable war, but we would lose our independence and our people would be massacred."[44] Thus the government resigned itself to accepting Munich "aware of the necessity to safeguard the nation and of the impossibility of any other decision," not without protesting to the world "against a decision taken unilaterally and without our participation."[45]

In the morning the ministers of Great Britain, France and Italy asked to be received by Krofta to learn the decision of the government.[46] Krofta received them at 12:30 P.M. "In the name of the President of the Republic and in the name of the Government," he said, "I declare that we are submitting to the decision taken in Munich without us and against us. Our standpoint will be expressed to you in writing. At this moment I have nothing to add." At the same time he asked the ministers to use their influence with the German government for the cessation of anti-Czech propaganda which would make execution of the Munich Agreement difficult. When the French minister attempted to address words of condolence to Krofta he was cut short by the foreign minister's remark: "We have been forced into this situation. Now everything is at an end. Today it is our turn, tomorrow it will be the turn of others."

The scene was poignant. According to Italian minister Francesco Fransoni, Krofta was at that moment a completely broken man and intimated only one wish, that the three ministers should quickly leave his room.[47]

The general public in Czechoslovakia got its first information about the Munich Agreement from foreign broadcasts. Only at 5:00 P.M. did Prime Minister, Jan Syrový, announce the decision of the government to cede: "Abandoned, we are in a certain respect a fortified place encircled by forces which are more powerful than we."[48] Prague—as an American newspaperman wrote—then became "a city hushed by grief."[49] Later crowds formed in the main Prague thoroughfare, Václavské náměstí, and demonstrated against the capitulation.

In this atmosphere of defeat, a period of feverish political activity opened. The most important events were the negotiations about the territorial changes imposed by Munich. At home it was imperative to watch closely the events in Slovakia where the extreme autonomists were louder every day. The anti-Munich politicians, mainly of the leftist groups and the representatives of the younger Czech political generation even pondered an attempt at a military coup which would install an anti-Munich government headed by General Krejčí.[50]

Another urgent problem was that of the head of the State. Transferred by a stroke of the pen into the orbit of Germany, Czechoslovakia could not afford to keep at her head a protagonist of the defeated political orientation, President Beneš. Prague noticed this change of atmosphere immediately after Munich, when the members of the Czechoslovak delegation at the International Commission started bringing messages and opinions from Berlin which left no doubts about this issue. Mastný assured Göring in vain that the new Czechoslovakia would modify her foreign policy and wanted to live in close friendship with the Reich. He met with an implacable German aversion to Beneš. The Nazi regime not only abhorred the representatives of a political philosophy which it considered forfeited, but Hitler himself felt a strong personal disgust for his consistent opponent. Göring advised Mastný officially that Germany could not tolerate Beneš as the head of Czechoslovakia. If Beneš did not resign immediately, Germany, in carrying out the Munich Agreement, "would proceed against Czechoslovakia with the utmost ruthlessness."[51] The representative of the Czechoslovak foreign ministry, Arnošt

Heidrich, heard the same words from the German State Secretary, Weizsäcker.[52]

The President was fully aware that under the changed circumstances he could not stay in office. In the first moments, under the depressing effect of the Munich Agreement, he dictated a letter of abdication; later, however, he decided to stay for the time being even though he sensed the hostility of the right-wing politicians. In the meantime he wished to settle the most urgent problems stemming from the capitulation.[53]

Before complying with the German demands, Beneš made some changes in the composition of his government which were required by the new situation. In the first place, his close collaborator Kamil Krofta was to be replaced by a more acceptable person. František Chvalkovský, the Czechoslovak envoy in Rome, was appointed as Krofta's successor in the Ministry of Foreign Affairs. Chvalkovský was known for his contacts with the Agrarian party, the largest Czechoslovak political party, and with its late leader, Antonín Švehla.[54] He viewed Beneš's foreign policy with ironical skepticism. His temperament and political background separated him as well from the professorial Beneš as from the grave and reserved historian Krofta.

General Syrový, Inspector General of the Armed Forces, retained the premiership and the post of national defense. It was again a nonpolitical cabinet of experts like Syrový's first government which was installed on September 22, following the acceptance of Franco-British proposals. There were two Slovak ministers. Politically inexperienced, Syrový had to rely in the all-important sphere of foreign policy on the judgment of Chvalkovský.

On October 5, President Beneš announced his resignation to the Prime Minister in a letter in which he noted that his person could endanger the necessary political changes at home and, what was even more important, the irreversible evolution which would follow Munich in the international domain. The same day he took leave of his countrymen in a broadcast address in which he declared: "I believe I am acting rightly in leaving so that our State and nation can develop quietly and undisturbed in the new atmosphere and adapt itself to the new conditions. This means that it should not renounce old friends and should gather new friends around it in a spirit of calm, of realism and of loyalty to all..."[55]

The departure of Beneš was a new success for Germany. The German press celebrated this event in officially inspired commentaries and revived the old anti-Czech propaganda. "The last man whose name is on the document of Versailles, and the youngest one, leaves his post at the age of 54. Today, when this epoch belongs to the past it is only logical that its representatives disappear," wrote *Frankfurter Zeitung* (October 6).

The organ of the National-Socialist Party, *Völkischer Beobachter,* in a harsh editorial on the same day claimed that Beneš was abandoning the public life of Europe "laden with a heavy historical error."

The day after his resignation Beneš took leave of the officials of his office. In the afternoon of the following day, at the end of his mental and physical forces he retired to his country residence at Sezimovo Ústí in southern Bohemia where he managed to overcome the nervous exhaustion of the preceding weeks.[56]

Berlin was, however, not content with his resignation and indicated that its intentions concerning Czechoslovakia could be only provisory while Beneš remained in the Republic. The Czechoslovak government thus had to recommend to him that he expatriate himself. In spite of his original intention to stay several more weeks at Sezimovo Ústí, Beneš left for London by air on October 22 and settled in the house of his nephew.[57]

CHAPTER I
IMPLEMENTATION OF THE MUNICH AGREEMENT

Negotiations with Germany

The principal members of the International Commission set up by the Munich Agreement arrived in Berlin in the afternoon of September 30. The Czechoslovak delegate, minister Mastný, left the Czechoslovak capital for Berlin in the afternoon. Accompanied by minister Rudolf Künzl-Jizerský from the Foreign Ministry, General Karel Husárek and three other military advisors, he landed in Berlin shortly before 6 P.M. and went directly to join the Commission, which was already in session. The other Czechoslovak representative on the International Commission, minister Arnošt Heidrich, visited the British, French and Italian ambassadors who were members of the Commission, and found them reserved.[1] The presence of the German generals and the Sudeten German representatives did not augur well for a moderate solution to the frontier problem.[2]

Mastný received for his mission short instructions from President Beneš concerning several technical matters (e.g. no plebiscites in the German enclaves as Brno and Jihlava, termination of anti-Czechoslovak propaganda). The Czechoslovak delegate had to point out the possibilities of a more free and calmer cooperation in the future and to invite the Germans not to encumber it by excessive harshness when liquidating the past.[3] The following days dispelled these Czech illusions.

The Commission opened its first session at 5:20 P.M.,[4] some time before the arrival of the Czechoslovaks. According to the presiding officer, German State Secretary Weizsäcker, the most urgent task was to organize the evacuation of the first zone. This area was a narrow strip in south-western Bohemia which was to be evacuated during the next two days, the 1st and 2nd of October. To this end, Weizsäcker proposed the immediate formation of a military subcommittee.[5] The subcommittee had to work very rapidly to give the instructions in time for the movement of troops into the four zones.[6] The Czechoslovak delegates endeavored to obtain as many concessions as possible. "The Germans were very polite, but very firm, and in almost every case refused to give an inch."[7]

The subcommittee reported its first decisions before the closing of the first session of the International Commission. After some minor changes, it was decided that the German troops would cross the border on October 1st at 2:00 P.M. Between the two armies there was to be maintained a neutral zone of at least three kilometres.[8]

The evacuation began on Saturday, October 1st, at Klein Philipsreuth. It started in the Bohemian Forest (Šumava), in the region where the ancient frontiers of Bohemia, Austria and Germany met. The occupation of this inaccessible and isolated mountain area was terminated on October 2nd, as prescribed by the Munich Agreement. On the same day the Czechs started the evacuation of the second zone, in northern Bohemia, including both banks of the Elbe, and the industrial area adjacent to the two norther salients of Bohemia. The occupation of this second zone was not yet finished when the German troops marched into the third zone containing the towns of Cheb (Eger) and Aš (Asch),[9] and the spas of western Bohemia. This operation took three days. At last, on October 6 and 7, the German troops occupied the fourth zone, the northern part of Moravia-Silesia with the towns of Krnov (Jägerndorf), Bruntál (Freudenthal) and Frývaldov (Freiwaldau).

From Berlin British and Italian military service attachés went to Czechoslovakia to watch over the transfer of the territory on behalf of the International Commission. They were not welcomed by Germans who did not like foreign officers circulating among mobilized German units.[10] Besides these officers about 30 British observers, ex-officers in mufti, responsible to Ambassador Henderson, were watching the transfer of the territory.[11]

Between October 1 and 10 there were several incidents in the neutral zone separating the two armies, the advancing Germans and the retreating Czechs, when localities were temporarily left without police after the Czech withdrawal.[12] However, according to the British reports there were no incidents or clashes between the troops.[13] The Czechs withdrew in good order. "The men were stolid and silent. There was no talk, no laughter, no singing."[14] In many cases the German troops overstepped the demarcation line either by mistake or deliberately and later the Czechoslovak delegate in Berlin Heidrich sent his German counterpart, Ambassador Herbert von Richthofen two long lists of such incidents.[15] In some cases the Germans withdrew, in others they stayed. When the British observer R.G. Coulson in one case appealed to German generosity, the local German commander looked at him in surprise and then remained "contemptuously detached."[16]

In the meantime, the International Commission held its sessions in Berlin. The military subcommittee was in charge of the technical side of the occupation. In addition, it dealt with the difficult problem of the evacuation of military material from the fortifications which the Czechs had to surrender. At the second session of the Commission it was agreed to divide the work among three subcommittees designated by the letters of the alphabet: A. the military subcommittee, which had already been in session since the beginning, B. the financial and economic subcommittee and C. the subcommittee for plebiscites and frontiers.[17]

The Commission did not meet on Sunday, October 2. Hitler used this occasion to call its German members in order to brief them on the last German zone to be occupied between October 7 and 10 (the "fifth zone"). According to him, its line had in principle to coincide with the Godesberg line. Hitler admitted only "some small revisions" in favor of the Czechs. He was especially interested in the north Bohemian industrial center of Liberec (Reichenberg), and in the region of Svitavy (Zwittau) in western Moravia. He was ready to renounce plebiscites in the language enclaves of Jihlava (Iglau), Brno (Brünn), Olomouc (Olmütz) and Konice (Konitz) in Moravia (as demanded in the Godesberg memorandum) provided that the Czechs would not insist on a plebiscite in the area with Czech population separating the German enclave of Svitavy from the German territory in Silesia. For this whole territory should—according to Hitler—fall to Germany in any event, even if the remaining German language enclaves were to be renounced.[18] The area in question was, however, of vital importance to Czechoslovakia, for it was crossed by important railroad lines connecting Bohemia with Moravia and the eastern part of the State (Praha-Brno, and Praha-Moravská Ostrava).

Subcommittee C (for plebiscites and frontiers) started its work the next day. It immediately became a center of dispute. Its Czechoslovak members, though unaware of the instructions given the preceding day by Hitler to the German negotiators, sensed the stiff atmosphere on the German side.[19] According to Czechoslovak minister Mastný the assistance of the French and British ambassadors proved weak and ineffective and the Munich Agreement was continuously interpreted to Czechoslovakia's disadvantage.[20]

During the period of October 3 and 4, the subcommittee held five sessions. The former German minister to Brussels, Herbert von Richthofen, presided. Originally it was hoped that the subcommittee would have a neutral chairman, for which office the British representative intended to propose the Italian delegate, Count Massimo Magistrati.[21] Czechoslovakia was represented by minister Heidrich and by General

Husárek. The British delegates were ready to make large concessions, but they were shocked by the atmosphere of the meetings. "The proceedings of the subcommittee were confused and frequently noisy, and the chairman was quite uncapable of maintaining order," says British ambassdor Henderson in his report. "It was not uncommon for four or five Sudeten Germans and the Czech representatives all to be shouting at once."[22] Another member of the British delegation speaks of a "shouting match."[23]

From the first session, the Germans declared the Godesberg line to be the only possible basis of discussion, whereas the British and French opposed it. The debate turned largely on what the percentage of the German population in the areas to be ceded should be, and which census should be used as the statistical basis. The Franco-British proposals of September 19 which the Czechoslovak government accepted on September 21, stated that the areas for transfer "would probably have to include areas with over 50 per cent of German inhabitants."[24] The Munich Agreement spoke of "the territory of preponderantly German character" without mentioning any percentage. In the subcommittee Czechoslovakia was offering to transfer areas in which the population was more than 75 per cent German, based on the Czechoslovak census of 1930. The Germans were asking for areas with only 51 per cent of German inhabitants, the statistics based on the Austrian census of 1910. According to them, the Czechoslovak censuses of 1921 and 1930 were biased from the national point of view. On the other hand, the Austrian census was to their advantage.[25]

The negotiations were deadlocked. The plenary session of the Commission held during the evening of October 4 was fruitless. Nothing came of the discussions, although they lasted three hours. It was impossible to reach an agreement on the two controversial questions: the percentage of the German majority, and the date of the census. The chairman of the Commission, Weizsäcker, suggested therefore that a restricted committee composed of the five heads of the delegations could perhaps deal better with these intricate problems. Even this intimate gathering led to nothing. According to Mastný there were very heated controversies.[26] The Germans remained intransigent and Mastný declared that he would break off the negotiations and leave if there was no will to compromise on the German side.[27]

French ambassador François-Poncet proposed as a basis for discussions the figures of 1918, to which the statistics of 1910 and 1921 were to be compared. This was, however, rather illusory, since there was no census taken in 1918 and therefore the figures could have been only a rough estimate. As to the German majority, he suggested the proportion of two thirds. Neither Mastný nor Weizsäcker accepted this proposal, but the Czechoslovak minister sent one of his subordinates to Prague to submit the French formula to the government.[28]

At this moment Hitler himself took action behind the scenes. The dragging pace of the negotiations and the unwillingness of the western powers and of Czechoslovakia to accept the German demands were in his eyes but maneuvers to deprive him of the gains of Munich. He got the news of the Berlin deadlock while he was on tour in western Bohemia. On October 4, in the evening, he was in Karlovy Vary. From Löbau in Saxony he returned to Berlin to deliver the speech inaugurating that year's *Winterhilfe* campaign and to urge the laggards on the International Commission to produce some results. That same night Ribbentrop expressed to the French ambassador the discontent of Hitler. François-Poncet was awakened in the middle of the night and called to the German foreign minister. Ribbentrop told him excitedly that Hitler had charged the British and French delegates on the International Commission with going back on the Munich decisions. According to him, the French obstruction might cause the reopening of the crisis which—as was thought—had been settled in Munich.[29] If Czechoslovakia did not agree before midday to the German demands (i.e. 1910 statistics and over 50 per cent German majority), Hitler was going to order German troops to occupy the Godesberg line.[30] François-Poncet protested against this attempt at intimidation and proposed to ask in London and Paris for the official interpretation of the Munich Agreement. Thus the peace restored in Munich was suddenly troubled and the diplomats had to strive with all their energy to avert a new crisis in Central Europe.

On the morning of October 5 all meetings were adjourned at German request and the delegations looked hurriedly for instructions from their governments.[31] Henderson saw François-Poncet, who told him about his talk with Ribbentrop. The two diplomats then met Italian ambassador, Bernardo Attolico, and Henderson suggested that the Italian try to intervene by seeing Ribbentrop.[32] The French ambassador telephoned French Prime Minister Daladier for his opinion on the two controversial points. Daladier replied that, according to his recollection and understanding of the Munich Agreement, the proportion of Germans ought to be 51 per cent and the population figures of 1918 were to be used as a basis. Henderson described to Halifax the tension created by Ribbentrop's ultimatum at 10:45 A.M. Two hours later London replied that Prime Minister Chamberlain agreed with Daladier.[33]

On October 5, early in the morning, Prague accepted the proposals of the French ambassador. However, when Mastný met François-Poncet at about noon, the French diplomat declared emotionally that the situation had been overtaken by the events of the last night, and told him what he had learned about Hitler's mood. He advised Czechoslovakia to accept the German *Diktat*.[34]

In the early hours of the afternoon Ribbentrop called the three ambassadors and persuaded them to yield to the German demands. Attolico and Henderson were without explicit instructions. Although Henderson disliked the methods used by the Germans on the International Commission, and although he protested against "the indecent haste," he accepted the German point of view because in his opinion the 1910 map was "at least better" than the Godesberg line.[35] It was agreed to adopt the 1910 census figures and—for the German preponderance—the proportion of over 50 per cent. The participants in the meeting, to which Czechoslovakia was not invited, signed a brief protocol and a map with the line demanded by the Germans. Ribbentrop intended to use this document, signed by the representatives of all the four Munich participants, as an instrument of pressure on the Czechs in the event they wished to procrastinate and refer the matter back to Prague.[36]

Later in the afternoon, after the signing of the protocol, a Czechoslovak delegation—still unaware of its existence—attempted to save what could be saved. On October 4, the Prague government decided to send two of its members, the Minister of Public Works, General Husárek, and the Minister of Propaganda (a newly created post), Hugo Vavrečka, to Berlin to announce the impending resignation of President Beneš and to take stock of the situation there.[37] By drawing attention to the imminent departure of the man who was the chief object of Hitler's ire, they apparently hoped to moderate the German demands. The two ministers accompanied by Mastný called on Weizsäcker. They stressed that the Prague government fully realized that Czechoslovakia, with her new restricted frontiers, could only pursue a policy of close cooperation with Germany. At the same time the two Czechs asked for considerate treatment of their people. On this occasion Weizsäcker acquainted them with the map on which the new border line was drawn.[38]

Shortly afterward, at 5:30 P.M., the three ambassadors, Henderson, François-Poncet and Attolico, joined with the Czechoslovak and German delegates.[39] The map with the new frontier was officially presented to the Czechs, who raised several objections. They objected that the new frontier would make the connection between Bohemia and the eastern regions of the state very narrow and economically intolerable. It was just at that point where there could be no tampering with the frontier line, replied the German representative. An exchange of population could be carried out but no amendment could be considered. All Czech objections remained in vain and the ambassadors, according to Mastný, "behaved with reserve."[40]

The Italian ambassador tried to soften the blow by proposing that certain railroad lines which were to be cut by the new frontiers should be crossed by the German troops as late as possible, but not later than October 10.[41] To break their opposition, the Czechs were confronted—on the instruction of Ribbentrop—with the four-power protocol showing that even France and Great Britain had already adopted the German standpoint.[42] At 7 P.M. the International Commission held a short, formal meeting. Weizsäcker reported the decision. There was no discussion.[43]

The two Czechoslovak ministers then reported the results of the Berlin negotiations in the night session of the cabinet in Prague. The cabinet examined the new situation in a session which lasted until 6:15 A.M. of October 6. There was no alternative under the given circumstances but to accept the decision of the International Commission.[44] The two delegates returned to Berlin in the morning of the same day. At 12:30 P.M. another session of the International Commission opened and minister Mastný declared that his government accepted with profound sorrow the new line.[45] The occupation started the next day and was completed on October 10.[46]

With the exception of the additional plebiscite area (marked in green on the Godesberg map) the line agreed upon on October 5 corresponded in general to the Godesberg demands of Hitler. It followed the nationality line systematically to the disadvantage of Czechoslovakia and cut deeply into the body of the country. North of Prague it approached the capital to about 25 miles. Plzeň, with its armament works, was almost on the border. Jindřichův Hradec (Neuhaus), originally claimed by Germany, though remaining in Czechoslovakia, was surrounded on three sides by German territory. Bohemia and Moravia were deprived not only of their natural border, but also of their modern fortifications built in the preceding three years.[47]

* * *

There still remained two problems: first, to determine the territories in which a plebiscite was to be held, and second, the final delimitation of the frontiers.

Czechoslovakia was against the plebiscites. In his instructions of September 30 to minister Mastný, President Beneš mentioned expressly the danger to the integrity of Czechoslovakia represented by plebiscites in Brno, Jihlava and other German enclaves. On the German side, Hitler was ready to dispense with a plebiscite in several German enclaves, provided that the Czechs would not insist on a plebiscite in the region between the Svitavy enclave and Silesia.[48] When the British ambassador saw Weizsäcker in this connection on October 10, he had the impression that there were forces at work in favor of the plebiscites with the view to including in the Reich further territories presumably in the Olomouc-Brno and Moravská area. At this point even Henderson lost patience and warned the State Secretary against new radical territorial demands. He said that personally he would never agree to such plebiscites. "Germany got all she wanted and if she could not behave with decency it would be useless to go on negotiating," declared the British diplomat.[49] On the same day his colleague, French ambassador François-Poncet, declared himself also against the plebiscites.[50]

We do not know precisely the evolution of Hitler's ideas at that time. The fifth zone was so favorable, Czechoslovakia was so paralyzed, that he probably thought it would be useless to complicate the situation further with the plebiscites. Maybe the outburst of the British ambassador and the French attitude also had their effect. While, on October 2, he did not entirely give up the plebiscites, on October 11, in his conversation with Ribbentrop, he declared himself against them.[51] Accordingly, on October 13, at the meeting of the International Commission, Weizsäcker announced that Germany was giving up the plebiscites, and the Commission decided unanimously to dispense with them.[52] The final delimitation was to be settled by bilateral negotiations between Germany and Czechoslovakia. The International Commission adjourned, leaving the Czechoslovak negotiators facing the Germans alone.

Berlin first drew up a summary of all German claims for frontier rectifications. It was so exaggerated that the Germans themselves acknowledged that it far exceeded what could be advocated or achieved.[53] The final version of the German claims was framed on November 3 and was submitted to Hitler on the 6th or 7th.[54] The chief demands concerned the region of Chodsko near Domažlice in south-western Bohemia, several areas in northern and eastern Bohemia (Liberec, Český Dub [Böhmisch Aicha], Jablonné [Gabel]) and Brodek, south-west of Svitavy in Moravia. According to the German calculations Germany would have thus acquired 26,000 Czechs and 6,000 Germans. In Slovakia, the Germans demanded Devín (Theben) near Bratislava.[55]

The demands did not seem to Hitler radical enough. He decided that, in principle, no territories which had been occupied by Germany were to be returned to Czechoslovakia. To his advisor's objection that some areas claimed by Germany were entirely Czech, Hitler remarked that a large number of Germans were still in Czechoslovakia, so that an exchange was not justified. The only concession, on a small scale, that could be made was in the case of territories which were purely Czech and whose population desired to return to Czechoslovakia. For this there would have to be at least a 90 per cent Czechoslovak population. The areas of Břeclav (Lundenburg) and Moravský Krumlov (Mährisch Kromau) and the environs of Jindřichův Hradec were not to be given back. In the neighborhood of Brodek the Germans should take as much as possible. Hitler did not, however, appear to desire particular pressure in this matter. He ascribed special importance to the extraterritoriality of a future superhighway, *Autobahn*, which he projected and which was to connect Breslau and Vienna across Moravia.[56] In return for this concession he was ready to accord Czechoslovakia the extraterritoriality of certain railroad lines which were cut by the new frontiers. According to Hitler's orders, it was to be intimated to the Czechs that Germany had been very modest in her demands, having, moreover, abandoned the claim to Brno and its surroundings. Hitler ended his instructions with a threat: Should the Czechs make difficulties, they were to be given to understand that they would do well to accept the proposals. "Otherwise the Führer would take up the matter personally and they might then fare far worse."[57]

Czechoslovakia presented her proposals for final delimitation ("the sixth zone") on November 2. In a private meeting Heidrich informed the German ambassador, Karl Ritter, about the Czech demands and gained the impression that at least some of them would be accepted.[58] Mastný had the same impression when he met Ritter four days later. According to Weizsäcker, some of them seemed reasonable, others impracticable.[59] The Czechs asked for facilities on the Brno-Břeclav railroad and in the last resort the return of Břeclav, for extension of Czech territory around Plzeň, the return of Český Dub and the railroad line Stará Paka (Alt-Paka)—Dvůr Králové (Königinhof)—Jaroměř, which had been cut on October 5 in several places by spearheads of German territory. They also asked for the spur at Ústí nad Orlicí (Wildenschwert). The most important of the Czechoslovak demands presented to Berlin concerned, of course, the area of Svitavy. However, the German foreign ministry maintained that any request for discussion of this area was to be refused.[60] For the time being the Germans refused to discuss the most difficult and delicate areas of delimitation, maintaining that they should be reserved until the end of the negotiations.[61] These hopes were, however, thwarted by a banal incident fully in line with the mentality of Adolf Hitler. A propaganda map had been printed clandestinely in Czechoslovakia, the French text of which charged that Hitler, by the occupation of purely Czech territories, had broken his word. The accusation was printed in red letters. This aroused Hitler's allergic sensitivity to printed criticism of his personality and his reaction was to stiffen the German demands.[62]

The meeting of the German-Czechoslovak frontier committee opened on November 10. Minister Richthofen presided. The Czechoslovak delegate, minister Heidrich, had the difficult task of defending the Prague demands and facing the German desiderata. The session was painful from the beginning. At the opening von Richthofen read a categorical statement according to which the decisions of the International Commission of October 5 and 13 awarded the Sudeten territory to Germany "once and for all." The Czechoslovak requests would lead to a complete alteration of the line of October 5 and 13 and their presentation—continued the German delegate—"caused the greatest surprise to the Reich Government." Germany not only did not intend to give up any part of the occupied areas, but still had certain claims to put forward. And Richthofen submitted to Heidrich a map with a red line marking the new German claims. According to Hitler's orders he stressed that it meant "a great sacrifice for the Reich government" to abandon several towns with a German population. Concluding, he asked the Czechoslovak delegation to give its assent to the projected frontier demarcation in a day or two.

Heidrich, in his reply, tried to refute the German arguments. He observed that from the beginning the line of October 5 was intended as a demarcation line, not as a final settlement of the frontier. The Czechoslovak desiderata were based on the ethnographic conditions and did not contain any deviation from the ethnographic frontier. All his objections were, however, in vain. Richthofen asked for an answer by Saturday, November 12. Accordingly, Heidrich decided to leave the same day for Prague to consult with his government.[63]

For Czechoslovakia, the new German territorial demands were like "a bolt from the blue." These words, indeed, were used by Mastný when he appeared the next day at the German Foreign Ministry to protest, on orders from Prague, against Richthofen's ultimatum. His intervention was in vain. Under State Secretary Ernst Woermann, who received him, confirmed the German standpoint and declared that the German demands "admitted of no bargaining."[64]

In Prague, Foreign Minister Chvalkovský, personally offended, did not dare to communicate the German demands to the cabinet and to the political leaders until the following day, November 11, in the evening. He delayed his presentation in order not to prejudice negotiations on internal politics which were to take place in the afternoon, and which dealt with the presidential election, the dissolution of political parties, and the new constitution.[65]

During the evening session of November 11, the government accepted the German proposals. Shortly before midnight, Chvalkovský's chef de cabinet, Hubert Masařík, and minister Heidrich appeared at the German legation to communicate the answer. Having taken note of the fact that the German government renounced the intention of making further demands,[66] Prague expressed the hope that Berlin would not turn down certain modifications of its demands where consideration for Czechoslovak national feeling appeared possible without disadvantage to German ethnic interests. Moreover, the Czechoslovak government stated that it had met the German claims "on the assumption that henceforth nothing more stands in the way of a German guarantee of the new and final frontiers of the Czechoslovak state."[67]

However, when Ribbentrop received the Prague answer he felt offended by the inference that Berlin had renounced further demands. He telephoned immediately[68] to make certain that no such declaration had been made by Germany, for he intended to present still other desiderata concerning especially the project of the Breslau-Vienna *Autobahn*, crossing Czechoslovakia.[69] On November 13, the Czechoslovak delegation was told that the question of new demands remained open, that the modifications asked by the Czechoslovak government could not be conceded, and that the frontier guarantee referred to by Prague could not be linked with the question of the frontier delimitation as Prague had suggested. The delimitation agreement could be signed only when the pending transportation problems (e.g. the *Autobahn* question) had been settled. On Ribbentrop's orders everything was to be ready in three or four days.[70] Later, Ribbentrop decided that the occupation of the new territories was to take place on November 24.[71]

If there was at the beginning a discussion—though unsatisfactory for Prague—about the delimitation of the fifth zone, the negotiations for "minor modifications" mentioned in the Munich Agreement turned into a pure *Diktat*. At all German places which Mastný contacted, he met with arguments stressing the inviolability of decisions made in the highest places. As to the British, French and Italian embassies "it needed no special mention"—as Mastný stated—that "beyond expressions of full sympathy there was not the least desire to undertake anything privately or to exert influence" on behalf of the Czechs.[72]

The protocol about the final demarcation of frontiers was signed at the German foreign ministry on November 20. Its chief part was a map with the final corrections.[73] On November 21, in the morning, the acting chairman of the International Commission, ambassador Ritter, informed British chargé d'affaires Sir George Ogilvie-Forbes that the Commission had been summoned to meet at 6 P.M. in order to sanction the new line agreed upon by the Czechs and the Germans. Ritter invited the British diplomat to call on him at 1 P.M. to see the map of the proposed line.[74]

He justified this haste by the fact that the new frontier was to come into force on November 24. Besides—certainly a welcome explanation—he hinted about the impending departure for Berchtesgaden of the French representatives on the Commission, accompanying the new French ambassador Robert Coulondre, who was to present his credentials to Hitler.[75]

Forbes consulted his French and Italian colleagues. The agreement had been signed on the preceding day, and there was no alternative but to indorse the fait accompli. In his report to the British Foreign Secretary, Forbes declared that "the case would have been different," had the Czechs protested and appealed to the International Commission.[76] Nevertheless, a few days earlier he himself had been very skeptical about obtaining territorial adjustments from the Germans.[77]

The session of the International Commission was short and formal. It started at 6 P.M. and ended at 7:30 P.M. Ritter read the memorandum signed on November 20. Mastný stressed the feeling of deep grief which filled the hearts of the Czechoslovak people and expressed the hope that the sacrifices made by Czechoslovakia would contribute to good neighborly relations with Germany. The Commission approved the minutes of November 20 and declared that the frontier marked on the annexed maps was "the final frontier within the meaning of paragraph 6 of the Munich Agreement.[78] The Italian ambassador declared that with the agreement on the delimitation of the frontier, the most important task of the International Commission was accomplished. The French and British chargés d'affaires associated themselves with these remarks and thus indirectly met the German wish to terminate the activities of this international body. Czechoslovakia would have preferred to maintain its existence and not to be left facing Germany alone. However, Germany dispelled any Czech expectations in this regard. Before the meeting of the Commission on November 20, Richthofen declared to Heidrich that any Czechoslovak attempt to extend the existence of the Commission would be considered by Germany as an intention to turn for help to England and France which would create displeasure in the highest places.[79]

There were few sectors where the final frontier line was changed to the profit of Czechoslovakia. The border line was altered in general to her disadvantage and only accentuated the bizarre meanders of the border fixed on October 5. Twelve new salients penetrated into Czechoslovak territory. Czechoslovakia had to abandon several areas in western and northern Bohemia. Near Plzeň a new salient gave to Germany the coal mines of Litice. In Moravia a long salient appeared in the area of Litovel. In Slovakia the German territory encircled Bratislava by including Devín at the confluence of the Morava and the Danube.

The fundamental objections of Czechoslovakia were not heeded. The border in the area of Svitavy was not revised in her favor. Břeclav was not returned. Jindřichův Hradec remained surrounded by German territory on three sides. Only a little over fifty Czech localities with 23,000 inhabitants were returned.[80] On the other hand, Czechoslovakia had to cede to Germany 110 new localities and villages in Bohemia, 17 in Moravia-Silesia, one in Slovakia. According to German calculations, Germany got 39,443 Czechs, whereas in the localities returned to Czechoslovakia there were only 263 German inhabitants.[81] These modifications were implemented on November 24, according to the wishes of Ribbentrop.[82]

The changes wounded the national feelings of both Czechs and Slovaks. The "Chod" country west of Domažlice is rich in historical traditions and reminiscences and the loss of the Chod villages was considered an offense to the whole nation. In these eight villages even in 1910 the German population formed only one per cent.

The Chods protested. As soon as November 2 they sent a deputation to Prague and two weeks later, at a meeting in Domažlice, they suggested a plebiscite in their region.[83] All in vain. The villages were occupied by the German *Ordnungspolizei* on November 24. The villages were like dead, people stayed at home. The occupation started at 10 A.M. At that moment in the unoccupied part of the Chod country the church bells started to peel. "At Domažlice there was just the annual fair. The main place was overflowing with people. When they heard the bells, they uncovered their heads and silently took leave of their brothers. On the Chod castle of Domažlice a black flag was hoisted."[84]

The German annexation of Devín, an important strategic point near Bratislava, had the same effect on the Slovak people as the loss of the Chod country. In prehistoric times, this site was Celtic; in Roman times, it was a Roman station near the *limes* and the town of Carnuntum. In the ninth century A.D. it became a bastion of Greater Moravia and the residence of its princes. In the Middle Ages a castle was built there, the ruins of which have been preserved until the present day. It was surrounded with legends which were revived by the literary romanticism of the last century.

On the German side, Devín was mentioned at the beginning of October. On October 7 Weizsäcker, in a memorandum to Hitler stated that the community of Devín had a German majority in 1910, that it was, however, separated from the German territory by two rivers and that there was no bridge. One day later, Hitler decided not to demand a plebiscite for Devín. In his opinion Devín had to go to Slovakia.[85] On October 25 he visited the Danube bridgehead of Petržalka (Engerau), recently annexed by the Reich, and saw on the spot the situation on the other bank of the Danube. Probably at this moment he decided to annex it. The German proposals of November 3 placed Devín on the list of German territorial demands.[86] One week later, when the Slovak minister František Ďurčanský called on Göring, a demarche was made on behalf of the Slovaks, and the leader of the "Carpathian Germans," Franz Karmasin, intervened asking that Devín should remain in Slovakia. "All Slovak history books would have to be burnt," Karmasin said to Göring, "if the Slovaks were to lose the castle." In his opinion German military requirements could be met by special agreements without the cession of the territory. Göring answered that these arguments were new to him and probably to Hitler also, and he promised to submit the matter once more to the Führer.[87] The German consul in Bratislava, Ernst von Druffel, also recommended that Devín should be left to the Slovaks. Although he believed that the historical background of the Devín legends was based only on a very weak historical foundation, he nevertheless emphasized that the German claims to Devín would doubtless contribute to driving the Slovaks into closer reliance on Prague and that the psychological effect of the loss of this place on the Slovaks would be very serious. According to Druffel, Devín was of importance to Germany only in view of the future Danube-Oder canal which Germany intended to build across Czechoslovakia. Also the undeniably natural character of the frontier justified, in his opinion, the abandonment of this demand.[88]

All these arguments were in vain. The annexation of the new bridgehead was sufficiently enticing to Hitler to overcome psychological considerations, and Devín was eventually occupied. Besides the community of Devín, the ruined castle and several installations important to Bratislava, Czechoslovakia lost the Kobyla hill, of strategic importance at the confluence of the Morava and the Danube. At the beginning of December, Germany decided to return to Slovakia the Danube island of Käsmacher with the pumping station of the Bratislava aqueduct. At the same time, however, Germany occupied a small area near Karlova Ves and a part of the northern slope of the Kobyla hill.[89]

Bohemia and Moravia-Silesia lost about 30,000 square kilometres (11,600 square miles) to Germany i.e. about 38 per cent of their area. Before Munich, Bohemia and Moravia-Silesia had 79,000 square kilometres (30,500 sq. miles); the later Protectorate of Bohemia-Moravia had only 49,000 square kilometres (18,900 sq. miles). In 1930 the Czech lands had 10,674,000 inhabitants. After Munich they lost 3,869,000 inhabitants (of whom 200,000 went to Poland), i.e. about 34% of the whole population. Some 2,806,000 Germans went to Germany (along with ca. 720,000–750,000 Czechs). About 234,000 Germans remained after Munich in Bohemia and Moravia-Silesia.[90]

Germany thus achieved the maximum of her territorial demands. Hitler pushed the ethnographic principle to the extreme in order to undermine the viability of what remained of Czechoslovakia, and to remove the potential threat to Germany's right wing in the event of future undertakings in the East. With the exception of the German enclaves in the Czech territory, he reached the Godesberg line. For the abandonment of the German islands in Brno and Jihlava, he was amply compensated by the occupation of the vital Svitavy region, where he could dominate the communications between the western and eastern part of the Czechoslovak state.

The two western European powers represented on the Berlin International Commission followed the amputation of the Czechoslovak Republic on the whole as passive onlookers. They assisted at the proceedings of the Commission with apparent disgust, but achieved practically nothing on behalf of Czechoslovakia. At the most they may have influenced Hitler's decision against the plebiscites. On the other hand, the British representative, ambassador Henderson, reminded Lord Halifax on October 7, that "it would be as unwise as it would be misleading to encourage the Czechoslovak government to believe that they have much to hope from the International Commission."[91] And on October 11 he warned that Czechoslovakia "by making difficulties over lost causes" risked losing still more.[92] According to the British sources, even the French attitude in this respect was "to do nothing to spoil the effects of Munich."[93]

Under these circumstances, the Czechoslovak minister in Berlin, Mastný, was perhaps right when he declared that it would almost have been better had Czechoslovakia not been represented on the International Commission at all.[94] For Germany remained intransigent in her demands regardless of who happened to be in power in Prague. In the Czechoslovak capital rumors circulated during the first days of October 1938 that it was only the fact that Dr. Beneš's still remained President which incensed Hitler and impelled him to increase his territorial demands. The protocol about the fifth zone was signed in Berlin at the very moment when the Prague radio announced Beneš's resignation. A few weeks later Berlin refused the slightest "prestige success" even to the new Czechoslovak Foreign Minister, Chvalkovský, who did not spare his assurances of loyalty to Germany.[95]

The detailed protocol dealing with the final frontier delimitation was to be signed in January 1939 in Dresden. All the documents were ready, but eventually the German delegation refused to sign them. It was apparent that Germany wanted to elude the promised guarantee of Czechoslovakia by thwarting the final action on frontiers. For, in the meantime, as we will see, Hitler had already issued his directions concerning the final dismemberment of Czechoslovakia, and the settlement decreed in Munich and implemented by the Berlin International Commission was thus destined to be only an interlude of brief duration.

* * *

The signature of the protocol of November 20 was followed by long negotiations on administrative and economic measures made necessary by the new delimitation of the frontiers. They dragged on and were not yet terminated when Germany occupied Prague in March of 1939. Other agreements were signed at the same time as the delimitation protocol: a treaty regarding nationality and option questions, a declaration on the protection of minorities and agreements on resumption of railroad communications and on the construction of an extraterritorial highway across Moravia and of an Oder-Danube canal.

The option treaty dealt with the questions of nationality in the annexed territory. According to it the Germans remaining in Czechoslovakia—with the exception of the German political refugees—could up to the 29th March, 1939, opt for German nationality. Vice versa, the Czechs who remained in the occupied territory could opt for Czechoslovak nationality.[96] More important, from the political point of view, was the declaration on the protection of minorities. The very term of "declaration" differentiated it from the other agreements. The German foreign ministry had prepared a draft of a special treaty dealing with this problem. However, at a conference in Heinrich Himmler's liaison office for ethnic Germans, *Volksdeutsche Mittelstelle,* on November 7, the representatives of the most interested German departments (Ministry of the Interior, Supreme Command of the Armed Forces, and Himmler's office) considered the plan for settlement by treaty to be premature. They did not wish to grant the Czech minority in Germany the position which they expected for the German group in Czechoslovakia. The intended declaration was to be couched in such general terms as not to commit Germany too deeply vis-à-vis the Czech ethnic group.[97] The final text reflects this standpoint. The declaration spoke of "preservation, free development and activities" of the minorities, but did not say how that protection would be guaranteed, leaving the decision on questions of principle and detail to a standing German-Czechoslovak governmental commission.[98] With these reservations on the German side, the protection of the large Czech minority in the Reich was illusory and the Czech population in the Sudeten territory was exposed to oppression.

Another important question for Czechoslovakia was the meaning of paragraph 2 of the Munich Agreement which specified that the evacuation should be completed "without any existing installations having been destroyed" and that Czechoslovakia would be held responsible for carrying out the evacuation "without damage to the said installations." The Germans tried to keep in the Sudeten territory the greatest possible quantity of products and raw materials whose shortage they already felt at home. When the International Commission took up this issue, it met immediately with difficulties. The Germans claimed not only the State and communal property but also that belonging to private Czech citizens. Finally they accepted, however, a compromise suggested by the Italian commercial attaché. According to the agreement signed on October 28, Czechoslovakia was to return the public and private property, the latter however only when it had previously served to public purposes.[99]

On October 27 a railroad agreement was signed, and on October 31 the railroad traffic between Germany and Czechoslovakia was resumed over some 50 frontier points.[100] A novelty which resulted from this agreement was German extraterritorial trains connecting Breslau and Vienna across Moravia. Czechoslovakia was compensated by the same rights of extraterritoriality for her trains crossing her former territory (e.g. in the Svitavy region).

In all these instances, Czechoslovakia had to retreat in the face of German pressures. The most revealing sign of the German attitude was, however, the way in which Germany forced upon Prague a convention on construction of an extraterritorial highway across Moravia.

As early as October 11, Hitler, in a conversation with Ribbentrop at Godesberg, gave him orders to sound out through ambassador Ritter at the Economic Committee of the International Commission, the possibilities of such an *Autobahn* which would follow the railroad Breslau—Brno—Vienna.[101] Two days later Ribbentrop discussed this proposal in Berlin with Chvalkovský who "agreed in principle."[102] On November 1, well ahead of the signing of any formal agreement, Hitler ordered Inspector General of German Highways, Dr. Fritz Todt, to prepare the construction.[103] Under Ribbentrop's prodding, the negotiations made rapid progress. On November 13, he demanded a quick, positive answer of Prague ("by tomorrow")[104] and the agreement was signed in Berlin on November 19.[105]

The highway was to be constructed by the German *Autobahn* company. Prague was to place the necessary strip of land at the German disposal free of all cost. The zone was to enjoy extraterritorial privileges while remaining under Czechoslovak sovereignty. From the moment of its opening the Reich would have in the zone all government prerogatives including the jurisdiction. The construction was to be in charge of the German government and the German company could use not only German but also Czechoslovak contractors, workers, materials, and tools, thus availing itself of the rich Czechoslovak economic potential at a time when the German resources were drained by an accelerated rearmament and the construction of the *Westwall*. According to the preliminary plan the highway was to be 78 km (about 48 miles) long and the construction was to be terminated in 1940. It did not materialize because of the war.[106]

Still another agreement was signed in Berlin on the same day: the German-Czechoslovak protocol on the construction of an Oder-Danube canal. Even this plan was thwarted by the war.[107]

The occupied Sudeten German territory was at first under military administration. On October 21, 1938, Konrad Henlein was appointed civil governor (*Statthalter*). The region extending from Furth im Walde in the Böhmerwald to Nový Jičín (Neu-Titschein) in Moravia formed the *Reichsgau Sudetenland*. Other parts of the annexed territory were attached to the adjacent German provinces. Liberec (Reichenberg) became the seat of Sudetenland administration.[108] On December 4, general elections were held in the *Gau*. Thanks to totalitarian methods the regime won 98.9% of votes. Forty one Sudeten German deputies were elected with Henlein and Karl Hermann Frank at their head.

The Czechs lost all their positions in the local Sudeten German self-government, all political parties were liquidated. Only one Czech newspaper was permitted, but it soon ceased to appear owing to lack of interest in a "streamlined" journal. Czech high schools were closed and only some elementary schools were maintained in agricultural localities with the Czech population. Numerous Czechs were arrested and the Czechoslovak legation in Berlin intervened in more than 300 cases of arrests from October to January.[109] From an area which was in the limelight of political interest in 1938 Sudetenland slowly sank to the status of a rather insignificant province administered by officials transferred there from the Reich. Its light consumer industry destined for export was in the later years of war effort less important for Germany than the heavy industry of Bohemia and Moravia to which Berlin payed by far a greater attention.[110]

Negotiations with Hungary

The negotiations between Prague and Budapest were of a different character. More than any other diplomatic talks originated in Munich, they reflected all problems and conflicts latent in this part of Europe. Thus, according to a Czech historian, "the eastern part of the Czechoslovak Republic became a point of intersection of power controversies, a diplomatic tilt-yard where Czechoslovak, German, Polish,

Hungarian, Rumanian, and Italian interests and indirectly those of other powers met."[1]

Militarily weak, Hungary had to rely more on the benevolence of the Axis powers than Poland. Moreover, Germany, having secured in Munich an overwhelming influence on Czechoslovakia, was not inclined to lose a territory over which she had just began to exert her control. Czechoslovakia, aware of the weakness of Budapest, was in no hurry to comply with its demands. Besides, her diplomatic personnel were engaged in other important negotiations and for technical reasons were not available for additional tasks. At the same time Prague was about to yield to Slovak and Ruthenian movement towards autonomy and had to devote its attention to the shifting situation in the eastern part of the state. Thus Hungary had to wait a full month for the implementation of the Munich clauses in the eastern part of Czechoslovakia. In the course of rather complicated negotiations she changed her line of conduct several times. On the whole her main support came from Italy, while Germany proceeded with a guarded reserve. For the first time, Berlin's ascendancy over Rome was becoming apparent. The British government warned Hungary against any harsh demands on Czechoslovakia.[2] Moreover, there were difficulties coming from Yugoslavia and Rumania. As early as October 1, Yugoslavia informed Hungary that she would not agree to the cession to Hungary of strictly Slovak and Ruthenian territory "as this might be dangerous for Yugoslavia" and the Rumanian government stated in Rome that it would have to reconsider its attitude should Hungary put forward claims to territory inhabited by a non-Hungarian population.[3] Rumania had an interest in direct land link with Czechoslovakia, a supplier of arms, "a secure line of communications with Central Europe," as King Carol explained to Hitler on November 24.[4]

On October 1st, to strengthen its position, the Hungarian government asked for the diplomatic support of the Reich to be able to increase its pressure on Prague. It got the German promise,[5] in reality, however, Germany assisted Hungary but to a limited degree. The line of German policy towards Slovakia, a matter of great consequence for Budapest, was crystallizing only in the first days of October. On the 6th the Supreme Command of the Armed Forces expressed the opinion that it was in the military interest of Germany that Slovakia not be separated from the Czechoslovak union but should remain with Czechoslovakia under strong German influence.[6] The following day this standpoint was repeated in a memorandum submitted by the Foreign Ministry to Hitler.[7] "The Hungarian solution" of the Slovak problem, expounded by the Hungarian envoy in Berlin, thus fell on deaf ears. Moreover, Hungary was just then dismayed by the advance of German influence to her immediate vicinity and made a futile demarche in Berlin to show her displeasure with the impending occupation of the Bratislava bridgehead of Petržalka by Germany.[8]

Though Italy was more inclined to listen to the Hungarian requests than Berlin, Hungary did not fare any better in Rome. The Hungarian minister there unceasingly repeated the demands of his government and on October 3, he revealed that Hungary intended to take over the whole of Slovakia. "An error, a gross error and I personally am against it," noted Ciano in his diary.[9] In Berlin, Attolico expressed to Weizsäcker the Italian opposition to the cession of Slovakia to Hungary.[10]

After the Munich conference, on October 1st, Hungary demanded the initiation of direct negotiations.[11] The Czechoslovak government, however, was still attempting to arrive at a solution within the framework of the Czechoslovak state and was delaying its decision. Consequently Hungary became more demanding. In a note delivered in the evening of October 3, she asked for preliminary acceptance of certain conditions: Czechoslovakia should immediately set free Hungarian political prisoners; make a token cession of two or three border towns which the Hungarian troops would immediately occupy. The note proposed to start direct negotiations at 4:00 P.M. on October 6 in Komárno.[12] Finally, however, it was agreed to start negotiations on Sunday, October 9, at 7:00 P.M.[13]

This postponement permitted Czechoslovakia to form an appropriate delegation. A Slovak autonomous government had just been formed whose members accepted the mission to plead the cause of Slovakia. Prime Minister Tiso was designated as chief of delegation. Sub-Carpathian Ruthenia was initially represented by Governor Ivan Parkányi and after the formation of the autonomous government of the region by minister Edmond Bačynśkyj.[14]

The Hungarian delegation was headed by Foreign Minister Kánya. Among its other members the most prominent were Count Pál Teleki, the Minister for Education, János Wettstein, the envoy in Prague, and Colonel Rudolf Andorka, the head of the army intelligence service.[15] Count Teleki, former Prime Minister, acted as the leading expert of the delegation. To the political motives he added his geographical determinism, and persisted in stressing strictly ethnographic principles without any regard for practical, especially economic considerations.[16] The delegation adopted a sharp tone ("not to negotiate, but to demand")[17] and scored its first success at the very beginning of the talks. The Slovak delegates agreed to an occupation by Hungary of the railroad station of Nové Mesto pod Šatorom (Sátoraljaújhely) and the town of Ipolské Šahy (Ipolyság).[18]

This "symbolic" occupation of the two places was the only point on which the two sides agreed. For the rest, agreement proved impossible. The first Hungarian proposals submitted on October 9 demanded an unconditional cession of territory "up to roughly the line Bratislava-Nitra-Levice-Rimavská Sobota-Rožňava-Košice-Užhorod-Mukačevo" which would have deprived both provinces of their most important towns and vital railroad connections. In addition the Hungarians were demanding plebiscites in two or three regions beyond this line.[19] The Hungarian memorandum presented to the Slovak delegation attempted once more to separate the Slovaks and the Ruthenes from Prague. It demanded self-determination of the Slovak and Carpatho-Ukrainian people and declared that Hungary harbored the warmest feelings for these alleged demands of both peoples.[20] It was of no avail. The Czechoslovak delegation retorted twice that the question of free disposition should lie outside the Komárno negotiations.[21] Simultaneously Ďurčanský declared to Göring in Karinhall that the Slovaks never wanted union with Hungary[22] and in Komárno Bačynškyj stressed the same day in his opening statement that the Carpatho-Ukrainian people had already made the decision about its fate: It wished to live as equal with the Czech and Slovak people in the Czechoslovak Republic.[23]

The Slovak delegation proposed on the 12th the cession of the Danube island of Velký Žitný ostrov with 1,840 sq. km and 105,000 inhabitants. Komárno—according to this proposal—would be declared a free harbor.[24] On the 13th, the Czechoslovak delegation made further concessions and offered a new line ceding to Hungary the southern part of Slovakia (Šamorin-Nové Zámky-Bálássgyarmat). On the whole 5,787 sq. km would be ceded with 400,000 inhabitants (320,000 Hungarians, 44,000 Slovaks and Ukrainians).[25] The Hungarians declared this offer unacceptable and in the evening of the same day their delegation finally broke off the negotiations.[26]

In the evening the Hungarian Council of Ministers deliberated over the next steps to be taken. The ministers decided to present the problem to the four Munich signatories and to order the partial mobilization.[27]

Another means of pressure was the agitation by the irredentist bands on the border. Hungary used such irregular troops (*Rongyos Gárda*, "Ragged Guard") after the First World War to combat the Austrians preparing to occupy the border region of Burgenland. In the spring of 1938 the idea of an irregular force was revived with the intention to use them in Slovakia and Sub-Carpathian Ruthenia. The volunteers of the free corps were deployed along the Slovak border in September, but played an active role only in October and November.[29] On October 1, Prime Minister Imrédy entrusted the former Minister of the Interior, Miklós Kozma, with their organization. Starting October 5 their small groups were crossing the border to Czechoslovakia where they committed several acts of sabotage and attempted to incite the population to insurrection.[30] According to Kánya up to October 12 about 700 to 800 men had been clandestinely sent over the border.[31] Several of them were taken prisoners. The Czechoslovak authorities then closed the frontier almost hermetically and proclaimed martial law in several districts of Sub-Carpathian Ruthenia. A few days later the whole frontier region between Bratislava and Košice was under martial law.[32] Czechoslovakia protested several times against these activities, but in vain.[33]

In her actions Hungary continued to rely strongly on the support of Poland. On October 6 Count Csáky visited Warsaw where he presented a rather curious proposal. He requested Polish aid in the Hungarian occupation of Sub-Carpathian Ruthenia. According to his request Poland should either participate in the occupation or carry it out herself and hand over the area to Hungary. It was a somewhat naive plan and Polish Foreign Minister Beck refused any military help. Poland, according to him, could support Hungary only diplomatically.[34] At the same time Poland, pursuing her aim of a common Polish-Hungarian frontier, urged Hungary ceaselessly to take energetic steps and even threatened that she would stop her cooperation if Hungary showed a lack of determination in this matter.[35]

In Berlin Poland was systematically backing the Hungarian demands and Ambassador Lipski tirelessly interceded for the annexation of Sub-Carpathian Ruthenia by Hungary. It was during a discussion of the future of that region on October 24 that Ribbentrop surprised him with the suggestion that in exchange for German support of Hungarian claims on this area the German-Polish problems could be solved in a radical way by the return of Danzig and the construction of a German extraterritorial highway across the Polish corridor.[36]

The diplomatic situation did not change after Komárno: indifference on the part of Germany, support, though limited, by Italy. Under these circumstances, Hungarian diplomacy increased its endeavors to get the support and approval of both its allies. When the partial mobilization was decreed, two prominent emissaries went to the Axis capitals to sound out their opinion about the Hungarian military measures and the whole of Budapest's demands. On the same day, October 14, former Prime Minister Darányi went to Munich and chief of the cabinet of the Ministry of Foreign Affairs, Count István Csáky, to Rome.[37]

Darányi met with Hitler's old aversion to the Hungarian nation which was strengthened by the wavering attitude of Budapest during the Munich crisis. The instructions that Hitler gave Ribbentrop in Godesberg earlier on October 11, provided only for a cession of regions with an incontestable Magyar majority. In principle Germany sympathized with Hungarian demands on Czechoslovakia, however, according to Hitler, she "could only draw the sword for German interests."[38]

Before he saw Darányi, Hitler received Chvalkovský and recommended to him a direct agreement with Budapest rather than a conference of Four as suggested by Hungary. In the presence of Darányi, Hitler could not, however, contain his bad mood, and the report of the meeting at which Keitel and Ribbentrop were also present is a long chain of anti-Hungarian polemic. Hitler reproached his visitor for the attitude of his country: he had given the Hungarians many warnings and told them that he would solve the Czechoslovak problem in October. The situation now was that, if it came to a conflict, "Hungary would be completely alone and the outcome would be very doubtful." As to the intention of Budapest to hold a plebiscite in the whole of Slovakia and Sub-Carpathian Ruthenia, Ribbentrop did not advise the Hungarians to do this, for the outcome was very doubtful. If the Slovaks and Carpatho-Ukrainians became independent, Hungary could then conclude a customs union or something of the kind with them, replied Darányi. Hitler thought this inadvisable and recalled the recent declarations of the Slovak leaders who "had been pestering the Germans with assurances that they did not want union with Hungary."

Hitler was against a conference of the four Munich signatories. Besides his contempt for the two western Powers, he undoubtedly did not wish their presence or interference in a matter which he regarded as purely of the German political interest. To Darányi he painted the outlook of such a meeting in black colors, without any hope of success. Instead he suggested bilateral negotiations between Prague and Budapest.[39]

While the results in Munich were meager, Hungary fared better in Rome. Csáky arrived there full of anti-German feelings and reproaching the Reich for having permitted the strengthening of Prague opposition. Mussolini approved of the Hungarian military measures and the suggestion to submit the controversy to a conference of four Powers. In his opinion the meeting could take place the following week on October 17 or 18 in Venice or on the island of Brioni, and would not involve the heads of government, but only the four foreign ministers.[40]

Even here the preponderant role of the Reich appeared in the functioning of the Axis. Under the effect of the harsh reception in Munich and from fear not to irritate Hitler still more, Hungary changed her attitude and later, the same day, Csáky returned to Ciano to inform him that Hungary was abandoning the plan for a four-Power conference and was accepting direct negotiations with Prague.[41] Thus the German standpoint won and the Italian moves on behalf of a four-Power conference were in vain. It left a disagreeable after-taste in Rome and Ciano complained in his diary[42] that for the first time Italy had been taken in tow.

Hungary had her own idea of direct negotiations. According to a memorandum sent to Berlin and Rome on October 17, it was up to Czechoslovakia to present a new proposal which Hungary would either accept or declare to be unsatisfactory. Hungary was requesting that Berlin intervene in Prague on behalf of this proposal. If the new Czechoslovak proposal were unacceptable, Hungary would ask the German and Italian governments to mediate or to arbitrate between Prague and Budapest.[43]

Before recommencing its negotiations with Hungary, Prague wanted to learn more about the attitude of the Reich, this time not through Chvalkovský, but through the representatives of the two provinces the most concerned about the Hungarian demands. The Slovaks, afraid that the Czechs were more compliant with Hungary than they, requested that Ribbentrop receive them. An official Slovak delegation, composed of Tiso and Ďurčanský and accompanied by the Carpatho-Ukrainian representative, Bačynškyj, arrived in Munich on October 19. The audience was granted at the request of Chvalkovský. Ribbentrop manifested an interest in the worries and aspirations of his guests and told them that he had instructed the German minister in Budapest to inform the Hungarians that they should renounce their claims to several towns which were vital for Slovakia. As for further negotiations, he recommended that they should be resumed in one or two days.[44]

Germany was reluctant to abandon large tracts of a state which she was preparing to occupy eventually and she suddenly seemed to side with her former adversary, Czechoslovakia. When Hungary proposed an arbitration by the Axis on October 20, Ribbentrop assumed a negative stand pretending that arbitration would end in displeasing both parties and that perhaps the Axis would have to impose its decisions by force. In the eyes of his Italian colleague he almost became "an advocate of Prague."[45] Only when he came to Rome on October 28 to press Italy to the conclusion of a military pact did he on this occasion yield to Ciano's arguments that a German-Italian arbitration would have its psychological effect on the other Balkan countries and would clearly demonstrate to them that Britain and France had finally vanished from the Balkan scene.[46]

Kánya qualified as "hard work" the talks which were taking place at those moments between the capitals of the Central European countries.[47] Hungarian patience was indeed put to a severe test owing to a partial reversal of the German attitude. A wave of irritation against the Reich was spreading in Hungary. In Rome, the only capital which was favorable to them, the Hungarians freely vented their indignation as shown in Ciano's diary.[48]

The new Czechoslovak proposals were submitted to the Hungarian minister in Prague on Saturday, October 22. Prague was ready to cede about 10,000 square kilometres, about 4,000 more than before, but less than 12,940 sq. km which Hungary demanded. The five towns demanded by Hungary, Bratislava, Nitra, Košice, Mukačevo, and Užhorod, would remain in Czechoslovakia.[49]

The Hungarian reply arrived in Prague on Monday the 24th. It expressed satisfaction with the agreement about an essential part of the Hungarian demands and formulated several counter proposals: 1. The Hungarian troops would occupy the undisputed areas within three days of October 27. 2. Disputed areas with the towns of Nitra, Košice, Užhorod, and Mukačevo were to be divided into eight sectors in which plebiscites based on the 1918 census were to be carried out by November 30 under international control. For Bratislava a special agreement was envisaged. Further, the Hungarian counter proposal asked for self-determination for all nationalities in Czechoslovakia. Without this Hungary could not guarantee the new Czechoslovak frontier. In case Czechoslovakia did not accept the proposed plebiscite, a decision was to be reached by arbitration between Germany and Italy with the inclusion of Poland for the eastern sector.[50]

On the following day, the Czechoslovak cabinet deliberated for more than eight hours. The Czechoslovak answer was handed over on October 26. It rejected the Hungarian demands for self-determination of all nationalities which veiled Hungary's aspiration for the recuperation of the whole of Slovakia and Sub-Carpathian Ruthenia. The note accepted the arbitrage by the two powers of the Axis. If they agreed to the participation of Poland, Prague would propose the inclusion of Rumania.[51]

Germany viewed the suggested Polish participation unfavorably. If accepted, the Polish presence could have meant complications concerning Sub-Carpathian Ruthenia the region where Germany intended to maintain her influence, at least temporarily. Consequently the inclusion of Poland was dropped. Under these circumstances the Czechoslovak suggestion to include Rumania as an arbiter also lapsed.[52]

The Hungarian answer, which was handed over on October 27, did not mention self-determination of the Slovaks and Ruthenes any more. Hungary accepted the suggestion that the arbitration should apply only to the disputed area with a Hungarian majority. Prague and Budapest then asked the Axis powers for arbitration. This was accepted and the place and date were fixed: Vienna on November 2.[53]

In spite of the fact that the omission of Great Britain and France was not entirely in the spirit of the Munich Agreement, neither of the western powers showed much interest in dealing with a tangled problem in an area which they were tacitly conceding to the influence of Germany. The French Foreign Minister indicated that he wished if possible to be left out of the matter.[54] According to his ambassador in Berlin a conference of four powers would be undecisive, as France would have to be on the side of Czechoslovakia, and Britain would support France.[55] As for Great Britain, she would have been ready to join in the discussion, but would have been happier if the problem were solved by the two Axis powers.[56]

The delegations assembled in Vienna on November 1st. Czechoslovakia was represented by Chvalkovský, the political director of his ministry, Ivan Krno, the Slovak General Rudolf Viest, the Slovak Prime Minister Tiso, the ministers Ďurčanský and Pavel Teplanský, and the Carpatho-Ukrainian minister Msgr. Augustin Vološyn.

In the morning of November 2 Ribbentrop had a preliminary talk with Ciano. He did not want to abandon even the three eastern towns (Košice, Užhorod, Mukačevo) and the discussion was at times quite animated.[57] The conference itself was opened at noon in the palace of Belvedere. After the introductory speeches of the two foreign ministers of the Axis, the two parties made their statement, minister Kánya for Hungary, Chvalkovský for Czechoslovakia. The Hungarian expert Teleki stressed the difficulties of the frontier line at Nitra and Košice; the Czechoslovak expert Krno pointed out that the magyarization had reached its culminating point in 1910. In the places where there was a Magyar majority in that year, the Slovaks were preponderant in, for instance, 1880. Teleki retorted by quoting the documents from the 18th century. Kánya intervened: The Munich Agreement had only one fault, namely that the period of three months for the solution of these questions was too long. In his final statement Ribbentrop did not fail to react to this remark of the Hungarian minister, reminding him that it was a result of the co-operation of the German and Italian governments with the two other powers at Munich that the question of the Hungarian minority had been brought near any solution at all.[58]

With the exception of Bratislava and Nitra, Ciano was able to carry through all Hungarian demands. Carpatho-Ukraine, however, remained in Czechoslovakia. As Ciano declares self-complacently in his diary, Ribbentrop's lack of preparation permitted him to cut in favor of Hungary the territorial zones which in reality could have been a subject of numerous and heated controversies.[59]

The text of the award was announced to the representatives of the two parties at 7:00 P.M. Chvalkovský grew pale, Kánya remained impassive and in a whisper expressed his satisfaction to the Italian diplomat

Magistrati. The Hungarian minister in Rome, Frigyes Villani, wept.[60] The text was a brief document of seven paragraphs. The evacuation was to begin on November 5, and to be completed by November 10. A Hungarian-Czechoslovak commission was to deal with the questions of nationality and option (par.4). Another commission was, among other things, to take special care of the Magyar ethnic group in Bratislava (par.5). The main part of the document was the map of the new frontier.[61]

In all, Czechoslovakia lost 11,833 square kilometers (4,569 sq. mi.) with 972,092 inhabitants (1930) of whom 53.9% were Magyars. Slovakia lost 10,390 sq. km (4,012 sq. mi.) with 854,217 inhabitants, Carpatho-Ukraine 1,463 sq. km (557 sq. mi.) with 117,875 inhabitants. Hungary acquired 347,849 Slovaks, Ukrainians and Czechs, i.e. 35.8% of the whole population ceded by Czechoslovakia. In Czechoslovakia only 167,737 Magyars remained. The Slovak population in Hungary rose to almost half a million.[62] Of the largest towns occupied, Košice had 70,000 inhabitants, Užhorod 27,000. Among the smaller towns ceded to Hungary were Nové Zámky, Levice, Rimavská Sobota, Rožňava, Mukačevo, and Berehovo. The area of Hungary increased by 13%, her population by 11.7%. The occupied territory was a rich agricultural region grown with grain and sugar beets. In its central regions were vast forests and important ore and coal deposits. The southern part of Carpathian Ukraine had famous vinyards. Czechoslovakia lost almost the entire railroad line Komárno-Bratislava and 150 km of the oldest railroad of ancient Hungary which connected Budapest and Vienna via Nové Zámky and Bratislava. The entire line Košice—Užhorod—Mukačevo—Berehovo, 200 km long, was also lost, leaving thus Ruthenia without any railroad connection with the rest of the state. Of the Danube bank, which before the Vienna Award formed the frontier in the length of 150 kilometers, only a short sector from Devín to Bratislava remained in Czechoslovakia. The harbor of Komárno, in which Czechoslovakia had invested 61 million crowns prior to 1936, went to Hungary. Komárno possessed a shipyard of the Škoda Works and was also an important military base.

The occupation started on November 5. At 10:00 A.M. all church bells in Hungary began to peal. The poorly equipped units of the Hungarian army crossed the Danube on pontoon bridges north of the towns of Györ and Magyarovár near the Hungarian-German border.[63] Komárno was occupied on the 6th and Regent Horthy, in admiral's uniform and mounted on a white horse, entered the recovered territory. Košice was occupied on November 10. Horthy made there a speech in which he thanked Germany and Italy for the Vienna Award and recalled the friendship with Poland. At the same time he assured "the brothers of other origin than Magyar" that "the love of the Hungarian hearts was awaiting them and guaranteed them full liberty of language and culture."[64]

Hungary lived in a festive mood. Lord Rothermere came to Budapest.[65] The old propagator of the revision of the Trianon Treaty took part in the entry in Košice of Regent Horthy. He was received everywhere with enthusiasm which embarrassed the Hungarian government, all too aware of the British-German tensions. The lord was discretely asked to send greeting telegrams to the Axis capitals to paralyze the uneasiness which could have been created by these Anglophile demonstrations.[66]

From the occupied regions news of the unfriendly treatment of the newly acquired minorities soon arrived. Almost at the same moment, when remarks made by Horthy in Košice were published, news of quite a different kind, about the measures against the Slovaks reached Bratislava. As early as November 15, the organ of the Slovak Populist Party, *Slovák*, stated that the intolerant spirit of old Hungarian bureaucracy and gendarmery persisted in Hungary: "The spirit of the great Hungarian father of fatherland Deák is constantly trampled down." The situation was, above all, tense in the Velký Žitný ostrov, where the Hungarians wanted to expel several hundreds of the Slovak families who had been there since 1919.

Several incidents occurred, the most serious one at Šurany at Christmas where the Hungarian gendarmes used firearms against the Slovak demonstrators.[67] The Slovaks even attempted to reorganize Hlinka's People's party in the region ceded to Hungary. The founding congress was to meet in Nové Zámky in the presence of Prime Minister Tiso on February 12, 1939. Budapest took a negative stand, however, and the meeting did not materialize.[68]

* * *

The Vienna Award left Carpatho-Ukraine (Sub-Carpathian Ruthenia), though amputated, in Czechoslovakia. The efforts of Hungarian and Polish diplomacy had failed. In spite of this, Hungary was not abandoning the hopes of securing her ends by skilfully creating trouble in Czechoslovakia and influencing her two Axis friends. At the cabinet meeting in Budapest on November 6, the occupation of Carpatho-Ukraine within the next two weeks was designed as the most urgent aim of the Hungarian foreign policy.[69] On November 15, Regent Horthy told German minister Erdmannsdorff that "in the event of an explosion" in Carpatho-Ukraine, Hungarian troops would march in and remain there "until the population was guaranteed the right of self-determination."[70]

On November 19, Germany notified Budapest of her opposition. The German minister stated that Germany objected to the action envisaged by the Regent. "If Hungarian action gave rise to difficulties, continued Erdmannsdorff, Germany could not support Hungary."[71] Similarly Italy opposed the Hungarian intentions. Ciano indicated clearly that Italy disapproved of the Hungarian plans and intended to proceed in this affair in agreement with Berlin.[72]

For the next move in their diplomatic efforts, the Hungarians used the German verbal note of November 19. Though this statement expressed clearly the German opposition to their plans, the Hungarians interpreted one of its sentences as a conditional approval. They concluded that they could act, without, however, expecting any help from Berlin. This interpretation then served as basis of the campaign started by the Hungarians in Rome.

On November 20 or shortly before, the Hungarian military attaché, Lieutenant-Colonel Vitéz Szabó, called on Mussolini and declared that the situation in Carpatho-Ukraine was becoming more and more untenable and that the Hungarian government was going to occupy the country within the next 24 hours. Szabó mentioned the German declaration and stated that his government had concluded that Germany did not in principle disapprove of this action, but was only apprehensive for Hungary.[73] Persuaded by these arguments, Mussolini promised to send air force units to support the Hungarian action. At first he had offered 12 fighter squadrons, but because of the lack of airfield accomodations, Hungary could accept only eight, i.e. 96 aircraft. Fifty aircraft were to have arrived on November 20, but fog reported from the Hungarian town of Szombathely prevented them from leaving Gorizia.[74]

Berlin learned quickly of Szabó's audience with Mussolini. The same day, November 20, Attolico called on Ribbentrop to sound out the Germans. The German minister manifested his strong opposition and declared that the Hungarian interpretation of the German statement was wrong. Attolico defended the Hungarians and stated that in that case they had obviously misunderstood the German message. Ribbentrop would, however, not even admit the possibility of a misunderstanding. In the afternoon he consulted with Hitler and handed over to Attolico a communication for Mussolini. The message stated that the German government was "extremely surprised at the interpretation of its reply to Hungary." Hitler was of the opinion that a Hungarian occupation would discredit the Axis powers whose decision Hungary had unconditionally accepted three weeks ago. "Hungary was playing a frivolous game if she intervened by force now and she would bear the full responsibility for all eventual consequences."[75]

Mussolini was thus in a serious imbroglio. He telegraphed to Berlin that he deeply regretted that an attempt had been made to depict to him the situation "completely at variance with the truth." He agreed with Hitler that the Hungarian action would seriously weaken the prestige of the Axis, and promised to join a German-Italian demarche in Budapest if Hitler thought it necessary.[76]

In Budapest, in the meantime, the preparations were culminating. Though November 20 was a Sunday, full staffs were on duty at the war ministry and the foreign ministry. The disappointment was not long in coming. In the morning of Monday, November 21, Ribbentrop handed over to Attolico the draft of a protest note to Budapest approved by Hitler and requested that Attolico ask Mussolini if he was ready to make similar representations in the Hungarian capital. About midday Ciano replied by telephone that Italy shared the German view and would make a demarche in Budapest. At the same time he complained that Hungary had not informed him correctly.[77] At Obersalzberg, Hitler himself was following the situation closely. A copy of the German note to Budapest was to be handed over to Polish Foreign Minister Beck.[78]

The demarche of the German and Italian minister in Budapest took place the same day, in the evening. The German note mentioned the Hungarian communication to the Italian government according to which Hungary intended to begin military operations for the occupation of Carpatho-Ukraine, and mentioned also the German misgivings expressed to Hungary earlier. It protested above all against the mistaken interpretation of the German step of November 19, and pointed out that Hungary by her signature in Vienna recognized the frontier of Carpatho-Ukraine as final. If she now used armed forces she might be placed morally in a very difficult position and would discredit the two arbitrating powers. "The German government therefore feels justified in expecting Hungary to abide by the Award." Berlin used still another argument: An incursion into Carpatho-Ukraine might meet with Czechoslovak armed resistance. "Judging by the relative strength of both armies, which is known to the German government, Hungary might in that case run into a difficult, not to say critical, military situation." And Germany would not be in a position to render assistance of any kind to Hungary. On Ribbentrop's instructions, Erdmannsdorff, in an oral commentary, expressed to Kánya Germany's astonishment at the Hungarian attitude. The Italian minister Vinci confined himself to delivering the note.[79]

The direct action had thus failed and Czechoslovakia kept her eastern province. Toward the end of November the Hungarian troops concentrated near the frontier were withdrawing.[80] Beck decided to leave a detachment of frontier-guards near the border. However, the tension continued and the Carpatho-Ukrainian territory was harrassed by the incursions of terrorist bands coming from Poland and Hungary to provoke troubles and perpetuate insecurity.

Negotiations with Poland

The Polish will to be treated as a Great Power and the feeling of independence toward the Reich had a serious impact on Prague in the difficult days of the September crisis. Munich was a decisive milestone in the controversy between Prague and Warsaw. As in the case of Hungary, Prague had to make concessions. In Munich, Poland was promised that her demands would not be forgotten, however, in the Polish eyes this success was of a rather dubious character. To shift the Polish demands to the last paragraph of the Agreement, to put them on the same level as the demands of Hungary, to postpone the implementation for three months, all this offended foreign minister Beck and led him to manifest all the more his energy and decision.[1]

In the morning of September 30 a conference on the situation created by the Munich Agreement was held in the office of President Mościcki. Besides Beck, Marshal Śmigly-Rydz, Prime Minister Felician Slawoj-Skladkowski and Vice-premier Eugeniusz Kwiatkowski were present. Beck would have liked to send General Bortnowski, commander of the Polish troops concentrated near the Czechoslovak border, immediately to the Těšín territory as a sort of protest against the proceedings of the Munich conference.[2] In the end it was agreed to send the Polish demands "in the categorical form of an ultimatum" to Prague. In the early afternoon Beck showed his closest advisors the contents of a note to be sent to Czechoslovakia the same day by air so as to reach Prague before midnight. "After which our troops will immediately enter Cieszyn."[3]

Shortly before 1:00 P.M., when the meeting deliberating with Mościcki was closing, the Czechoslovak answer to the Polish note of September 27 was handed to the minister of Poland in Prague. Czechoslovakia assured Poland that the frontier would be rectified and the controversial territory ceded regardless of the development of the international situation. The territory would be transferred at the latest on December 1, i.e. one month earlier than the delay set at Munich.[4] The note, sent by airplane, reached Warsaw at 5:30 P.M.

Given the mood in the Polish capital, the Czechoslovak answer could not have been satisfactory and did not change the stand adopted in the morning in the office of President Mościcki. Returning at 10:00 P.M., the same plane brought the second Polish note to Prague. On Beck's order it was to be delivered to Krofta before midnight. In his instructions for the Polish minister Beck ordered: "Please do not accept any discussion on the substance of the note. It is a demand *à prendre ou à laisser*" (in French in the text).[5] Papée delivered the note to Krofta at 11:40 P.M.

The note rejected the Czechoslovak answer as "completely insufficient and dilatory" stating harshly that the Polish government could no longer place faith in Czechoslovak declarations. The note therefore demanded that the town and the suburbs of Těšín be evacuated in the 24 hours starting at noon, October 1 (i.e. practically speaking within 12 hours). The remainder of the territory was to be ceded within ten days following October 1. Until noon of October 1, Warsaw was expecting "an unequivocal answer accepting or rejecting the Polish demands." To accentuate her demands, Poland announced the same day unofficially to Prague that she was concentrating ten divisions in the neighborhood of Těšín.[6]

Beck stayed up the greater part of the night, going to bed only toward the morning[7] and the chief of his cabinet, Count Michal Lubieński, took over the duty. The atmosphere was tense. The report of the British ambassador, Sir Howard Kennard, speaks with irony of officials in the Polish foreign ministry looking ostentatiously at their wristwatches "as if at five minutes past twelve the whole of Poland's might would be unleashed."[8]

Germany, in this delicate situation, was maintaining a friendly attitude. Beck, in spite of his disappointment over the Munich results, expressed to Berlin his thanks for the interest shown in Munich in the Polish demands. At the same time (in the evening of September 30) he asked for a benevolent attitude on the part of Germany in case of an armed conflict between Poland and Czechoslovakia.[9] At about noon on October 1st, when the delay set by the Polish ultimatum to Czechoslovakia was expiring, Ribbentrop promised the Polish ambassador that in the case of such an armed conflict, the German government would maintain a friendly attitude toward Poland.[10] Göring, whom Lipski saw immediately after his meeting with Ribbentrop, was more ebullient. "Overjoyed by the results of the Munich conference," he asked Lipski, with regard to the Polish ultimatum to Prague, why Poland was asking for so little, and why she did not want to annex Moravská Ostrava.[11]

The Polish pressure threatening to upset the precarious détente achieved at Munich raised concern among other signatories of the Munich Agreement. On October 1st British ambassador Henderson expressed to Lipski the misgivings of his government, pointing out the disastrous consequences military action against Czechoslovakia would entail for Poland during such a delicate international period.[12] Immediately afterwards Lipski was called by Italian ambassador Attolico, who "was hurt and accused us [Poland] of undermining Mussolini's work: the result of Munich, which had saved peace."[13] Italian foreign minister Ciano ordered the Italian ambassador in Warsaw to warn Beck against unnecessary impatience. "They [the Poles] have waited twenty years, they can wait another day or two and avoid an incident which might make the situation difficult again."[14]

In Warsaw, early in the morning of October 1, the ambassadors of Great Britain and France made urgent démarches to recommend patience. Kennard offered British mediation and advised against any hasty military measures.[15] Léon Noël, the French ambassador, declared that the Polish measures were "particularly inadmissible and full of risks for Poland in the future" and drew attention to a possible Soviet reaction.[16] Lubieński made the impression on Noël that his government was beginning to be uneasy about the possible consequences of its gesture. The orders were given to the Polish army to cross the border at noon if Czechoslovakia did not cede at that time, he declared. However, Lubieński added, if the train has left, it was perhaps still time to stop it on the way.[17]

When Beck rose in the morning of October 1, Lubieński reported to him the demarches of the two ambassadors. At 11 A.M. he sent Kennard a message saying that Poland could not accept the British offer of mediation "as it is too late." With a certain amount of irony, Kennard asked Lubieński, who delivered the message, whether he seriously wished him to wire this to London. At this moment Beck asked Kennard by telephone to visit him.

In the course of the audience, which lasted half an hour, Beck, as Kennard reported later, changed his stand three times. At first he refused categorically British mediation on the ground that it was too late. Then, when Kennard protested, he became more moderate. At that stage he was called to the telephone. When he returned he announced that the Czechoslovak government had requested a one-hour extension of the deadline, and that he had granted it. The conversation with the British diplomat then ended on a cordial tone.[18]

In Prague the cabinet thought it impossible to start a conflict with Poland while the German troops were marching into other parts of Czechoslovakia and recognized the necessity to cede the territory demanded by Poland. Simultaneously with the session of the cabinet, President Beneš was discussing the problem with the representatives of the political parties. The discussion led to the same conclusion. At 11 A.M. the cabinet met with the President presiding and decided to accept the ultimatum, asking at the time for a one-hour extension.[19]

The Polish minister in Prague got the text of the Czechoslovak answer at 12:30 P.M.[20] and transmitted it to Warsaw by telephone at 12:50

P.M.[21] The note, signed by Krofta, was relatively brief. It stated that Czechoslovakia agreed to a much shorter time-table than fixed by the Munich Agreement. The Prague government considered its offer of the preceding day as just and equitable. Forced by circumstances it accepted, however, the Polish proposals and suggested an immediate meeting of military experts to reach agreement about the procedure to follow. At the same time Czechoslovakia was asking for maintenance even after the occupation of the traffic on the railroad line Bohumín-Žilina, the only means of communication between the two halves of the state.[22]

The evacuation began as agreed on October 2. The troops halted on the first day when they had occupied a circle about 18 kilometers in diameter around Český Těǎín.[23] On October 10 the Polish troops entered Orlová and Karvinná thus ending the occupation. There was great nervousness everywhere and there were some local incidents.[24]

The case of Bohumín (Oderberg), an important railroad junction in the territory to be ceded by Czechoslovakia, was somewhat complicated. During his talks with Hitler on September 20 in Berchtesgaden, Lipski claimed this place, "prolongation of railroad communications until the railroad station of Bohumín-Oderberg."[25] On the map accompanying the Godesberg memorandum Bohumín was, however, situated in the territory marked in red, i.e. as the area to be ceded to Germany on October 1. The part of the region of Těšín to the west of the line Moravská Ostrava-Frýdek was designated as the plebiscite area. According to Ribbentrop's instructions of October 3, the Poles were to be told that the inclusion of Bohumín in the Polish zone would present Germany with a new situation.[26] Eventually Germany changed her stand and Hitler declared on October 5 that he had no interest in Bohumín.[27]

Poland, however, was afraid that the local German *Ordner* units might seize Bohumín before the Polish army and for that reason, in spite of the German good will, she preferred to act quickly. In the morning of Sunday, October 9, the Polish troops entered Bohumín, though according to the original plans the town was not to be occupied until two days later.[28]

Warsaw acquired at this stage two districts, Fryštát and Český Těšín, where according to the Czechoslovak census of 1930 there were about 227,000 inhabitants, of whom 121,000 were of Czechoslovak nationality and 76,000 of Polish origin.[29] Eight per cent were Germans. Czechoslovakia lost eight coal mines representing 45% of her total coal production (63.5% of the production of the Ostrava-Karvinná basin). Besides this, Poland acquired five of ten local cokeries. Their quality equalled the best German coke and was welcome to Poland whose metallurgy lacked the coke appropriate for her iron-poor ore.[30]

Thousands of refugees without money and shelter flocked to Moravská Ostrava after the occupation and the authorities had to organize public kitchens for the poor. From the town of Těšín not only the Czechs but also the Germans were fleeing. The number of refugees and expellees was variously estimated from 20,000 to 34,000 persons.[31]

Until October 24 the area was under military administration. The governor (*wojwoda*) of Silesia Michal Grazynski sent his deputy Léon Malhome as a civil delegate who started a harsh regime directed against the non-Polish population. Only Polish sign posts were allowed and not one Czech school remained in the region. All Czech associations were dissolved and their property confiscated.[32] This comportment in the occupied territory gave raise to several protests from both the Czechoslovak and German sides.[33]

The Polish claims, however, were not yet fully satisfied. On the day following the end of the occupation, Beck summoned his advisors to discuss new demands to be put to Czechoslovakia. Poland was once more claiming the border regions of northern Slovakia in Spiš and Orava which had been refused to her after the First World War.[34] The territorial claims that Beck tried to resuscitate were of a rather delicate nature. They concerned the territory of Slovakia whose feelings Warsaw wanted to spare with regard to future possible developments. The Polish policy following the occupation of the Těšín territory was by no means clear.[35] Like other problems in this part of Europe even the Polish-Slovak relations were developing under the shadow of the growing German power. Warsaw would have welcomed an attachment of Slovakia to Hungary or an independent Slovakia leaning on Poland. A Slovakia remaining in close connection with Prague in a state increasingly dominated by Germany was the least satisfactory settlement for Poland. When after Žilina it became clear that it was just this third solution which prevailed, Beck's policy was somewhat taken aback and had to adapt to the given situation.

When Beck gave Papée new instructions on October 11 he recommended that he proceed according to the developments of a delicate situation and to decide with whom he would deal—with the Slovaks or with the Prague government. In the first case the demands should be limited. On the other hand, if he negotiated with the Czechs, he had to put forward maximum demands. "Treat the Slovaks with much prudence in order not to repel them," were Beck's instructions.[36]

In spite of this reserve the Polish demands met with violent resistance in Bratislava and caused deep despair. While at the beginning of October there was some talk in Žilina about the federation of Slovakia with Catholic Poland,[37] a few weeks later the Slovaks were faced with territorial demands of their potential ally. The old adherent of Polish-Slovak co-operation, Karol Sidor, went therefore to Warsaw on October 19 to negotiate. He was received by Under-Secretary Jan Szembek to whom he exposed the principles of the policy of new Slovak government. He explained the intention to build an entirely independent Slovak state and suggested making it "a sort of political and military protectorate of Poland." However, he warned Szembek, that the Polish demands in Spiš and Orava were damaging the pro-Polish sympathies of the Slovak people. The Polish diplomat was plain-spoken: "If we have to deal with an independent Slovak state this question will not present any difficulties, because we will have no territorial demands on an independent Slovakia." It was difficult to convince Sidor, who reproached the Poles for wanting to tear from Slovakia "a piece of live flesh" and asked for adjournment of the debate on this issue.[38] Sidor's visit did not change the Polish standpoint and on October 22 Papée presented new demands in Prague.[39]

In the course of negotiations in the last days of October, Poland added other demands in the region of Těšín, in the neighborhood of Slezska Ostrava.[40] Later, however, she gave up all claims in this region and insisted only on the rectification in the mountaineous areas on the northern border of Slovakia.[41] The tone of the Polish interventions was as harsh as during the negotiations for the Těšín area. On October 29 Warsaw asked for "an immediate realization" of its demands and warned that it would not hesitate to use "the most energetic means" to satisfy them.[42]

Papée summed up these demands to Chvalkovský on October 31 at noon and asked for an answer by 5:00 P.M. of the same day. The following day, on November 1st, shortly before the departure of Chvalkovský for Vienna, he came again and brought a note with the final Polish demands. Chvalkovský ordered an immediate reply which repeated verbatim the Polish requests and accepted them almost to the full extent. The Czechoslovak minister was in a great hurry. The negotiations were for the most part verbal and Chvalkovský took the pertinent documentation with him to Vienna to show it to Ribbentrop.[43] Apparently he was trying to avoid in Vienna the reproach that the dispute with Poland had not yet been settled. He also wanted to gain a free hand in the settlement of Hungarian demands, while attempting to improve the Czechoslovak position. On the Polish side, the same striving for an independent action was apparent on the eve of the Vienna Award as in the days of the Munich crisis.[44]

The Polish note was a lengthy document enumerating in detail all the new rectifications. The suggested frontier line followed the Oder from Bohumín (already in Polish hands) to Hrušov which—as well as Slezská

Ostrava—remained in Czechoslovakia. In Slovakia two areas were to be ceded to Poland. The first one north of Čadca, an important railroad junction, which remained on the Slovak side of the new border. The second sector was the mountain massif of Javorina. Moreover, there were other small rectifications farther east.[45] By November 30 all territorial adjustments were completed.[46]

The occupation was accompanied by several incidents. The Poles were accused of some minor faits accomplis. So the Slovak News Agency reported on November 26 that shots were exchanged between Polish and Slovak soldiers when the Polish units crossed the demarcation line on the creek of Černianka and occupied the village of Čierné near Čadca in the Slovak territory. At Oravský Podzámok the Slovaks erected a barricade on the route of the autobus transporting the Polish demarcation commission. On November 27 there were incidents when Javorina was occupied, and Prague had to offer its excuses in Warsaw.[47]

The Slovaks were offended by the conduct of the Poles, and the populist organ, *Slovák* stated that they would keep it in painful memory. The mutual relations cooled off and this change did not escape Warsaw. On November 22, *Kuryer Warszawski* stated in its editorial that the columns of the *Slovák* did not contain articles favorable to Poland as frequently as before. The Polish paper deplored it and considered it as an unfortunate sign of the new situation that the Slovak poet Andrej Žarnov, a known translator from the Polish, had broken with the Polish poets as a result of the Polish conduct. In the view of the British minister Newton Poland was faced with a hostile and disillusioned Slovakia which was turning for assistance not to Warsaw, but to Berlin.[48] In the German campaign against Poland in 1939, western Slovakia became one of the bases of the German attack.[49]

CHAPTER II
THE NEW CZECHO-SLOVAKIA

A Painful Balance Sheet

After the territorial surgery of October and November 1938, Czechoslovakia—or according to the new spelling: Czecho-Slovakia—lost almost one-third of her area and one third of her population. In her new frontiers she had 99,579 square kilometers (38,060 square miles) with about ten million inhabitants. Above all, the ratio of nationalities which gave Hitler the justification for his moves was changed. The German minority fell to less than 444,000, the Hungarian minority was considerably diminished (168,000) and the number of Poles was almost nonexistent (5,500).[2]

The loss of the industrial regions of the Sudeten borderland meant a considerable weakening of the economic potential of the country. Czechoslovakia lost about 40% of her industrial capacity. In the industrial regions of western and northern Bohemia ceded to Germany, light industry had predominated and thus these losses were heavier than those of heavy industry. Textile production suffered severely (60.6%), especially in the field of exportation. Further losses were: half of the paper production, more than one-fourth of the beer production, one-fourth of the fruit trees, and one-fourth of forests. Czechoslovakia lost 54.7% of her coal, 93.2% of the lignite production, 35.3% of coke and 17% of iron ore production.[3]

A disquieting phenomenon was the unemployment. In the course of the winter of 1938–39 it more than doubled (77,000 end October, 104,000 in November, 148,000 December, 187,000 January, 172,000 February 1939).[4] About 146,000 persons fled from the border areas, among them 125,000 Czechs, 11,600 Germans and 7,500 Jews. An Institute for the Care of Refugees was founded in November to find shelter for the newcomers, to integrate them in the economic life and to facilitate emigration of those intending to leave the country. Toward the end of January about 12,000 refugees were in mass shelters in castles, camps and other places. In the very first weeks of the Institute's operation about 4,000 persons emigrated.[5]

The international public opinion manifested a great interest in the fate of the refugees. In Great Britain several organizations collected considerable sums to support them. The Lord Mayor of London, Sir Harry Twyford, and the League of Nations High Commissioner for Refugees, Sir Neill Malcolm, arrived in Czechoslovakia to distribute first aid and to try to solve the problems of the future of the refugees.[6]

Germany demanded the immediate return of the German refugees who had fled the Nazi regime in the years before Munich, were residing in the occupied zones on October 1 and then had escaped to Czechoslovakia. It seems that at first the Czechoslovak authorities were returning them within 48 hours to the Sudeten territory. Sir Neill Malcolm, accompanied by John W. Wheeler-Bennett and the chief of the French military mission, General Louis Faucher, tried to intercede with Prime Minister Syrový, but without success.[7] However, as from October 15, the American minister, Wilbur Carr, saw that in spite of the inflexible attitude adopted by Syrový during his conversation with Malcolm, the subordinate organs had apparently received the order not to apply this measure in the cases when the life of the refugees would be imperiled. The German democratic circles estimated that about two or three thousand persons could be in serious danger, including women and children.[8]

The economic situation and the problem of the refugees forced Prague to seek financial aid abroad. Negotiations of a loan were initiated by the Czechoslovak government with London in October. On October 2 Prague appealed to Great Britain: The new Czechoslovakia had to assist her citizens coming from the occupied territory without delay, at a moment when her economy was weakened by loss of the Sudeten areas.[9] To meet these needs the government was asking for a loan of 30 million pounds. This demand was received favorably at first in London then in Paris. Lord Halifax recalled the old proverb "He who gives quickly gives twice," and on October 15 an advance of 10 million pounds was agreed.

On October 15, Prague sent a memorandum on a larger financial assistance to London and Paris.[10] In the meantime, however, the situation had changed unfavorably. First doubts were expressed freely in the British Parliament and press: Will not the money granted to Czechoslovakia eventually profit Germany on which Czechoslovakia was apparently more and more dependent? On the other hand, wasn't there a possibility of an anti-Semitic policy in Prague? The financial negotiations then in progress could be used to force Czechoslovakia to moderation and to assist the Jewish minority to the same degree as the refugees of the German nationality. On October 18 the Czechoslovak negotiators in Paris appeared discouraged to find the view gaining ground in France that Czechoslovakia must now "inevitably become a German protectorate."[11] Two weeks later the Czechoslovak minister,

Štefan Osuský, reported from Paris that Great Britain was putting on the brakes and that the negotiations were deadlocked.[12] On November 3, Bonnet told Osuský that France was ready to grant financial assistance to a neutral Czechoslovakia, not to a country gravitating so visibly towards Germany.[13]

At the beginning of December, London decided against any new financial assistance and against exportation credits. The negotiations scheduled to begin at mid-December were to limit themselves only to the matter of which part of the advance was to be taken for a free gift. In agreement with Paris the British government decided that 4 million out of the advance should be treated as such. The remaining 6 million would be a loan guaranteed by London and Paris. Czechoslovakia was to undertake to provide certain sums of foreign exchange for all refugees who emigrate "without discrimination on religious, political or racial grounds."[14]

Czechoslovakia was disappointed. She had hoped—as remarked Dr. Ivan Krno, chief of the political division of the foreign ministry—to the British minister Newton—that the British government "would show their interest and practical sympathy not only for the Jews and the German Social Democrats but also for the Czechs and Slovaks."[15] When the assistance was promised in October, Czechoslovakia hoped she would be able to use it for her economic reconstruction and in the 10 million pounds she saw the first installment which could later be enlarged. The arguments presented in this respect by the Governor of the Czechoslovak National Bank, Dr. Jaroslav Pospíšil, had a stimulating effect,[16] and on January 27, 1939, a British-French-Czechoslovak agreement was signed at the Foreign Office in London. The British government considered as a free grant to Czechoslovakia 4 million pounds of sterling out of the advanced 10 million. This sum of 4 million was to be paid into a special account and to be used to provide foreign exchange for refugees. According to the same agreement the French government took over from Czechoslovakia responsibility for the interest on the 5% Czechoslovak loan of 1937–42 and its repayment. The nominal value of this loan issued in France amounted to 700 million francs (4 million pounds sterling). The interest Czechoslovakia would have to pay was also to be used to provide foreign exchange for the refugees.

The total financial assistance given by Great Britain and France to Czechoslovakia amounted to approximately 16 million pounds. About 8 million pounds (4 million from Great Britain and 700 million francs representing the French loan) were granted as a free gift and set apart to refugees who intended to emigrate. The remaining 8 million, the proceeds of the guaranteed Franco-British loan, were to be used for the relief and settlement of refugees in Czechoslovakia and, so far as not required for that purpose, they were to be utilized for the economic reconstruction. Thus the aid for this purpose was minimal.[17]

Bohemia and Moravia (The Czech Lands)

Munich created unprecedented confusion in the minds of the Czech people. Not understanding the underlaying causes and circumstances of the catastrophe, people were led in many cases to hasty conclusions about alleged culprits and past errors. In this agitated state of mind they were prone to rejecting their traditional values and their past representatives only because they had temporarily failed. Detailed news was scarce and it was at times difficult to distinguish the truth from mere rumors.[18] "I feel as if a herd of runaway bulls had trampled over me," said the Czech author Karel Čapek.[19] The American minister in Prague, Wilbur J. Carr, spoke of "a nation in bereavement but momentarily benumbed by the magnitude of the situation."[20]

The right-wing press reacted to the Munich defeat with violent attacks on outgoing President Beneš and the traditions which he represented.[21] Some rightist circles, formerly opposed to Beneš, entertained vain hopes that the relations between Prague and Berlin would at last clear up and a peaceful co-existence would emerge after the era of the uncompromising Beneš policy. They imagined that their moment had come and that the events were vindicating their doubts about the former direction of Czechoslovak diplomacy.

A series of minor symptoms indicated the new situation. The representatives of the fallen regime retired or were dismissed. The Czechoslovak minister in London, Jan Masaryk, resigned on December 5 after fourteen years of service in London as counsellor and as minister.[22] October 28, the twentieth anniversary of the foundation of the Republic, was not a holiday, but a working day observed by manifestations of sad sobriety.[23] At the beginning of November some young conservative students of Charles University overturned the statue of Thomas Garrigue Masaryk in the building of the Faculty of Philosophy in Prague. The portraits of the first two presidents were to be removed from the schools and sent to the archives or storage rooms. Only toward the end of the year did the authorities decide that the portraits of Masaryk could be placed among those of the great personalities of the nation on the walls in the schools. The offenses directed against the person of Karel Čapek during the three months after Munich prematurely broke the frail body of this master of the younger literary generation with whom T.G. Masaryk entertained friendly relations.[24]

On November 6, the Prague paper *Národní Politika* reported that former minister, Josef Matoušek, a right-wing senator representing the former National-Democratic Party, proposed to the speaker of the House of the Deputies, Jan Malypetr, to create a commission to investigate the causes of the Munich capitulation. On November 9, Matoušek stated in *Národní Listy* that there was no question of superfluous recriminations or personal quarrels or even persecution: "The role of the commission will only be to find out how these things happened."[25]

The questions which the subcommittee was to submit to Beneš and his chief collaborators concentrated upon two main points: Why did Czechoslovakia not reach an agreement with Germany and Italy and how had the territorial cession been brought about. Some of the questions were based on unsubstantiated rumors. The proposal also suggested enquiry on the activities of several top Czechoslovak diplomats to investigate whether their personal actions or erroneous information were not detrimental to the state.[26]

Independently of this proposed enquiry the Czechoslovak envoy in Paris Osuský asked for the appointment of a similar commission to investigate the causes of the "national catastrophy." The government viewed his demand as too broadly formulated and refused it. In the session of November 11 it decided to set up a commission to investigate only the official activities of minister Osuský in Paris, especially in the last months before Munich. This decision reflected the opinion of some political quarters in Prague convinced that Osuský let himself be surprised by the turn of the French policy so that the Prague government had not been duly informed about the changed situation. Osuský opposed such a limited investigation and refused to accept the commission as proposed by the government. Even Matoušek's initiative failed. At the moment when it was necessary to follow with close attention the intentions of Berlin—there had just arisen the problem of the so-called sixth zone—it seemed not appropriate to analyze the causes which led Czechoslovakia to Munich and Vienna.[27]

At the same time some small groups which before Munich were vegetating on the periphery of political life began to stir. Their political influence was minimal, but their vociferous propaganda fostered the oppressive atmosphere in post-Munich Czechoslovakia. The fascist group of the former General Rudolf Gajda joined the newly founded Party of National Unity in November, but it tried to preserve some freedom of action. Later Gajda attempted to approach Marshal Göring. The German legation in Prague, however, described him as a Czech chauvinist and his friendship for Germany as opportunism and advised against the meeting. In Berlin the counsellor of the legation, Günther Altenburg, head of the Austrian and Czechoslovak desk in the Foreign Ministry, declared in a report to Weizsäcker that Gajda's character was too unsteady and pronounced himself equally against the contact.[28]

Another fascist group which launched into a noisy propaganda campaign was the "Vlajka" (The Flag), an organization founded in 1930. It propagated a corporative state after the Italian pattern and fiercely attacked even the pallid remnants of democracy still existing in Czechoslovakia. Jews, free masons and marxists, real or imaginary, were the main targets of its attacks. The group attempted to enter into contacts with the German legation. However, even in this case the Germans did not trust the exalted nationalism of the "Vlajka" and the legation did not recommend its support.[29] These attempts to undermine its authority did not escape the government and on November 11 the offices of the "Vlajka" were sealed and its papers prohibited.[30]

The third ultra-conservative group tilting toward the fascist ideology was "The Action of National Renascence" (*Akce národní obrody*, ANO). Its followers too were strongly anti-Semitic, against free masons and against all slogans "alien to the spirit of the nation" and were opposed to even the slightest dose of parliamentary democracy. The government was busy suppressing their propaganda and namely prohibited their advertsisements seeking Aryan "observers" for Jewish businesses and helpers for the fight against "the Jews, free masons and old abuses."[31]

This group, too, tried to make overtures to the Germans. Its representative, the secretary of the armament industry's association, Miroslav Hlávka, called on Altenburg on October 20, and asked for moral support of his movement. Even in this case the Germans observed reserve. Later, in a special memorandum, the ANO group denounced the Prague government to Berlin for its "insincerity toward Germany" and proclaimed itself in favor of the German and Italian political philosophy.[32]

The new regime in Prague paid special attention to the most extreme group on the left, the Communist party. On October 9, the party's activity was suspended in Slovakia; on the 20th Prague did likewise.[33] Some days later Sub-Carpathian Ruthenia followed. At the end of the year a part of the German communists, about one thousand persons, left Czechoslovakia for Britain. The chairman of the party, Klement Gottwald, left for Moscow on November 9 and his deputy, Rudolf Slánský, followed in December.[34]

The central government, in agreement with the left-wing parties, did not wish to yield hastily to the wave of totalitarianism then flooding Central Europe, but tried to conserve at least some appearance of democracy. The changed situation, however, led it to simplify the party system. Eventually two major parties emerged: the Party of National

Unity, and the National Labor Party.

The first of these groups was constituted in November when five majority parties of the center and right merged. Its largest component was the Agrarian party led by the deputy Rudolf Beran. In Parliament the new group had about one-half of the seats. Though against totalitarianism, the party nevertheless leaned toward political patterns then current in Central Europe and its program approved on February 16, 1939, recommended corporative organization of public life.[35]

Having previously withdrawn from the Second International, the Social Democratic party announced its dissolution on October 28 and the foundation of a new party of the working people, the National Labor Party. It was composed of Social Democrats and some National-Socialist deputies (former party of Dr. Beneš) who had not entered the Party of National Unity. The new group was to be only loosely connected with the dissolved party. In its program, as published in February 1939, there was not a word about socialism, class struggle or revolution.[36] It was meant as a loyal opposition, in reality its position was hopeless and uneasy. The waning of parliamentary traditions in Czechoslovakia was not favorable to its policies. "It will not be allowed to win an election, it will not be able to pluck the fruit of its victory," in these words a competent political observer summed up the bleak chances of the new leftist party.[37] In February Beran assumed an unfriendly attitude towards it, and one of his papers, the *Večer*, on February 25, stamped its very existence as a danger to the state. At the same time the rightist press began to ventilate the presumed advantages of the one-party system.

The press was submitted to rather strict censorship since the government was afraid of international complications should there be open criticism of current affairs.[38] For its information it had to rely primarily on the official sources. Any expression of resentment against the new situation could be but very indirect and timid. Thus the newspapers which had been supporters of the first two presidents, were but pale reflections of their former selves.

Only slowly did the large masses of population realize the extent of the losses. The new government afraid of demonstrations which might serve as a pretext for further German pressure or intervention was but gradually releasing information about the negotiations of the International Commission in Berlin. Only when the decisions about the fifth zone were known, did the people become aware of the calamitous changes. It was not until December 9 that the authorities permitted the publication of maps showing the new frontiers. To avoid comparisons with the previous frontier line the maps could show only the new borders; maps with both frontier lines were forbidden.[39]

Slovakia and Subcarpathian Ruthenia (Carpatho-Ukraine).

It would exceed the frame of the present work to try to analyze the background of the autonomist trend in Slovakia and the psychological and social differences dividing the Czechs and Slovaks. The exposition will be limited to the situation of 1938, about one year before the final disintegration of the Czechoslovak state.[40]

The Slovak Populist party lost its leader, Andrej Hlinka, in the summer of that year. The death of the man who under the Hungarian domination dared to defend his people against oppression was an irreparable loss to the party. There was no successor worthy of his heritage, and the presidium of the party decided late in August to leave the post of the chairman vacant. His functions were to be carried out by the vice-chairman of the party, Msgre Josef Tiso. He was, however, to function only as acting chairman until September 1939 when the congress of the party was to settle the question.[41] The new leader belonged to the moderate wing of the party and was no newcomer to politics. He had been a deputy in the Prague Parliament and the Minister of Health in 1927–28.

Much more dynamic than this elderly prelate was the leading journalist of the party, Karol Sidor (born in 1901). A scholarship granted by the Prague ministry of foreign affairs sent him to Poland in 1926. The semi-authoritarian regime of this Catholic Slav country appealed to his own political philosophy and thus Sidor, after his return, supported the polonophile trend in his party and entertained close relations with Poland.[42] He cooperated with a group of young radicals leaning to separatism, Ferdinand Ďurčanský, Matúš Černák and Karol Murgaš, whose aspirations were encouraged by various German agencies, in the first place by the Nazi dignitaries in Vienna.

At that time, Professor Vojtěch Tuka, the most radical of the Slovak politicians and a pronounced separatist, was still living outside Slovakia, in forced residence in Plzeň in Bohemia. The most talented political mind of the Slovak separatist group, he alone was able to coordinate their vague and disconnected aspirations. He had, however, to wait for his release on the aftermath of Munich to deploy his activities.

The Populist party laid down its demands in June 1938 and presented them to Parliament on August 17. The bill proposed: 1. Recognition of the national individuality of the Slovak people. 2. Exclusive use of the Slovak language in Slovakia. 3. Creation of an autonomous Slovak Diet. 4. Immediate transfer of the executive power into the hands of the representatives of the Slovak Populist party.

When the domestic situation became tense in September the extremist members of the party were unwilling to deal with Prime Minister Milan Hodža. As he had done in the case of the Sudeten Germans, President Beneš entered into direct contact with the Slovaks. On September 22, after the acceptance of the British-French proposals, a new cabinet was formed with General Syrový as premier. The Slovak Populist Party was represented by a radical autonomist, a young high school professor, Matús Černák. The same day President Beneš submitted to Tiso his own proposals containing substantial concessions to the autonomists.[43] The proposals coincided only partly with the Populist party's demands and did not amount to a full autonomy as the party demanded. Though the populists were not completely satisfied they nevertheless accepted the Beneš plan as a basis for further negotiations. In all the Slovaks had three representatives in the Syrový government. To Vladimír Fajnor, the President of the Supreme Court, were now added Černák and a little later Professor Imrich Karvaš, a Social Democrat leaning to the former agrarian Prime Minister Hodža.[44]

The critical days preceding the Munich conference brought confusion into the Slovak populist ranks. Under the depressing impression of Chamberlain's speech of September 27 about "a quarrel in a faraway country" the leaders of the party decided to seek Polish assistance to protect the Slovak nation against the threatening deluge. Influenced by Karol Sidor the executive committee of the party framed a resolution expressing readiness to federate Slovakia with Poland or—should such an eventuality arise—to join a trialistic state consisting of Poland, Hungary and Slovakia. The declaration was handed over to the Polish minister in Prague, in the evening of September 28.[45]

This was, however, but a momentary mood and after Munich the Populist party concentrated its endeavors on autonomy within the framework of the republic. When the negotiations were resumed the weakening of the Prague government strengthened the extremists. On October 3 Černák demanded the immediate transfer of the executive power in Slovakia to the representatives of the Populist party and threatened that he would resign if the demand was not accepted by noon of October 4. The Prague government rejected his radical demands and Černák left the cabinet.[46]

The changed balance of forces became apparent when the executive committee of the Populist party met in Žilina on October 5 to deliberate the political future of Slovakia. The result of the Žilina talks was an agreement between the Populist party and other Slovak political parties (with the exception of Social Democrats) about the Slovak autonomy as conceived by the Populists. The executive power was to be transferred immediately to a Slovak government composed of five ministers which were to be nominated by Tiso as vice-chairman of the party. A bill about the decentralization of the state was then approved. From the competence of the Slovak government were to be excluded foreign affairs, defense and public debt, and loans for the common needs of the state.[47]

The Prague government, just then astounded by the cession of the fifth zone to Germany and assailed by Polish and Hungarian demands, was forced to cede even here. On October 6 it appointed Tiso minister for the administration of Slovakia, and on the following day the other Slovak ministers were appointed: Černák (Education), Teplanský (Agriculture, Public Works, Commerce and Finances), Lichner (Communications), and Ďurčanský (Justice, Social Welfare and Health).[48] On November 23 the House of Deputies and the Senate in Prague passed a law of autonomy of Slovakia (and Subcarpathian Ruthenia).

Slovakia became a country of a single political party. At the beginning of November, the Slovak branch of the Agrarian party and other Czech and Slovak political groups merged with the Populist party, which was to be "the real and sole representative of the will of the Slovak people." The Communist party was dissolved on October 9. On November 23 the activities of the Social-Democratic party were suspended. Likewise the existence of the Slovak National party was terminated. This group, though autonomist, did not wish originally to join Hlinka's unique party, however, a few weeks later, even it surrendered.[49]

Having gotten rid of all opposition, the Slovak government proceeded without delay to general elections. Only one list was permitted, that of Hlinka's Populist party, headed by Tiso, with Sidor in second place. The elections were held on December 18, in the plebiscitary style current in the totalitarian regimes. The voter had to answer one suggestive question: "Do you want a new, free Slovakia?" The Jews and in some places the Czechs were forced to cast their ballots in separate boxes. When a Czech senator protested Tiso retorted that this was an internal Slovak issue. According to him Prague should not interfere. The government got about 98% of the votes. Out of 63 elected deputies, 2 represented the German minority, one was a Magyar; there was no Czech deputy.[50]

Another sign of changed times was the formation of a storm-trooper organization of the Populist party, the Hlinka Guards. Its nucleus was a similar organization founded in the twenties by Tuka, the *Rodobrana*. The Hlinka Guards were created on the initiative of Alexander Mach in June 1938 as an avant-garde of the autonomist movement. Their members were to serve as political militiamen of the party. After Munich their membership rapidly increased. Its by-laws were approved by the Slovak government in December 1938. At the same time all gymnastic associations were dissolved and the Hlinka Guards were gradually taking over their property, especially of the "Sokol", the gymnastic organization of Czech origin. The supreme commander of the Hlinka Guards was Karol Sidor.[51]

While the western part of the state, the Czech lands, (Bohemia and Moravia) proceeded with the political reorganization slowly and hesitatingly, the Slovak government started its activities with energy and enthusiasm. "When one arrives in Bratislava from Prague where one breathes an unspeakable sadness, one is somewhat astonished to be immerged from the beginning in an atmosphere of juvenile exuberance and total jauntiness," wrote a French observer. "The *joie de vivre* seems to have fled indeed to the capital of the autonomous Slovakia."[52] An American observer, George F. Kennan, the second secretary of the legation in Prague, viewed the situation in Slovakia much more severely in a report from January 14, 1939. He did not pass over the psychological errors made by the Czechs in Slovakia, but he expressed doubts about the achievements of the new Slovak leaders: "In cultural matters, as in economic, the endeavors of the new Slovak government have produced more negative than positive results. The only guiding principle has been linguistic chauvinism in its most petty and shortsighted form."[53]

The regime organized anti-Czech manifestations and Tiso declared in Prievidza on December 11: "Slovakia to the Slovaks. The Slovak bread belongs in the first place to the Slovaks."[54] In Prague, the central government proposed to withdraw 9,000 Czech government servants from Slovakia and to create 4,000 Slovak officers in the army.[55] At the same time three Slovak state secretaries were appointed to the central ministries (Foreign Affairs, National Defense, and Finance).[56]

Despite this nationalistic effervescence there were prominent Slovak voices warning against anti-Czech excesses and campaigns. The evangelic bishop, Dr. Vladimír Čobrda, termed anti-Czech slogans ingratitude and indecency of which the Slovaks should be ashamed.[57] Likewise the Slovak author, Elena Šoltésova, declared shortly before her death in February 1939 that nothing could break the Slovak brotherhood with the Czechs. "Do not pay attention to what is going now," she warned a Czech visitor.[58] The words of the leading Slovak scholar, Dr. Josef Škultéty, were in the same vein.[59]

The new masters of the Slovak political life were strongly anti-Semitic. It was an anti-Semitism with socio-economic overtones rather than the rigidly racist variant of the Nazi model. There were several anti-Semitic excesses in which the Hlinka Guards played their role. The Slovak government, though more active in this field than Prague, had nevertheless to observe a relative moderation out of regard for the reaction in the United States from where much needed money remittances of the

Slovak emigrants were coming. On January 23, 1939, a commission for the solution of the Jewish question was formed and one of its members, senator Dr. Anton Mederly, framed a bill which would practically have relegated the Jews back into the ghetto.[60]

* * *

In the east, in Sub-Carpathian Ruthenia, the evolution was similar. In this most eastern part of Czechoslovakia, smaller and less populated than Slovakia (12,644 square kilometers, i.e. 4,880 sq. miles with 725,000 inhabitants according to the census of 1930) the situation was still more complicated. In the times of the Austro-Hungarian monarchy this was one of the most backward regions of the empire from the point of view of economic as well as social and cultural development. More than half of the inhabitants were illiterate. There was a vast emigration to America and from this trans-Atlantic branch of the population came the initiative to join the future Czechoslovakia. The Treaty of Saint-Germain attached the territory to the new state (Chapter II, art. 10) on the condition that Sub-Carpathian Ruthenia will get "the largest autonomy compatible with the unity of the State."

The conditions in the region at the time of its incorporation into Czechoslovakia were, however, far from amenable to the implementation of this clause without reserve. As long as its inhabitants had not reached a certain degree of political maturity, as long as the most glaring signs of economic misery inherited from the past were not eliminated, political life was impossible in a country where the national idea was alive only in a narrow circle of local patriots, predominantly priests. The local scene was presenting characteristic traits of an underdeveloped country, in the social, economic and political sphere.

The linguistic fluidity only heightened the problems of the region. From the national point of view Sub-Carpathian Ruthenia was experiencing what might be called an embryonic stage of national development.[61] The Russian orientation competed with the Ukrainian. According to the Russophiles the inhabitants were part of the Great-Russian people. Even the Russophile group was, however, differentiated into several shades of opinion. The strongest fraction was for a moderate form of autonomy within the frame of the Czechoslovak Republic (Edmond Bačynśkyj, Petr Židovský). The group around the deputy Štefan Fencik was under the Polish influence. The local Ruthene group, led by Andrej Bródy, entertained close contacts with Budapest. The Ukrainophiles argued that the region was the most western settlement inhabited by the Ukrainian people. The Ukrainian camp led by Msgre Augustin Vološyn, concentrated the local Ukrainian intelligentsia and Ukrainian emigrés from Galicia and the Soviet Ukraine.[62] There was even a third current of opinion suggesting that the local population, the Rusyns, were a separate Slavic nationality. The confused Czechoslovak authorities wavered periodically between the Russophile and Ukrainophile orientation.

The first move towards autonomy was made in 1937 with a law extending the powers of the governor, the head of the local administration. The following year Prague negotiations with the Sudeten Germans had an impact even in this remote area. Talks with Prime Minister Hodža took place and at the beginning of October 1938 an agreement between the Russian and Ukrainian camp was reached in Užhorod with a view of creating an autonomous government.

The government was appointed of October 11. At its head as "minister for the administration of Sub-Carpathian Ruthenia" was the autonomist deputy, Andrej Bródy, representing the Russophile orientation. The government had three ministers (Fencik, Julian Révay, Bačynśkyj) and two state secretaries (one of them Vološyn). Bródy's group was predominating.[63]

The truce between the two factions was but of a short duration. The Ukrainian fraction led by Vološyn and Révay was dissatisfied with its share in the government and was seeking support in Germany.[64] There were contacts in the first days after Munich and on October 10, a Ukrainian delegation asked the German Secretary of State Weizsäcker in a telegram for protection against Hungarian revisionism and at the same time complained that the Prague government was ignoring the self-determination of the Ukrainian people.[65]

These arguments were supported by the fact that the attitude of the two representatives of the Russophile orientation, Bródy and Fencik, was not beyond doubt. Fencik oscillated between Poland and Hungary and Bródy was even receiving financial subsidies from Budapest.[66] Less than a week after the formation of the first autonomous government, minister Révay warned Chvalkovský against Bródy and his contacts with Budapest.[67] A few days later, accompanied by Vološyn, he denounced Bródy and Fencik at the German legation. At the same time the two Ukrainians demanded a government formed solely by the Ukrainian elements. Only a man whom Germany trusted could be—according to them—its member.[68]

The crisis came into the open on October 23. Budapest had been pressing Bródy to demand self-determination in a way which, in the Hungarian view, was to be but an intermediary stage leading up to annexation by Hungary.[69] When the central government in Prague discussed the latest Hungarian proposals, Bródy and Fencik, following the instructions from Budapest, declared themselves in favor of a plebiscite in Subcarpathian Ruthenia. Révay and Bačynśkyj opposed their proposal and offered to resign in protest. On October 26 Bródy was arrested and detained until February 1939.[70] Fencik fled to Hungary and from there carried out the propaganda campaign for the reunion of the region with Hungary.[71]

The new government was appointed on October 26. It consisted of Prime Minister Vološyn, the Minister of the Interior Bačynśkyj and Minister of Transportation and Economy Révay. This setup was maintained even in the Beran government installed on December 1. The seat of the third minister remained vacant. On November 22 the constitutional amendment about the autonomy was published and became effective on December 16.[72] When Užhorod, the capital of the region, was occupied by Hungary the seat of the government was transferred to the small country town of Chust.[73] The Ukrainian orientation prevailed and in December, Ukrainian was proclaimed the official language.[74] All Czech inscriptions in Chust had to be changed into Ukrainian by December 10.[75] On January 2, 1939, the autonomous government permitted the use of the name of Carpatho-Ukraine. Hitherto only the official denomination of *Podkarpatská Rus* (Sub-Carpathian Ruthenia) as established by the peace treaties, was authorized.[76] On January 22, all political parties were dissolved and only the party of the National Ukrainian Union was permitted.[77] On February 12 the elections of the first Diet of the autonomous Carpatho-Ukraine were held. Like in Slovakia, the government ticket got 93% of the votes.[78]

In the affairs concerning Carpatho-Ukraine Germany had an important say. For the time being, Hitler wished to keep in his hands the card represented by this small mountainous province. In this he was supported by the opinion of his military experts. On October 6, the Supreme Command of the Armed Forces sent a memorandum to the minister of foreign affairs according to which annexation of the province by Hungary, a common Hungarian-Polish frontier, was undesirable.[79] This thesis was reiterated in a memorandum prepared by Ribbentrop for Hitler in view of the Komárno negotiations. The part dealing with the Carpatho-Ukrainian question stated that an independent Carpatho-Ukrainian state without the support from outside was at present hardly viable. This solution would, however, have the advantage that it would create a nucleus for a greater Ukraine in the future. The most natural solution for the present was an autonomous Ukraine oriented toward Slovakia or Czechoslovakia. Orientation of the autonomous region to Hungary was to be definitely rejected, for a common Polish-Hungarian frontier thus created would facilitate the formation of an anti-German bloc.[80]

Hitler agreed and stated that Germany should interfere as little as possible in the question. He declared himself in favor of an autonomous Ruthenian area with orientation toward Prague, "which of course would only be a temporary solution until the final separation."[81]

At the beginning of November, Oberführer Behrends of the *Volkdeutsche Mittelstelle* was instructed by Ribbentrop to take charge of the underground activities in Carpatho-Ukraine.[82] Germany established a consulate in Chust. At the end of November, Hofmann, the press attaché of the German legation in Prague, was sent on a special mission to Carpatho-Ukraine to report on the situation. He summed up his impressions by stating that the province was viable, especially if foreign help were available for reconstruction.[83] Later, Révay and Wilhelm Keppler, the State Secretary for special duties in the German foreign minstry, signed a memorandum laying down a program of economic collaboration between Germany and the Carpatho-Ukraine, particularly to develop the production of raw materials, the construction of railroads and roads, the conservation of forests, and the building of a suitable capital for the country. At the same time the Carpatho-Ukrainian government signed over to a German company all the prospecting rights for minerals and their exploitation.[84]

The German Minority

In post-Munich Czechoslovakia the German minority, the source of all the changes that at a rapid pace radically transformed the situation in central Europe had a special position. Their number fell to about 444,000 (according to some sources to 390,000 of which about two-thirds lived in the western part of the state.[85]

In Parliament the Sudeten-German faction ceased to exist. In its place was organized a "club of national-socialist deputies and senators" (*Parlamentarischer Klub der deutschen national-sozialistischen Abgeordneten und Senatoren*). It was presided over by deputy Ernst Kundt, one of the leading Sudeten German representatives who negotiated with Czechoslovak authorities in the months preceding the Munich Agreement. Kundt, whom Berlin considered an expert on Czechoslovakia, stayed in Prague and became the spokesman of the remaining German population.[86]

Outside Parliament the reorganization of the German minority was as yet not finished. On Kundt's initiative a "German Office for Liquidation and Reorganization" (*Deutsches Arbeitsamt für Liquidierung und Reorganisierung*) was set up with its seat in Prague and chapters in six other cities. It was to look after the interests of the German minority, to reorganize it and to secure for it "an appropriate political status" in relation to the Czechoslovak government.[87] It gathered information and complaints, real or imaginary, of the German population which Kundt used later as arguments against Prague.[88]

At the beginning of October the German government put at the disposal of Kundt the sum of 10 million crowns to help those Germans who were affected economically by the recent events.[89] In January, he asked Berlin for a supplementary sum of 1,000,000 marks (10 million crowns) for his protégés.[90] The Germans remaining in the rump-Czechoslovakia were suffering along with the Czechs from tearing up the centuries old economic unity. However, even the German chargé d'affaires had to admit that many alarming reports reaching Berlin on the position of the remaining Germans were often exaggerated, if not invented, and designed to persuade the Reich to occupy additional areas inhabited by the German minority.[91]

The Presidential Election—The Beran Government

The most urgent problems stemming from the Munich Agreement and the Vienna Award settled, there remained one more formality—the election of a new President. At first, around November 11, the name of the Foreign Minister Chvalkovský was mentioned, but he eventually refused. Forced by his ungrateful office to constant and rather unsuccessful contacts with Germany, he felt that he was not popular enough among his countrymen. Besides this, the long years spent in the diplomatic service abroad alienated him from the problems of the domestic policy.[92]

Then the name of Jaroslav Preiss, president of the largest Czechoslovak bank, the "Živnostenská banka", was put forward. At the same time the Party of National Unity proposed several university professors and leading public servants, in the first place Dr. Emil Hácha, first president of the Supreme Administrative Court; followed by Dr. Vladimír Fajnor, president of the Supreme Court of Appeals; and Dr. Bedřich Horák, president of the General Accounting Office. The Minister of Agriculture, Ladislav Feierabend, suggested the distinguished historian Josef Šusta.[93]

Eventually Hácha was offered the office in agreement with the Slovaks and the representatives of the National Labor Party. On November 24, the newspapers announced on the front page that Hácha was chosen by all Czech, Slovak and Ruthene political groups as the only presidential candidate. The election took place on November 30, much later than prescribed by the constitution. Of 312 votes, Hácha got 272. The Communists (35 votes), the German National Socialists (4) and one

Hungarian deputy handed in blank cards.[94]

The third President of the Republic was a distinguished jurist, but a man who so far had had no direct contacts with politics and whose physical forces had begun to decline. He was little known to the population and the official press service went to great lengths to make him appear in a more attractive light. Born in 1872, he followed a peaceful career in the magistracy in the Austrian monarchy. He was a pure jurist, a conservative without any marked political profile; however, a highly cultured man mastering the German and English languages in their most minute details. With his brother he translated into Czech short stories by Rudyard Kipling and a humorous novel by J.K. Jerome. He was an expert on English self-government and he wrote a monograph on this subject. He was interested in literature and fine arts, probably as an escape from the monotony of the juridic career. His health was not perfect. In his youth he was an ardent mountaneer and swimmer. Now he was suffering from insomnia caused by abuse of tobacco, and his mental forces were threatened by progressing cerebral sclerosis. The death of his wife in the spring of 1938 disheartened him and from then on he aged rapidly.[95]

After the presidential election, the Syrový government resigned and on December 1, a new central government was formed with the chairman of the former Agrarian party Rudolf Beran as prime minister. The Slovak autonomist Sidor was appointed vice-premier and minister for Slovakia. Chvalkovský retained the ministry of foreign affairs, General Syrový the ministry of national defense.

Beran had until then directed the party from behind the scenes. He was a man of natural inborn intelligence and a skilful political tactician. He had dealt for the most part with problems of domestic policy and his knowledge of foreign policy was limited. He did not speak any foreign language, not even German. Like several other contemporary European statesmen—of a much greater stature than himself—he believed in pacific coexistence with national-socialist Germany hoping that a conciliatory attitude would be much more profitable to his country than the rigid line of Beneš. In 1938, in the New Year's issue of the agrarian newspaper, *Venkov*, he argued that the Sudeten German party could no longer be ignored in the political life of the country. Subsequently, in February and March, he twice met the German minister in Prague, Dr. Ernst Eisenlohr, and cautiously sounded out the prospects of a rapprochement with Germany. With Beran, appeasement under the duress of the situation became the predominant line in Czechoslovak politics.[96]

The political team which succeeded the former pre-Munich coalition of right- and left-wing parties was by its nature conservative. It acted in the atmosphere of national defeat, in the constant fear of new and radical German demands. Under the ever present pressure from Berlin to adapt to new conditions and to eradicate all traces of the former regime it was forced to take many measures in marked discordance with the traditions of the recent past. "What I am to do? If I do not conform to what is wanted, not only I but perhaps my country must pay the penalty," complained Chvalkovský to the American minister, Wilbur Carr.[97] A new regime was emerging which Beran in an interview with a French newspaperman called vaguely "the authoritarian democracy."[98]

Though not totally abandoned, the democratic institutions were slowly fading away. Public opinion in general was not against a simplification of the party system; however, the mode and circumstances under which this metamorphosis materialized was not a good omen for the future of political freedom in the truncated state. The House of Deputies held nine sessions in November and December, devoted primarily to passing government bills. There were some speeches critical of current events, especially of the behavior of the autonomous Slovak government, but on the whole the discussions were muted and reserved. Trying not to complicate the difficult situation the deputies avoided discussions of the calamity which befell the state and practically rubber-stamped all government bills. Nevertheless, two deputies, Ladislav Rašín, Beneš's oponent before Munich, and the former Social-Democrat, Jaromír Nečas, called for a halt in the attacks on the fallen regime.

One of the most important among the government bills was the enabling bill passed after the presidential election, on December 15. To expedite as quickly as possible the urgent tasks of reconstruction and to prevent unwelcome, though rather mitigated criticism of unpopular measures, the government preferred to by-pass the normal parliamentary procedure. On the basis of the enabling law it could govern two years by decrees, without Parliament. The law also gave the President power to make certain amendments to the constitution by decree.[99] The two years of its validity were the time deemed necessary for the return to normalcy. Some members of the government hoped, however, that the transitional period would not be so long and on December 6 Prime Minister Beran enumerated among the most pressing tasks of the government the framing of the new constitution and the new electoral law. Beran's mouthpiece, *Venkov*, even predicted on January 1, 1939, that the new parliament would be elected within the next few months.[100]

Changes in Foreign Policy

The same country whose first foreign minister was sometimes

reproached for a policy that was beyond the dimension of the state, lost almost all initiative in this field after Munich. All controversial problems of the territorial character being settled for the time being, activity in the field of foreign relations was limited to two questions: to maintain good relations with Germany, and to obtain the international guarantees promised by the Munich Agreement.

When Beneš in his valedictory statement advised his countrymen to adapt themselves to the new situation, he stated that it did not mean to give up former friends: "We will look around for new friends, quietly, objectively, with loyalty toward all."[101] Since the very moment of its formulation, however, this advice was proving impracticable. In negotiations in Berlin former friends were showing their passivity, new ones could not be gained.

In Prague, the critics did not spare either France or Great Britain. They reproached France for breach of the alliance treaty, Britain for her ill-advised political initiative. The prestige of these two western powers fell to zero. According to a British historian, "to return to Prague after Munich was, for an Englishman, a most humiliating experience... The Czechs were not in general openly hostile but they were, which was worse, contemptuous. They did not hesitate to say that they had been betrayed, and who could blame them?"[102]

The advances of cooperation which Prague did not spare in order to protect itself against any renewal of brutal moves by the Reich were ignored. As early as September 30, German chargé d'affaires Hencke was told at the Czechoslovak Ministry of Foreign Affairs that the Prague government hoped that "the former enmity would give place to the coexistence of the great German and the small Czech people, inspired by mutual respect."[103] On October 5, the new Czechoslovak ministers, general Karel Husárek and Hugo Vavrečka, asked State Secretary Weizsäcker in Berlin for "considerate treatment of the Czechoslovak people."[104] They attempted to support their demand by stressing that the resignation of President Beneš was but a matter of a few hours away. Similarly, the new premier, General Syrový, hoped that Beneš's resignation was a concession without which Germany would continue "her subversive maneuvers and attacks."[105] With Beneš or without him, the result was the same and on the very evening of the President's resignation the agreement on new territorial concessions to Germany ("the fifth zone") was published.

For the new Foreign Minister, František Chvalkovský, the news of the agreement on the fifth zone had an ominous ring. By character an opportunist, he hoped that the friendly relations which he had built up in Italy would help him in his new office when he faced the other partner of the

Axis. His first thought after his appointment was to contact the German leaders directly, above all Ribbentrop, and if possible Hitler himself. The nomination reached him at his post in Rome. Before his departure from Rome he called on the German ambassador, Hans Georg von Mackensen, and asked him to enquire in Berlin if he could be received by Ribbentrop and—"if he were accessible"—by Adolf Hitler. On his arrival in Prague, he renewed his demand in a conversation with the German chargé d'affaires Hencke.[106]

His demand was accepted. Not only Ribbentrop, but Hitler himself agreed to receive the new minister.[107] Before his journey to Germany, Chvalkovský prepared for his visit by reassuring Hencke of his loyal attitude. He proposed "to do everything in his power to establish good neighborly relations with the Reich" and assured that the Czechoslovak government had "nothing in common with France."[108] Berlin learned with satisfaction that Chvalkovský was coming "with the firm intention of effecting a radical change in Czechoslovak policy."[109]

Chvalkovský used the same arguments in the course of two conversations he had in the following days in Germany: on October 13 in Berlin with Ribbentrop, and on the fourteenth in Munich with Hitler. At the time when all frontiers of the state were in motion and nobody knew exactly where the things would stop, his principal aim was to gain the goodwill of his German hosts and even to anticipate their wishes.

If, during his conversations with Ribbentrop, he was able to formulate his pledges in a more comprehensive way, he had to be even more concise during his audience with Hitler. Even here, however, he maintained his leitmotif and repeated in Munich his words about "a complete *volte-face* of the Czechoslovak policy" which he had pronounced a day ago in Berlin.[110] Hitler took notice of his statement, but warned Chvalkovský that Germany would immediately take energetic action and would settle the fate of Czechoslovakia with lightning speed in eight hours if she were to make even the slightest move to renew her efforts to act as an enemy of Germany.[111] In spite of the favorable impression he had made,[112] Chvalkovský did not gain any concessions; on the contrary, he was to cope in November with several new territorial demands by Germany.

Similarly, Prime Minister Beran did not miss any occasion to declare a fundamental change of foreign policy. So in his declaration in the Chamber of Deputies on December 13, he used loyal words in the address to both Germany and Italy. When he spoke also about maintaining former relations with two traditional friends of his nation, Rumania and Yugoslavia, and when he mentioned the continuation of relations with France, Great Britain and the United States, his words were rather a mere rhetorical figure of speech than an expression of the real situation.[113]

Even before his accession to the premiership Beran attempted to contact Hitler's deputy Rudolf Hess and Marshal Göring. Four unofficial representatives of the former Agrarian party appeared in Berlin in November and December, some of them admirers of the Nazi regime. Only one of them, Viktor Stoupal, an influential agrarian politician from Moravia, was able to reach the higher echelons of the German hierarchy. He was received by Weizsäcker on November 10, but not exactly in a friendly way. Weizsäcker reproached his visitor that "there was still something amiss in government circles" in Prague with respect to good neighborly relations. When Stoupal attempted to allude to border problems (Germany had just on that day submitted her proposals concerning the "sixth zone")—he was, in Weizsäcker's own words, "brutally" snubbed.[114] Nor was the journey of the agrarian newspaperman Vladimír Krychtálek at the beginning of December any more successful. He was received only by a subordinate official of the Ministry of Propaganda who, however, did not answer any of his questions (e.g. the return of the Chod villages that Czechoslovakia lost in November and German intentions concerning the promised guarantees).[115]

There was almost no discussion of foreign political problems either in the Council of the Ministers or in the Parliament. Chvalkovský was afraid of leaks and especially he did not trust Révay and Sidor. To the first he reproached his frequent contacts with the Germans; the latter reported to the Slovak government in Bratislava what he had heard in Prague and the Germans were subsequently informed about everything by way of Slovakia. Decisions in the field of foreign policy were made in close deliberations between Beran, Chvalkovský and the minister Jiří Havelka, one of the chief advisors of President Hácha. When necessary, other leading Czech ministers were informed. The Slovak ministers entertained their foreign contacts without regard for the central government and they did not notify Prague of their moves (e.g. Sidor's journey to Warsaw or Ďurčanský's visits to Germany).[116]

The government did not submit the Munich Agreement to Parliament. It wanted to indicate in this way that it considered the given situation as a temporary one, not agreed to in a constitutionally prescribed way. A week consolation, but not without some legal significance.[117]

From the Slovak side there were some unsuccessful attempts to influence the foreign policy. Minister Sidor criticized in two speeches at the beginning of December the continuence of the treaty with the Soviet Union and inveighed against the League of Nations ("the Geneva Jewry" in his words).[118] When Tiso alluded to the treaty with Moscow in the Council of Ministers, Chvalkovský retorted that even Germany had not asked for its abrogation, and the Slovak leader accepted the explanation.[119]

The treaty system, which before Munich was to guarantee the security of the state, belonged to the past. When a former member of the French legation in Prague, Jean Henri Daridan, visited Prague towards the middle of December, the chief of Chvalkovský's cabinet, Hubert Masařík, informed the German legation without delay. Daridan tried to convince Prague that the French government continued to feel the greatest sympathies for Czechoslovakia and wished to help her in her difficulties. He warned Prague against collaboration with Germany and recommended strengthening relations with Poland. According to German sources the answer was quite clear: Czechoslovakia's foreign policy should—especially after the experiences with France—be oriented above all towards Germany.[120]

In November, Poland, too, tried to ameliorate her relations with Prague. General Kazimierz Sosnkowski declared to Czechoslovak minister Slávik that "it would be an error of Czechoslovak policy not to count on the Polish safety valve in its present relations with Germany. Only a sincere agreement with Poland could permit Czechoslovakia from becoming a complete vassal of Germany."[121] At the same time a delegation of five Polish politicians came to Prague. It was headed by a member of the Foreign Affairs Committee of the Polish Parliament, formerly an adversary of Czechoslovakia, Jan Walewski. The group stayed in Czechoslovakia one week and met among others six Czechoslovak generals including General Syrový. The aim of this belated attempt was to bring about some degree of military cooperation of the two states to ease the Polish army in the war with Germany which these Poles considered inevitable. The Poles wished to bring together Prague and Warsaw and indicated that Poland would be uneasy if Czechoslovakia sold her soul completely to Germany. Chvalkovský, however, refused to receive them, and Masařík informed the German chargé d'affaires that the Polish advances had been repudiated.[122]

Relations between Prague and Moscow were becoming cooler. According to the Czechoslovak minister in Moscow, Zdeněk Fierlinger, the Soviet minister in Prague, Sergei Alexandrovsky, complained toward the end of January that Chvalkovský avoided every encounter with him.[123]

Under existing conditions, the principal ally from pre-Munich times, France, began to evacuate her positions. In November the French military mission was dissolved which had been since its arrival in Prague in 1919 one of the most visible signs of the alliance of the two nations. When on December 16 the last chief of the mission, General Louis Faucher, was leaving Prague with military honors, a chapter of French policy in central Europe was closed.[124]

Another position from which French influence disappeared was the "consortium" of the Škoda works. The works, founded in 1899, had been the greatest and the most modern armament factory of the Austro-Hungarian monarchy, reputed above all for its artillery material. In 1919, the works came under the French influence and the French group Schneider-Creusot acquired its newly issued shares. The vassalisation of Czechoslovakia by Germany naturally had its echo in an enterprise whose absorption into the German sphere of influence was welcome to Berlin, especially at a time when German war production was pushed to the extreme. In November, rumors spread that the French capital would be soon withdrawn.[125] A conference took place at the Ministry of Finance in Prague on December 16. The representative of the French holding company, *Union Européenne,* declared that the French group was in a very difficult situation: It would be impossible to participate in a production which was arming Germany. The Czechs suggested three solutions: first, the French group could conclude an agreement with the German government according to which the Škoda Works, while conserving other markets, would work both for France and Germany. The second solution was the sale of the Works to a Czechoslovak consortium. The difficulty of this alternative consisted in the high price asked by the French. The third alternative was, of course, sale to a German group. From these, the second alternative—sale to a Czechoslovak consortium—was realized.[126]

The preliminary protocol was signed in Prague on December 23, 1938. The 315,000 shares of the Škoda Works were transferred to a Czechoslovak consortium headed by the Anglo-Czechoslovak Bank and the Prague Credit Bank. The price was 9.5 million U.S. dollars to be deposited at Barclay's Bank in London within nine months.[127] Later the Škoda Works passed into the sphere of the German *Hermann Göring Werke.*

In the changed situation, the Czechoslovak government was envisaging the sale of the surplus armaments. Although its dependence on Germany was increasing almost every day, the government thought it advisable to withhold from Germany all that could be saved, and decided to sell the heavy material to France and Great Britain. A similar offer was made to Rumania. The answer from London arrived in the second half of October. The British military attaché even got a list of what Prague was ready to cede. At the same time the Škoda Works was discussing with Britain the delivery of artillery material. In the middle of November, the British Secretary of War sent two specialists to Czechoslovakia to inspect the material.[128] The talks, however, dragged out. It seemed that the British (as well as the French) representatives were in no hurry, convinced that the war would not break out before 1941.

At the beginning of November a French military mission visited Czechoslovakia to get information about the artillery material and the protective equipment used against chemical warfare. For the time being, the French army bought some 305 guns and material against gas warfare. On December 27, Ambassador Léon Noël asked the Polish Under-Secretary of State Szembek for permission to transport these arms through Gdynia.[129] Great Britain, too, bought some military equipment in Prague, tanks, which were also to be transported by way of Gdynia.[130] Bulgaria wanted to buy a large part of the Czechoslovak military equipment to lessen her economic dependence on Germany. And later she sought to send fifteen students from a Bulgarian military school for training in the Czechoslovak air force.[131]

Germany was naturally equally interested. Under German pressure, Beran and Chvalkovský decided to invite Germany to send an expert to negotiate the transaction.[132] Toward the end of 1938, a German mission arrived and bought some artillery material. The agreement was signed on February 11, 1939. The Germans did not take over the bought material and after March 1939 they simply confiscated it.[133]

The Guarantee—French and British Hesitation

The guarantee promised in Munich was meant to assure the base of the reorganized state weakened by its great territorial losses. The promise was an essential part of the Franco-British propositions of September 19 and it played a decisive role in making Czechoslovakia accept the compromise. To contribute to the pacification of Europe the Franco-British memorandum addressed to Prague on September 19 expressed the will "to join in an international guarantee of the new boundaries of the Czechoslovak State against unprovoked aggression." One of the principal conditions of such a guarantee, stated the paragraph VI of the memorandum, would be "the safeguarding of the independence of Czechoslovakia against unprovoked aggression in place of the existing treaties which involve reciprocal obligations of a military character."[134]

Lord Runciman, too, returned from Prague with the idea of a guarantee. He recommended not only that Czechoslovakia remodel her foreign relations, but also that the principal powers give her guarantees of assistance in case of unprovoked aggression.[135]

In the annex to the Munich Agreement, Britain and France declared that they were standing by the offer of their memorandum of September 19. Besides these guarantees Germany and Italy were to give theirs when the question of the Polish and Hungarian minorities in Czechoslovakia had been settled.

In the general euphoria in the aftermath of Munich the guarantee seemed sufficient compensation for the treaty system which had just been destroyed. As early as October 3, Home Secretary Sir Samuel Hoare expressed in the House of Commons the belief that such a guarantee "would make the new Republic as safe as Switzerland had been for many generations past."[136] On the following day, Minister for Coordination of Defense, Sir Thomas Inskip, even declared that his government "felt under a moral obligation to Czechoslovakia to treat the guarantee as being now in force."[137]

In spite of the bad experience Prague had just had with its allies, it nevertheless seized this opportunity to ensure the survival of the state. Prime Minister Hodža, in the aftermath of the Franco-British ultimatum, as well as President Beneš, on September 30, both advised—though in somewhat sceptical terms—not to underestimate the value of the offered guarantee.[138] The new foreign minister, Chvalkovský, made his first steps while still in Rome. Then, throughout the tenure of his office he unrelentingly pursued this goal and he regarded its implementation as his most important political task.[139] He raised the issue during the farewell visits on the eve of his departure to Prague. He mentioned the question to the British ambassador, Lord Perth. Mussolini assured him of his willingness to give a guarantee as soon as Polish and Hungarian claims had been settled.[140] German ambassador, Mackensen, pointed out, however, that it depended "on prior complete settlement of outstanding questions taking place.[141]

Hitler's reaction when Chvalkovský raised the issue during his first visit to Germany on October 14 was vague: Czechoslovakia should realize that British and French guarantees were as worthless as the treaty of alliance with France or the pact with Russia had been during the crisis and that "the only really effective guarantee was that by Germany."[142]

On November 11, Chvalkovský resumed his endeavors. The representatives of the Czechoslovak foreign ministry, Masařík and Heidrich, informed the German chargé d'affaires in Prague that the government accepted the new German demands (those of November 10 relating to the so-called sixth zone) and expressed the hope that there was nothing more standing in the way of a German guarantee of the new frontiers.[143] The reaction of Berlin was sulky, and two days later Ribbentrop declared that the question of the guarantee must not be linked with that of frontier delimitation and depended on further political developments in general.[144]

The French attitude was also evasive. According to Alexis Léger, the Secretary General of the Quai d'Orsay, things should not be hurried with the exception of an immediate danger. France, not seeing such a danger, did not want to act with precipitation. Asked by minister Osuský, Léger replied on November 21 that he could deal with his demands only if Czechoslovakia were threatened by new territorial losses. Therefore he asked Czechoslovakia to give new details to support her demands. The conversation took place in the presence of minister Bonnet. "I had an unfavorable impression," Osuský reported to Prague. Bonnet was more reserved, while Léger was talking openly and sincerely. "After all, it amounts to the same thing."[145]

On November 23, when the chapter of territorial changes was finally terminated by the protocol signed in Berlin on November 21, Chvalkovský informed the representatives of the four powers in writing, and in a verbal commentary indicated that in these circumstances the question of the guarantee was the order of the day. The German answer was negative. Following Ribbentrop's instructions, the German chargé d'affaires in Prague reiterated again that there was no direct connection between the two questions, the guarantee being a separate matter.[146]

As to France and Britain, Chamberlain and Halifax were meeting Daladier and Bonnet in Paris on November 24 to undertake a *tour d'horizon* on the eve of the signature of the French-German declaration. The discussion touched even the new situation in Czechoslovakia and in the first place the promised guarantee.

According to the British, the guarantee should only come into force as a result of a decision by three of the four powers. The French objected that this would reduce its value, because actually there would never be three powers against one, but always four against none, or two against two: France and Great Britain against the two Axis powers. But the British did not give in. Chamberlain considered the guarantee only as "an extra assurance to the somewhat suspicious Czechs." Halifax pointed out that "there was perhaps some danger in establishing a position where a future Czechoslovak government might look to France and Great Britain for support in pursuing a policy not entirely in conformity with German wishes." He thought that that would constitute "a certain element of provocation" to Germany. A situation therefore should be avoided when two Western powers alone should be helping Czechoslovakia like in September, but this time in a far worse position, with a weakened Czechoslovak army and an important German road to cut the Czechoslovak territory. The best way to handle the problem would be through Prague.[147]

Berlin was informed soon about the discussion. When Ribbentrop came to Paris on December 6 to sign the French-German declaration he easily raised doubts about the guarantee. He tried to induce Bonnet to give up the French interests in Central Europe, including

Czechoslovakia, and to abandon that area to Germany. Such was the German version of the conversation. On the other hand, Alexis Léger declared that nothing similar was said. According to the German minutes, Ribbentrop stated that Germany regarded this part of Europe as being definitely within her sphere of influence. He especially resented a British guarantee of Czechoslovakia. As he told Bonnet he did not understand what England was now seeking in Central Europe where so far she had not wished to be engaged.[148] And he explained in detail "how favorable it would be for the future reconciliation of differences between the authoritarian states and the democracies, and particularly between Germany and France and Britain, if this German sphere of influence were respected in principle."

Bonnet answered in vague terms. He only said that since Munich the situation had changed basically. When he raised the question of the guarantee for Czechoslovakia, the German minister was evasive.[149] Germany intended only to await developments, for her guarantee depended on the solution of the other minority problems and on German-Czech relations. Czechoslovakia should not "fall back into the Beneš rut once again." According to Ribbentrop, a four-power guarantee would mean a certain temptation for Czechoslovakia to follow once more the old paths of the Beneš policy. In the further discussion Ribbentrop added that the idea of such a guarantee would not be favorable to the course of understanding just embarked.[150] Thus the Paris conversations on this point were not satisfactory and Ribbentrop only promised to examine the problem again after his return to Berlin.[151]

During this impasse the two western powers were preparing to answer the Czechoslovak note. The guarantee appeared to them less and less opportune. In Paris, as well as in London, it seemed that the promise of September 19 was a somewhat hasty gesture, and that the guarantee was useless and even dangerous since the German impact on Czechoslovakia was increasing daily. Such a reluctant approach was not new. It had filled Chamberlain—in his own words—with apprehension since the very beginning when the idea of a guarantee was broached. According to him a truncated Czechoslovakia would be an unstable state and there would be no means by which Great Britain could implement the guarantee.[152] How could one guarantee a state which was compared by the opposition leader Clement Attlee to a chicken, a victim of a fox? How could one guarantee the frontiers of a state whose eastern half was coveted by greedy neighbors? Didn't the Czechoslovak minister in Berlin, Mastný, complain to the French ambassador Coulondre that his country wasn't anything but a mere German province?[153]

In his report of December 8, the British minister in Prague analyzed the situation of the post-Munich state and openly expressed the question of whether Czechoslovakia as such could continue to exist. Another report of the British diplomat spoke about the guarantee with open skepticism and reviewed the facts which, according to him, had since the beginning of October weakened the independence of the state. Above all, according to Newton, the proposed *Autobahn* across Moravia would be a further nail in the coffin of the independence which Czechoslovakia lost in Munich. Germany had a legal right to take direct interest in the treatment of the German minority, the possibility of a customs union was always lurking in the background, the loss of Sub-Carpathian Ruthenia was possible, Slovak separatism could be observed. A memorandum by the military attaché, Major G.A.C. MacNab, recently appointed to Prague, supported Newton's arguments about the end of Czechoslovak independence. The only power capable of guaranteeing Czechoslovakia was Germany. "The sooner, therefore, she gives the guarantee she promised at Munich the better, and any action on our part which might delay it or make Germany suspicious of Czech intentions would only be harmful to Czechoslovakia," stated Newton.[154]

On the same day when Newton was writing his pessimistic report, he was instructed by Halifax to find out the Czechoslovak views on the question of guarantee. It was in line with the decisions of the Franco-British conference of November 24 in Paris, when the two western allies, embarrassed by this problem, tried to shift the decision on to Prague's shoulders.[155]

Newton saw Chvalkovský on December 10. The Czechoslovak minister declared that his government had done its part in the full, had promptly executed the Munich Agreement, and now looked to the four powers to do theirs. According to him, the four powers should settle amongst themselves how they would implement their promises. "Any kind of guarantee would be welcome and the broader the better," declared Chvalkovský, adding that, "we would like this guarantee as soon as possible." In view of the slight British interest in the whole issue it is not surprising that Newton—according to the Czech version of the talk—repeatedly stressed that Czechoslovakia might be satisfied with a guarantee solely from Germany.[156]

In Berlin, ambassador Coulondre called on Weizsäcker on December 21 to ask whether there was anything new on this question. The answer was negative. When the ambassador insisted, the Secretary of State replied smiling: "Could not this thing be forgotten? Given the predominance of Germany in this area, would not the guarantee by the Reich be sufficient?" The French diplomat then mentioned the recent Franco-German declaration: "How can you expect that our agreement of

December 6 will inspire confidence in France if you do not observe an agreement signed by you a few months ago?" After the Vienna Award the conditions set for the guarantee were fulfilled. *"Alors, qu'attendez-vous?"* asked Coulondre. However, nothing could overcome Weizsäcker's opposition to the four-power guarantee. Czechoslovakia, in his words, belonged definitely to those territories, which had to be regarded as German domain. Nothing other than a German guarantee had any significance for Prague.[157]

To break this vicious circle, Chvalkovský wanted to sound out Rome. He probably relied on his previous good contacts in Italy, and maybe also on the anti-German feelings always present on the banks of the Tiber. Toward Christmas he announced to Rome that he would like to go there at the beginning of the year. Ciano's answer was evasive; the visit could take place only in February. At the same time the Italian foreign minister informed Berlin that in this affair Italy wished to act in concert with Germany.[158]

The exchange of opinion between Great Britain and France proceeded at a rather slow pace. On December 22, London informed Paris that it was now proposing to approach the German and Italian government on this subject. When Chamberlain, accompanied by Halifax, stopped over in Paris on his way to Rome in January, it was agreed to raise the question of the guarantee both in Rome and Berlin.[159]

However, Mussolini, when he received the two British statesmen on January 12, did not manifest much eagerness to deal with the affair, and his proposals were rather evasive. He declared that he was not unfavorable in principle, but that he did not think the time had come yet. To be effective, the guarantee should be given by the neighboring powers. Other powers might later come in, but their effect would be moral rather than material. Before a guarantee could be considered, three questions should be settled: 1) the internal constitution of Czechoslovakia itself, 2) the establishment of her neutrality and 3) the demarcation of her frontiers on the ground, not on the maps as was still the case.[160]

Before his journey to Rome, Halifax sent an aide-memoire about the British standpoint to Paris on December 22, and asked France for her latest information on the subject. The Quai d'Orsay answered only three weeks later, on January 13, and stated that there were grounds for hastening the implementation of the guarantee. A common Franco-British demarche in Berlin was therefore recommended.[161]

The demarche took place on February 8, 1939. Coulondre delivered a verbal note asking the German government to state its views on the guarantee as soon as possible.[162] It sounded out the German government on its intentions, and pointed out that Mussolini, in the course of Chamberlain's visit had indicated the conditions on which, in his view, the guarantee depended. While the French note mentioned this detail in a fleeting way, the British note enumerated point by point Mussolini's three conditions, thus weakening the weight of the note and stiffening the German attitude.[163] For, as Coulondre said later, "the eel was already under the stone."[164]

* * *

At the beginning of the negotiations the western powers were thinking also of the participation of other states which could join the four signatories of the Munich Agreement. However, these efforts failed. In the first place, there was the question of Soviet participation. The French representatives proposed it as early as September 18, in the course of their talks in London.[165] The Franco-British plan of September 19 suggested explicitly that the existing treaty arrangements between Czechoslovakia and France, and Czechoslovakia and the Soviet Union should be converted into a system of guarantees, which implied the Soviet Union, too.[166] On October 3, British Home Secretary Sir Samuel Hoare indicated that he envisaged a guarantee by all great powers and declared: "We do not in any way contemplate the exclusion of Russia." Two days later, Chancellor of the Exchequer Sir John Simon went still further and said that it was very important that Russia join in the guarantee.[167]

With the changing situation in Europe, the two western powers were, however, becoming skeptical about the Soviet guarantee. At the Franco-British conference in Paris on November 24, it was made clear that France did not wish to assume alone the responsibility for excluding the Soviet Union. The conference therefore left the decision to Czechoslovakia.[168] As early as the beginning of December, Chamberlain was inclined to abandon the Soviet guarantee if it would lead to the absence of the two partners of the Axis.[169]

However, the Soviet Union itself was not much disposed to grant the guarantee. The period between Munich and the fall of Maxim Litvinov in May, 1939, was a time of hesitation in the foreign policy of the Kremlin, and this attitude was reflected even in this issue. At the beginning of October, Czechoslovak minister in Moscow Fierlinger asked the Commissar of Foreign Affairs, Litvinov, and his deputy about this matter several times. Litvinov replied that he saw "no sense in the guarantee of a state which was becoming an appendix of Germany." In a note delivered to Fierlinger on October 9, he asked whether Czechoslovakia herself wished such a guarantee. Like the western powers, Moscow was leaving the decision to Prague. The answer of Chvalkovský was prompt and negative: Only the signatories of the Munich Agreement were competent to decide about the admission of new guarantors.[170] Berlin had been hostile to a Soviet guarantee since the beginning.[171]

CHAPTER III
THE UNEASY INTERLUDE

The harshness with which Berlin forced the implementation of the Munich clauses and the tensions which appeared among the partners who had only recently assembled at the conference table did not augur well for the future. Czechoslovakia found herself in a situation all the more alarming because her eastern part was far from stabilized. Germany was aiding and abetting the Slovak separatist elements, and in the Sub-Carpathian Ukraine, the Polish and Hungarian campaign for a common frontier threatened this far-away province with political liquidation.

The International Situation in Winter 1938–1939[1]

In the course of the winter 1938–1939 the illusions created by Munich were disappearing one after another and Europe asked with anxiety how long the capital allegedly gained in Munich would last. Though not liquidating Czechoslovakia entirely, Germany by the Munich Agreement totally paralyzed her former adversary. France and Britain were tacitly recognizing German predominance in Central Europe.[2] Even in the Berlin-Rome Axis the German preponderance was felt and it was Germany which on several occasions set the tone.

The dominating figure on the European scene was Adolf Hitler. The German dictator had brought from Munich a most negative impression of the western statesmen. In his eyes they were but "little worms" (*Würmchen*), and Chamberlain was an old man whom "he could put into his pocket." In a village in southern Bohemia, on October 20, he freely gave vent to these animosities. He wouldn't tolerate anything any more, he boasted; Germany was strong enough and could withstand any stress.[2] At that moment he was not yet decided where to turn next. Even Ribbentrop ignored what his master's intentions were.[3] The way to attain his nearest objective, total destruction of Czechoslovakia, had not yet fully crystallized in his mind. The final goal was, however, clear: domination over Europe and the world. "The pacifist record has worn out" (*die pazifistische Platte* [*hat sich*] *bei uns abgespielt*), he declared on November 10.[4]

In the aftermath of Munich, Britain and France, still full of optimism about the prospects of a peaceful cooperation with the Axis powers, tried to capitalize on the conciliatory spirit presumably found at the conference. British Premier Chamberlain, still in Munich, signed a declaration with Hitler on September 30 expressing their decision to deal in the future with questions concerning their two countries through consultation.[5] The French followed. On December 6, Ribbentrop and the French Foreign Minister Georges Bonnet signed a declaration in Paris aimed at terminating the ancient rivalry between the two countries, and insuring, after centuries of bloody struggles, peace on the Rhine.[6]

The Franco-German declaration was a belated fruit of the Munich euphoria and materialized in an unfriendly political climate. In the meantime tensions had appeared and especially German-British relations were slowly deteriorating. The British intention to remove deficiencies in the national defenses, shown in the course of the Munich crisis, ran counter the plans of Berlin and provoked an angry reaction. If England wanted to take action against Germany, let her try, Hitler declared on November 24. He was ready. If Britain rearmed, he would rearm twice as fast. They could never catch up with him.[7] Similarly British voices criticizing the policy of appeasement irritated Hitler and in two public speeches, in Saarbrücken on October 9 and in Weimar on November 6, he fiercely attacked the alleged British "war mongers."

The relations of the other members of the Axis, Italy, with the two western democracies, followed an inverse pattern. On November 16 the Anglo-Italian agreement of April 16 came into force and London recognized the conquest of Abyssinia. On November 19 France followed suit and the new ambassador, François-Poncet, presented his credentials to "the King of Italy and Emperor of Abyssinia." While Italian relations with Britain seemed outwardly satisfactory, tension was increasing with Paris in spite of this conciliatory gesture. Mussolini, judging France severely weakened by her retreat in Munich, was trying to force her to accept several Italian demands. This ill will found its expression on November 30 when in the course of Foreign Minister Ciano's speech a demonstration broke out in the Chamber of Deputies in the presence of Mussolini and the deputies loudly claimed Tunis, Corsica, Nice and Savoy.[8]

The French reaction was an emphatic refusal. On January 26, 1939, Daladier replied in the Parliament to all Italian demands with a categorical "No." The same day Foreign Minister Bonnet refuted the charges that France by her agreement with Germany of December 6 abandoned her eastern allies. He stated that the declaration did not affect the relations of France with any part of eastern Europe and did not destroy the agreements which France had contracted in that area with the Soviet Union and Poland.[9] Berlin immediately grasped the meaning of these words and Ribbentrop subsequently warned France several times against "this relapse into the so-called Beneš policy."[10]

Thus in the first months of 1939 the optimism born in Munich passed away. The two camps were watching each other with increasing suspicion. "The word 'peace' is in the mouths, but the fear of war has penetrated all the souls," with these words even the architect of French appeasement, Minister Bonnet, characterized the international situation in January, 1939.[11] Chamberlain himself was worried by the failure of Hitler to make "the slightest gesture of friendliness." Nevertheless the British Prime Minister was not abandoning his desire for a détente with Germany and decided to send two ministers, Oliver Stanley, the President of the Board of Trade, and R. S. Hudson, the Secretary of the Department of Overseas Trade, to Berlin by mid-March to sound out the German leaders on economic, and if possible even political matters.[12]

Speculations about the future direction of German dynamism abounded. Would it be the East, the Ukraine, or the West? The press in the western world and the reports of the western diplomats were full of these conjectures. In mid-January rumors about a possible German attack on Holland spread and the British resolved to speed up their military talks with France.[13]

However, despite these alarming signals, there was still a strong dose of optimism in the West. In London it was strengthened by the reports of the British Ambassador in Berlin, Sir Nevile Henderson, who was prone to believe Ribbentrop's assurances that nobody in Germany was thinking of anything but peace.[14] On February 18 Henderson even reported as his "definite impression" that Hitler did not contemplate any adventures at that moment.[15] Briefing newspaper correspondents in the Parliament on March 9, Chamberlain outlined in general an optimistic picture of the situation. "Europe is settling down to a period of tranquility," the Premier assured the journalists.[16] The same optimistic note appeared in a speech of Home Secretary, Sir Samuel Hoare, in Chelsea on the following day who set forth his rosy hope for a "five years' peace plan" which would lead in time to the creation of "a golden age."[17]

Similar illusions were still prevailing in France. In a speech of February 26 Bonnet expressed the hope that the declaration of December 6 would prove the first step toward the establishment of confident relations between the two countries. The French ambassador in Berlin, Coulondre, himself a critical observer of the German scene, believed at the end of

February that the moment was favorable for improving Franco-German relations and that the German government was well disposed.[18] Events following a few days later demonstrated clearly the profound futility of these British and French illusions.

Hitler's Plans—Relations between Prague and Berlin

The relations between the Reich and Czechoslovakia continued to be unsatisfactory. The loyal declarations of Prague got little response in Germany and the new territorial demands put forward by Berlin in November showed that Chvalkovský, in spite of his compliance, did not fare any better than Beneš.

At the time several projects were formulated in Germany which not only served to consolidate the territorial gains achieved at Munich, but to reach far beyond them. These plans were nothing new. They dovetailed as well with Hitler's ambitions as with the narrow nationalism of the Sudeten German leaders. Before Munich the Sudeten German party worked out a plan (*Grundplanung OA*) stating that the Reich had a historical right to the Czech lands, that the Czech language was to be pushed back, and the Czech territory Germanized.[19] The proposals formulated after Munich followed approximately the same vein, but were marked by an increasing radicalism. Around the time of the Munich conference or shortly afterwards, the Sudenten Germans proposed to Hitler special ties of Czechoslovakia with Germany and submitted a plan which already indicated the future solution: a "protection" (*Schutz*) of Czechoslovakia by Germany (quoting the relations of France and Monaco and the treaty between Britain and Transvaal).[20]

The Sudeten German leader, deputy Kundt, shortly after Munich recommended attempting to gain the trust of the Czech people to show that the National Socialism respected the national feelings of other nations,[21] but at the same time he reserved to the Czech people only a seeming sovereignty (administrative autonomy).[22] Similarly his colleague, the deputy Hans Neuwirth, in a memorandum for the German foreign ministry stressed that the goal of German policy must be securing of the Bohemian area for German interests. His proposals were one of the blueprints for future events. As one possibility Neuwirth mentioned the support of the Slovaks and Ukrainians up to the separation from the Czechs. Then, under the pretext of disorders and difficulties that would arise, the Czech lands should be annexed and put under the direct German administrations. Only out of consideration for the possible impact on smaller nations of south-eastern Europe which Germany had been trying to win, the authors of these proposals refrained for the time being from more radical measures and suggested only gradual moves.[23]

Berlin kept silent on its intentions. Its plans could be guessed only indirectly. The thoughts of Hitler, in his Obersalzberg retreat, were already reaching beyond the success of Munich. In his speculations he followed the same line adopted in the months preceding Munich: to be able to take the offensive while others were still preparing their defenses. It was necessary, according to Hitler, to preceed as quickly as possible, for time worked against Germany and "in two years the others will be much stronger than we."[24] His morbid preoccupation with his own health was another reason for prompt action.[25] He wanted to settle his territorial differences with Poland and thus prepare the way for a successful *Drang nach Osten.* Ribbentrop set forth these German plans to the Polish ambassador on October 24. Hitler repeated them on January 5, 1939, and on January 26, Ribbentrop exposed them again during his visit to Warsaw: the return to Danzig to Germany, an extraterritorial German railroad line and throughway across the Polish corridor. For the success of this policy, and to be guaranteed against a possible collision with the West, Germany had to be protected on her southern flank even better than by the Munich amputation of Czechoslovakia. Though powerless, Czechoslovakia had to be liquidated.

Munich deprived Hitler of the possiblility of a quick war which would have radically settled the fate of Czechoslovakia. A few days after Munich Dr. Schacht overheard Hitler saying: "That fellow (apparently Chamberlain—the author's note) has spoiled my entry into Prague."[26] The Franco-British capitulation in Munich made it difficult to start hostilities. The mood of the German population seemed to be against the war and this was probably one of the reasons which had made Hitler opt for the peaceful settlement. According to him "the solution of Munich could be only temporary." He was convinced that Germany could not tolerate on her flank "an abscess" of an independent, thought small, Czechoslovakia.[27] And on October 20, on a visit to southern Bohemia, he did not hide his plans for the incorporation of Bohemia and Moravia into the Reich.[28]

This stand of Hitler was known even to foreign observers. So the French ambassador, François-Poncet, knew not long after the meeting of Munich that the Führer, far from feeling happy about the success, thought that he was a victim of the cunning of his partners and blamed them for having prevented him from occupying the whole of Czechoslovakia.[29] The ink was hardly dry on the Munich Agreement when Hitler already spoke of a near and total liquidation of the Czech problem."[30]

The tension continued. On November 21, Hitler declared to the

Belgian Ambassador, Jacques Davignon, that he would not hesitate to intervene with armed forces "should Czechoslovakia have a point directed against Germany."[31] According to State Secretary Meissner, Hitler regarded the Czechs as worse enemies than the Poles. They ought to be extirpated before the solution of the Polish problem.[32]

On the other hand, the opinion of the military also had its weight. The Chief of Staff of Supreme Command of the Armed Forces, General Wilhelm Keitel, estimated that in the event of war Czechoslovakia could even after Munich pin down some 25 German divisions at the beginning. According to Keitel, Germany should arrive at the point where, in any conflict between Germany and the western powers, Czechoslovakia would no longer be of importance as an opponent of Germany. "The ideal would be voluntary military neutralization, something like the system in Luxemburg, whereby Czechoslovakia could retain about three divisions."[33]

Berlin was of course opposed to the building of a new Czechoslovak system of fortifications facing Germany which would force her to take reciprocal measures thus wasting her resources. Chvalkovský during his visit to Berlin in October promised Ribbentrop that Czechoslovakia was planning no new line of fortifications against Germany and that she would have only "quite a small army."[34] From Hitler he heard that strategic considerations were of no value for Czechoslovak security and that under these circumstances "a large army was an absolutely superfluous luxury for the country."[35]

On October 21, Hitler issued a directive to the Wehrmacht, signed by himself and countersigned by Keitel. According to it the Wehrmacht should be prepared for three eventualities: 1) Securing the frontiers of the Reich and protection against surprise air attacks; 2) liquidation of the remainder of Czechoslovakia, and 3) the occupation of Klaipeda (Memelland). "It must be possible to smash at any time the remainder of the Czech State, should it pursue an anti-German policy," says the preamble. The preparations should be considerably less in extent than those for the operation *Grün* of April 22. On the other hand, they should guarantee a high state of preparedness. The instructions showed clearly the predilection of Hitler for lightning actions to paralyze the enemy. The organization was to be prearranged for a surprise assault "so that Czechoslovakia herself will be deprived of all possibility of organized resistance." And further: "Quick and decisive success must be assured."[36]

Two months later this directive was completed, probably under the influence of German-French exchanges and the particularly advantageous stand of Germany in Prague. Whereas the first version envisaged a military action, the second directives issued on December 17 were preparing only a police action: "Outwardly it must be quite clear that it is only a peaceful action and not a warlike undertaking. The action must therefore be carried out *only* with the peacetime Wehrmacht, without reinforcement by mobilization."[37]

Parallel to this action initiated personally by Hitler and organized by Keitel there were preparations made in the German foreign ministry in the context of Chvalkovský's upcoming visit to Berlin. Ribbentrop, with the aid of German chargé d'affaires in Prague Hencke, elaborated several treaty projects to be submitted to the Czechoslovak minister. The mainstay of this treaty system was to be formed by a "Treaty of friendship" (*Freundschaftsvertrag*) which would have subjugated Czechoslovakia completely to Berlin, approximately like Belgium was to be attached to Germany in the case of a German victory in the First World War. The preamble of the draft stated that it was advisable for Czechoslovakia to look to Germany for political and economic support. Germany was to guarantee the inviolability of the Czechoslovak territory (art.1). The Czechoslovak government was to obtain the agreement of the German Reich in all questions of foreign policy. Czechoslovakia was to regard her former treaties of alliance as "obsolete" and "superfluous" and was not to conclude such treaties with third powers in the future (art.2). She was to adapt the futture organization of her army to the military interests of Germany (art. 3). And the two governments were to negotiate immediately their future economic relations (art.4).[38]

This basic document was to be accompanied by two complementary protocols dealing with military and economic matters. A military protocol the text of which was proposed by the Supreme Command of the Wehrmacht on December 3 stipulated close cooperation of both armies which in reality would have made the Czechoslovak army subordinate to Germany. No fortifications or barriers were to be built on the Czechoslovak-German frontier. The Czechoslovak armed forces which were to be of minimum size, were expected to lean on Germany and break off connections with other countries. Any proposals as to the strength, organization, and armament of the Czechoslovak army were to be submitted to Germany for approval. Arms and munitions were to be standardized on German pattern. There was to be no intelligence service against Germany, and Czechoslovakia was to be forbidden to tolerate intelligence service by third powers against Germany on her territory.[39]

In the field of economic relations Germany was rather circumpsect. Though eager to exploit the economic potential of her former adversary, she was not inclined to a closer union which could bring new burdens to her strained economy. As early as before Chvalkovaký's first visit to

Germany in October a memorandum which the German Foreign Ministry prepared for this occasion pointed out that in the case of a customs or economic union a foreign body (*Fremdkörper*) would be much in evidence in the German economy. In the view of its author, ambassador Ritter, an economic union would force Germany to provide Czechoslovakia with raw materials, such as iron ore, metals, textile raw materials, etc. Germany, having just acquired 10 million new customers, could carry such a new burden only with greatest sacrifices. According to Ritter, she could attain her economic goals in Czechoslovakia in other ways without burdening herself with deliveries of raw materials.[40] Hitler turned down the entire proposition on the ground that the Czechs could not be trusted. His final decisions made all these projects superfluous and they were shelved. Chvalkovský's proposed visit materialized late in January in a changed atmosphere when Hitler's plans for future actions were assuming their final form.

Simultaneously, the speaker of the German minority in Czechoslovakia, deputy Ernst Kundt, was raising his voice inventing new complaints against Czechoslovakia in spite of the Czech concessions. He warned his countrymen against the exercise of the right of option and against any decision which could weaken the German position in Czechoslovakia. In a memorandum submitted to Ribbentrop on December 16, Kundt stated that the Germans in Bohemia and Moravia were "in a really diastrous social and economic situation" and that the Czechs were "getting bolder again."[41] In a speech delivered in the first session of his *Arbeitsamt* at the beginning of January, 1939, he condemned the Czech efforts after Munich to build a purely national, Czech state. "This space is in the middle of a great political empire of the German people, so that Czechoslovakia will have to adapt accordingly in the very near future her relations to the German Reich, the German people and the German community remaining here," he declared.[42]

On January 17, in his press bulletin, he exposed under the title "What we want" the six points of the demands of the German minority: 1. Political activities of the Germans should be absolutely free from the point of view of program as well as of organization and exterior forms. 2. The Germans should stay in their present employment. 3. The German schools should be maintained and have a greater autonomy. 4. The Jews should be removed from all German-Czech relations. 5. Harmonious relations should be assured between the Czechs and the German people not only in the economic, but also in the political sphere. 6. Harmonious relations between the Germans of Czechoslovakia and the Czechoslovak government should prevail.[43]

In another speech, on February 15, he complained again that the Germans in Czechoslovakia were worse off than before and on February 17 he resumed the old favorite German slogan of the Germans as the *Kulturträger.* He even went so far as to declare that "today was no longer the era of Goethe, it was the Hitler era," and he warned that Czechs against half-measures, for the National Socialism, according to him, knew no compromise on principles.[44]

Kundt's statements aroused the indignant protest of the Czech press. "At this moment we should ask," wrote *Svoboda* in Brno, "that the Germans do not interfere with our domestic affairs. Kundt does not facilitate his task by resuming the ancient tone." "The old mentality of our Germans is not suitable to new circumstances," said the Catholic *Lidové Listy* on January 18. "The attitude of Germans must change in the new Czechoslovakia," wrote *Národní Politika* the same day. "The Germans are in our state not against their will . . . Those who remain here stay voluntarily and with the consent of the Reich. Therefore they should cease to present extremist claims."[45]

To a British observer Kundt's speeches were painfully reminiscent of the situation preceding Munich and he was surprised to find Chvalkovský "not unduly perturbed or pessimistic" about reaching an agreement with Kundt.[46] Chvalkovský, however, feigned optimism only in talks with the Prague diplomats. In a closed conference he declared bluntly that the minority problem had not disappeared in Czechoslovakia, only on Henlein's place was now Kundt and he was openly supported by the Reich.[47]

Still another symptom showed the interest of the Reich in the fate of the Germans remaining in Czechoslovakia: Hitler decided against the transfer of the German university in Prague to Germany and on January 11 the university was solemnly reopened.

* * *

When Chvalkovský met Ribbentrop on the occasion of the Vienna Award, the German Foreign Minister expressed his intention to receive him in Berlin in the near future,[48] however the decision about the date of the second visit dragged. These delays apparently mirrored Hitler's hesitations about which course to take. At last, on January 21, 1939, Chvalkovský made his second trip to Berlin. The recrudescence of the demands of the Sudeten Germans was not very auspicious for his visit. Only a few days earlier he had to complain of a whispering campaign, evidently emanating from the former Sudeten-German party, that the incorporation of Czechoslovakia in the Reich was imminent.[49] Indeed, German preparations for the visit foreshadowed a changed attitude toward Prague. There were to be no negotiations. The drafts of treaties prepared less than two months ago were pushed aside and Chvalkvovský was to be confronted with a long list of alleged German grievances. When Mastný inquired two days before Chvalkovský's arrival about probably themes of the forthcoming talks Weizsäcker refused to discuss any agenda.[50]

During his long talk with Ribbentrop in the morning and his audience with Hitler in the late afternoon, Chvalkovský was pressed into the posture of a petitioner overwhelmed with reproaches, thinly veiled threats and increased demands.[51] If he wanted to settle the question of guarantees or the rectification of frontiers, he was disappointed. If he wanted to learn the German attitude toward the new Czechoslovakia, he was submerged by a flood of argumentation which could not satisfy him. He did stress several points which were essential for Prague, but in vain. The answer was a long string of Ribbentrop's reproaches: Czechoslovakia did not seem stabilized, far from that. There were symptoms of a reawakening of earlier tendencies which made it seem as if a disguised Beneš policy were being pursued. According to German information, 90 percent of the followers of Beneš in the administration still held their posts. The *Maffia*, too, the well-known secret Czech political organization of the war years, was apparently springing up again. In a section of the Czechoslovak press and even in papers close to the government, a tone had been adopted which to Germany seemed extremely strange, said Ribbentrop. He quoted the passages of two Czech newspapers of January 20, *Venkov* and *Národní Hlas,* which said that the present situation could not be looked upon "as unalterable and permanent." The Germans were dismissed from factories producing strategic material, continued Ribbentrop. German university clinics were boycotted. Berlin learned that the official documents still used the expression "occupied territory" for the Sudeten German districts.

The audience with the Führer was full of the same grievances. There had been no thorough clean-up of the followers of the policy of Beneš. They had in reality strengthened their position of late. The Czechs seemed to Hitler like "drowning people" who in their extremity were grasping at a straw and pinning new hopes on it. "Much of what one reads in the papers was quite incomprehensible. He—Hitler—had the impression that these people in Czechoslovakia were waiting for the great miracle which would, however, never come." "It was incomprehensible to him," Hitler continued, "that any dreams still existed in Czechoslovakia of a new Czechoslovakia extending beyond her present frontiers." No power in the world would send even one soldier to save Czechoslovakia. All hopes of a "new return" were chimerical. Hitler considered the tendency of pronouncements in the Czechoslovak press a dubious symptom and advised Chvalkovský "to eliminate everything that could foster this tendency."[52]

The Chancellor and his Foreign Minister wanted to suppress all opposition, to break the least attempts to resist to the Reich, as for instance in the case of the demands formulated recently by the representative of the German minority, deputy Kundt. Should these tendencies persist, they would one day lead to "catastrophic consequences," according to the words repeated twice by Ribbentrop. Hitler threatened to call an "energetic stop" to the Czechoslovak question, if he were to be convinced that Czechoslovakia intended to rise at the first outbreak of conflict in Europe. "If Czechoslovakia," said Hitler, "ever thought of being a weapon against Germany, that would be catastrophic not for Germany, but for Czechoslovakia. Czechoslovakia should realize that her destiny was interwoven with that of Germany. It would be madness to think that great power politics could still be played in Prague today. The only solution is to live together with Germany on the closest terms."

The embarrassed Chvalkovský stressed to Ribbentrop that he had purged his ministry of the "worst" representatives of the old political trend. For a stricter control of the press, where, according to Chvalkovský Jewish influence was still strong, Czechoslovakia would set up an office on the pattern of the German propaganda ministry. On the other hand he complained to Hitler that the loan accorded after Munich by Great Britain favored Jewish emigration above all. Further he enumerated the achievements of the new regime in the three months of its existence: The Communist party was wiped out. Relations with the Soviet Union had so cooled that Soviet minister Sergei Alexandrovsky did not visit him any more. The Social Democrats had been driven into the background, the newly founded leftist Labor Party would not be admitted to the government in any case. Complete freedom of action for the German National-Socialist Party in Czechoslovakia had been established by a special decree of Czechoslovak cabinet. The Hitler salute and the wearing of the swastika were not objected to by the Prague authorities. Chvalkovský intended to create a special section in his ministry for dealing with the question of the German minority and he promised Ribbentrop to drop the expression "occupied territory" which was still used in Czechoslovakia for the Sudeten German districts and to which Ribbentrop took exception.

Among these explanations and promises Chvalkovský attempted to insert his demands. Of these the most modest was the return of the seven Chod villages. Ribbentrop stopped him immediately: "In no circumstances could he enter into a discussion of the German-Czechoslovak frontier."[53]

Much more important was to explore the intentions of the Reich with regard to the guarantees of the frontiers. Chvalkovský could raise this issue only at the end of his talk with Ribbentrop. When the German minister inquired about the reorganization of the Czechoslovak army, Chvalkovský replied that the army estimates had been cut by half, that the demobilization had been completed, but that no precise plans existed for the reduction of the army: everything depended on the frontier guarantee. "If the frontier of Czechoslovakia were guaranteed, she could consider herself a neutral state and could do with a very small army," declared Chvalkovský.

Ribbentrop's reaction was negative. He admitted no connection between the reduction of the army and the question of the guarantee, and changing the subject, he recommended to Chvalkovský that he "eliminate the influence of the Jews." According to the German minister, the impression sometimes prevailed in Germany that Chvalkovský stood quite alone.

In the afternoon, when he received the Czechoslovak minister, Hitler raised the military issue, too. Referring to the Dutch and Danish example he tried to show the importance of the absolute neutrality of the small states, which could content themselves with but a small army. If Czechoslovakia's attitude toward Germany were decided by mutual trust, an army of 10,000 or 20,000 men would suffice. Therefore Czechoslovakia should reduce her army, because it didn't count anyway. Unable to wage a war with her arms, Czechoslovakia could, according to Hitler, at the best only equip fortifications and a few forlorn posts, but could not oppose a modern army like Germany's. Without even mentioning the question of the guarantee, Hitler undermined all hopes of success Chvalkovský might have entertained.

The last favor Chvalkovský could ask in Berlin was some sign of good will towards the weakened Czechoslovakia. "A good word from Germany would work wonders," he told Ribbentrop. He repeated this theme to Hitler: "That from time to time the Führer could say a good word to the Czechoslovak people. That might work wonders." If he would state publicly that he wished to cooperate with the Czechoslovak people, not with the foreign minister, Chvalkovský shrewdly insinuated, that would demolish the entire structure of foreign propaganda. These remarks terminated the audience with Hitler who took leave of his visitor with the words: "Let's hope for the best."[54]

In spite of this optimistic remark, Chvalkovský returned to Prague worried and with a feeling that the atmosphere in Berlin was not favorable to his country. All his attempts to secure a better understanding had failed. Moreover, the Germans presented new demands.

The depression of Chvalkovský and his companion, the chief of his cabinet, Hubert Masařík, after their return, did not escape foreign observers. The British chargé d'affaires, J. M. Troutbeck, who visited Masařík shortly afterwards, summed up his impression in the following words: "I cannot say that I found Dr. Masařík in buoyant spirits. Indeed, rather the contrary. He opened the conversation by saying that it was impossible to conceive the difficulties of conducting the foreign policy of his country in the present conditions." Masařík gave the British diplomat a precise picture of the Berlin meeting, passing over in silence the unsuccessful step regarding the guarantees. Of this Troutbeck took notice and thought it suitable to report to London that the word "guarantee" was not mentioned either by Masařík or by himself throughout the conversation.[55]

Chvalkovský, too, tried to hide his uneasiness. During a conversation with the French minister he enumerated the German demands and attempted to present them as German pre-conditions for granting the guarantee. De Lacroix in his report summed up the German demands in ten points. Some of them, though important, are not contained in the memoranda of Hewel and Schmidt (e.g. the withdrawal from the League of Nations or the transfer of a part of the gold reserve). According to minister de Lacroix, the German demands consisted of the following points:

1. Complete neutrality of Czechoslovakia.
2. The foreign policy of Czechoslovakia must be brought into line with that of the Reich; adhesion to the Anti-Comintern Pact is deemed advisable.
3. Czechoslovakia must immediately leave the League of Nations.
4. Drastic reduction of military effectives.
5. A part of the gold reserve of Czechoslovakia must be ceded to Germany. A part of the Czechoslovak industries having been ceded, a part of the gold reserve must accordingly pass into the hands of Germany.
6. The Czechoslovak currency from Sudetenland must be exchanged for Czechoslovak raw materials.
7. The Czechoslovak markets must be opened to the German industries of Sudetenland. No new industry may be created in Czechoslovakia if it competes with an industry already existing in Sudetenland.
8. Promulgation of anti-Semitic laws analogous to those of Nuremberg.
9. Dismissal of all Czechoslovak government employees who may

have given Germany any grounds for complaint.

10. The German population of Czechoslovakia must have the right to carry Nazi badges and to fly the National-Socialist flag.[56]

Ferment in Slovakia and Carpatho-Ukraine

The ample autonomy achieved in Žilina appeared insufficient to the radical elements of the Slovak Populists. It only reinforced the separatist trend of the extreme right wing, represented by a group of young radicals such as Ferdinand Ďurčanský, Matúš Černák, Alexander Mach and Karol Murgaš who were hostile to the Czech orientation even before Munich.

This group of men, without any practical political experience, probably would not have been able to exercise—in spite of a favorable conjecture—any considerable influence on the Slovak political life had it not found a leader and organizer in the person of Professor Vojtěch Tuka, a man of a rather varied political past.

Born in 1880 in Piarg, Slovakia, Tuka declared himself Hungarian since his youth. Before the First World War he was a professor of international law in Budapest. In 1916 he was appointed professor at the Hungarian Academy of Law in Bratislava (the Presburg). In that year he published a theoretical treatise in Magyar, *A Szabadság* [*About Liberty*] in which he advocated the then current Hungarian opinion that the nationalities living in Hungary had no right to an independent national life, but had to be assimilated to the uniform Hungarian nation. In the census taken in Czechoslovakia in 1919 he declared his nationality and mother tongue as Magyar and only later proclaimed himself Slovak. At the end of 1920 he sought contacts with the Slovak society and even joined Hlinka's Populist party. He made a good impression on Hlinka and was entrusted with the task of drawing up the autonomist program of the party. In 1922 he became editor-in-chief of the party's daily organ, the *Slovák*. According to a contemporary witness he was working at that time in favor of the Hungarian legitimist circles whose aim was to create on the debris of Czechoslovakia a Habsburge empire comprising Bavaria, Austria, Slovakia, Hungary, Slovenia, Croatia, and Dalmatia.

In 1925 Tuka was elected to the Prague Parliament. In January 1928, he published an article in *Slovák* entitled "Vacuum iuris." There he affirmed that toward the end of the war it was agreed in Turčianský Svätý Martin that Slovakia would be attached to the Czech lands only for a trial period of ten years, after which a plebiscite would settle her relations with Prague. Since the plebiscite had not materialized, there was according to him a legal vacuum, and the Slovaks should decide whether they wanted to stay united with the Czechs in a common state and under what conditions.

At that time the Slovak deputy, Milan Ivanka, accused Tuka of collusion with the Slovak irredentist Fratišek Jehlicska, who was active abroad on behalf of Hungary against Czechoslovakia. In October 1929, Tuka was condemned to 15 years in jail. In 1937, President Beneš remitted the rest of his prison terms and Tuka was sent to a forced residence in Plzeň in Bohemia.[57]

After Munich he was released from detention, transferred to Piešťany in Slovakia on October 23, and handed over to the Slovak Minister of Justice, Ďurčanský, on condition that he would be well guarded and not permitted to go to Bratislava.[58] These terms were, however, not observed. At the time of the Vienna arbitration Tuka was in Vienna pleading for Slovak independence. He was disappointed when he was told by the Germans that Germany, for the time being, was in favor of Slovakia remaining in the frame of the Czechoslovak state.[59] In the middle of November he was in Germany again, this time protesting against the occupation of Devín.[60] At last, on December 6, he appeared in Bratislava. He was welcomed by Tiso himself and by Ďurčanský and attended a parade of the Hlinka Guards. He immediately started a radical separatist campaign and a few days after his arrival he stressed the necessity of an independent Slovak state. In the New Year's issue of *Slovák,* he urged the Slovak people not to be satisfied with autonomy any more, which according to him was but a presage of greater changes.

His words fell on fertile ground. A week later Mach declared in the same paper: "We wished and wish more." Another paper of the party, *Slovenská Pravda,* wrote: "Tuka was right ten years ago. He was right in proclaiming the truth which is prevailing today and which after our revolutionary times will find its expression in a Slovak state. The words of Tuka about the Slovak state do not frighten us."[61]

In spite of the weakened position of Prague, the Slovak separatists would not have been able to attain their aims by their own strength only. They had to look for help abroad. Hungary, of course, would have considered a voluntary return of Slovakia together with the Sub-Carpathian Ruthenia to be the most practical solution to the Slovak question, but even the most radical separatist could not think of it. The memories of the past were still alive and it was impossible to present such a proposal to the Slovak people.

The only acceptable option was the aid coming from Germany. Both the sympathy for the German totalitarian system as well as endeavors to gain German aid against the Hungarian revisionism played a decisive role at this juncture. For the Slovaks the enemy had been traditionally

Hungary, not the Germans or Germany. Thus in the opinion of the Germanophile wing of the Populist party an "unconditionally friendly cooperation with Germany" was to be one of the pillars of the Slovak policy.[62]

The Carpathian German party (*Karpathen-deutsche Partei*), a branch of the Sudeten-German party in Slovakia, which had been suppressed on October 5, resumed its activities on October 9 under the new name of the German party (*Deutsche Partei*). On October 9, its leader, the deputy Franz Karmasin, was appointed by Tiso State Secretary for the affairs of the German minority in Slovakia. Subsidized financially by Germany, he acted as liaison between the radical separatists and the leading German circles in Vienna. Through his offices Ďurčanský was received by Göring on October 12.[63]

The Germans turned their attention to Slovakia immediately after Munich. As early as October 6 the Supreme Command of the Armed Forces addressed a memorandum to the Foreign Ministry stating that it was in the German military interest not to separate Slovakia from the other parts of the Czechoslovak state, for the rump-state would of necessity depend to a considerable extent on Germany.[64] On October 7, the director of the ministry's political department, Ernst Woermann, drafted a memorandum for Hitler on the situation in the eastern part of Czechoslovakia. As for Slovakia, he mentioned four alternatives: total independence, autonomy within the Czechoslovak state, autonomy oriented toward Hungary, and autonomy oriented toward Poland. The memorandum rejected the last two possibilities, for Germany had no interest in any form of union of an autonomous Slovakia with Hungary, and the Slovaks themselves strongly rejected any solution of this kind. Germany was interested even less in a Slovak orientation toward Poland. By her acquisition of Těšín, Poland had already considerably increased her power in this area, and the addition of Slovakia to the Polish economic sphere would have put considerable difficulties in the way of German economic expansion in the south-east. Thus there remained only the first two alternatives. The economic viability of a completely independent Slovakia was doubtful, but was possible if Germany provided support. An independent Slovakia would best further the German penetration in the East and would be the point of least resistance in that area. The memorandum declared that Germany could tolerate "for the present" the solution just reached in Žilina. A complete separation between Bohemia and Slovakia would always be possible later. Hitler chose the Žilina settlement and on the following day he informed Ribbentrop that he thought it opportune to support that alternative of the Slovak autonomy within the framework of the Czechoslovak state.[65]

When Ďurčanský, accompanied by Mach, called on Göring on October 12 to ask his protection against Hungarian territorial demands, the Slovak representative declared that his people never wanted union with Hungary, but full independence, with very close political, economic, and military ties to Germany. Göring gained the impression that these efforts for independence should be suitably supported, for a Czech state without Slovakia would be even more at German mercy. According to him, an air base in Slovakia for operation against the East was very important.[66]

Shortly afterwards, on October 19, Ribbentrop received a larger delegation in Munich consisting of Tiso, Ďurčanský and Bačynśkyj. The Slovaks again defended their interests against the Hungarian questions, Ribbentrop privately invited Tiso and Ďurčanský to his hotel in the evening to ask them confidentially how they envisaged their future relations with Prague. Of the two Slovaks, Tiso was the one who was more reserved. According to him, the future depended on how Prague would respect the Žilina agreement. If Prague did not adhere to it, complete separation would soon follow. Ďurčanský, according to the German minutes,[67] seemed to be striving rather for a complete independence, possibly in union with Carpatho-Ukraine. Ribbentrop wanted to know if an independent Slovakia would be viable. Tiso replied that culturally and economically, she could maintain independence as long as she was helped militarily by guarantees of the great powers. She would be unable to form a modern army for the defense of her frontiers.

On November 11, Ďurčanský visited Germany for the third time in one month. He again called on Göring, above all to plead against the German aspirations concerning Devín. The marshal remained "cautious." He declared that at the moment the Slovak (and Ukrainian) question could be dealt with only "within the framework of the Czechoslovak state." An independent Slovakia was, however, the goal of the German policy.[68]

It seems that this contact of Göring with the Slovaks was not approved of by higher places in the Reich. On November 17, the chief of Göring's cabinet, General Karl Heinrich Bodenschatz, was informed on behalf of Ribbentrop that at the moment political negotiations with the Slovaks were not opportune. "The Führer had decided that at present the question of the separation of the Slovaks should not be touched upon, either in a positive or in a negative sense." The decision depended in part on the negotiations which had to take place "during the next few days" between Ribbentrop and Chvalkovský. The visit of the Czechoslovak minister came, however, two months later and in the meantime the Slovak problem was left virtually on a sidetrack.[69]

These visits of the Slovak leaders to Germany were not ignored in

Prague. President Hácha and Prime Minister Beran hoped nevertheless that a friendly settlement was still possible. The government decided that Hácha should visit Slovakia after Christmas to talk with Tiso about the outstanding problems. The President left Prague on December 26 for the mountain resort of Tatranská Lomnica in the Tatras. "I am leaving with the best will," he declared, "and I am convinced that Tiso as a Catholic priest will proceed in the same way and as sincerely as I." The negotiations ended to the satisfaction of the President. Tiso reaffirmed his loyalty to the republic and promised to remove the extremist elements and not to tolerate the intrigues against the integrity of the state.[70]

Thus the year 1939 began in a favorable atmosphere. The opening of the first Slovak Diet on January 18 indicated that the separatist elements were retreating and that moderation was prevailing. On this occasion, in the presence of Beran, several Slovak speeches were made in favor of coexistence in a united state. Tiso spoke of Hácha and Beran as of "personalities with a sense of reality." Two days later, two moderates, Mikuláš Pružinský and Josef Sivák, entered the Slovak government, while the extreme separatist Černák was removed.[71]

Nevertheless the separatist agitation continued and found expression in several speeches of the leading radicals. On February 5, Murgaš, in the village of Rišňovce near Nitra, declared himself openly for an independent Slovakia.[72] These moves had their repercussion in some Prague government circles. The Minister of Transportation, General Alois Eliáš, who knew well the situation in Slovakia, urged the demotion of the Tiso government. Concerned about the agitation of the radical elements of the Slovak Populist party, he summoned a private meeting of some Czech ministers in the neighborhood of Prague on February 12. The ministers decided to propose to Beran and Hácha an immediate dismissal of the Slovak government. A few days later a private session of the Czech ministers, under the chairmanship of Beran, took place. Beran, however, rejected Eliáš's initiative and remarked that in politics one must always be patient. Chvalkovský declared that the official German policy did not support Slovak independence, and he, too, refuted the proposal.[73]

* * *

Whereas in November Hitler apparently hesitated regarding what line to take with respect to Slovakia, a month later, in December, there were indications of his renewed interest. He called his economic advisor and minister for special duties, Wilhelm Keppler, and directed him to prepare himself to go as a political observer to the Slovak area.[74] His final plans probably crystallized in the last days of January. From his visit to Warsaw, Ribbentrop reported a negative attitude of Poland toward the German demands, and Hitler decided to settle his dispute with Poland by use of arms. It was, however, necessary to remove from his right wing the potential danger represented by Czechoslovakia.[75] As early as January 15, his remarks to the Hungarian Foreign Minister, István Csáky, indicated that he was examining the possibilities of a territorial—and no more ethnic—settlement with Czechoslovakia.[76] Hence his stronger support of the Slovak separatism.

Toward the end of January, Hitler called several chief officials of the Secret Service to a conference and declared that "the foreign policy of Germany demanded that the Czechoslovak Republic be broken up and destroyed within the next few months." The officials were ordered to prepare moves which could make possible the setting up of an independent Slovak state by the middle of March. Hitler stressed the secret nature of his orders: no other government department was to know of it.[77]

In the middle of February—according to Keitel—Hitler declared to him and to General Brauchitsch that he was ready to launch a military operation against Czechoslovakia which he designed as a "pacification action." He motivated his projects by the situation of the German minority in Czechoslovakia which according to him was "unbearable."[78] The audience which he granted to Tuka on February 12 was a sign of this changed attitude.

On February 2, Tuka was received by Göring, to whom he expounded his views. Göring advised him to repeat his statements to Hitler.[79] This audience took place in the newly inauguarated *Reichskanzlei* in Berlin. It lasted one hour and was a clear sign of decisions made by Hitler in the preceding weeks. The Slovak separatism was to be used to completely disrupt the Czechoslovak state and thus create the first stepping stone to further actions in the east. Though a private person—he was neither a member of the cabinet nor even deputy of the Diet—Tuka seemed to the German leaders the ablest man to accomplish this end.

He came accompanied by the State Secretary for German affairs in Slovakia, Karmasin. He addressed Hitler in the German way as *Mein Führer.* According to him, Hitler was the first to acknowledge the dignity of the Slovak people. The Slovaks wished, under the leadership of the Führer, "to fight for the preservation of European civilization." If they were still part of the Czechoslovak state, it was only because the present government was considered as a provisional phase. However he, Tuka, and his fellow-combatants were determined to follow the wishes of the Slovak people and to create an independent Slovakia. "I lay the destiny of my people in your hands, my Führer; my people await their complete liberation by you," said Tuka.

Then Hitler spoke and lost himself, as was his custom, in an endless monologue. He stated that up to six months ago he had been under the impression that Slovakia desired reunion with Hungary. It was only in his conversation with the Hungarian Prime Minister, Béla Imrédy, in September that he had realized that it was not so. In a veiled way Hitler indicated that the fate of Bohemia was already sealed, for the "Beneš mentality" was coming to life again. If this trend continued he would act quickly and ruthlessly as he had said to Chvalkovský. If it came to a far-reaching solution of the problem, Germany would not remain alone, for then Poland and Hungary would certainly join in. No difference then would be made between Czechia and Slovakia, as they were still conceived of as a unit. There was a German proverb "Cling together, swing together" (*Mitgefangen, mitgehangen*). Had the Slovaks declared their independence at the time of the [Munich] crisis, the position would have been very simple for Germany, who would have guaranteed the Slovak frontiers at once.

Hitler summed up his conclusion in three points: 1) He regretted that he had not known earlier of Slovakia's struggle for independence. 2) Further, he regretted that the situation then was not clear, for otherwise the solution would have been much simpler for all concerned. 3) If Czechia would not content itself with its natural destiny, he saw dark days ahead for Slovakia, too.

To this Tuka replied that he knew that the Czech future was dark. Therefore the Slovaks should free themselves from Czechoslovakia. Hitler then closed the conversation by declaring that it would be "a comfort to him to know that Slovakia was independent."[80]

In Slovakia more radical winds were blowing now than only a few weeks ago when the session of the Slovak Diet was opened in the presence of Czechs. In the government declaration made by Tiso in the Diet on February 21, the Prime Minister spoke only of the Slovak state.: "We shall build our state, our new state, our Slovak State . . . The Slovak people is about to build the state as an organ of its national sovereignty and guardian of its interests."[81] On the following day the propaganda chief Mach examined in the *Slovák* the possibilities of the Slovak independence. In his view the Slovak nation was "capable of creating a state"; this was not only its right, but its national duty. To a French newspaperman he declared that the Slovak ideal was "a total independence, the sovereignty of the Slovak state."[82]

In the following critical weeks Germany, however, turned to Tiso, and Tuka remained in the background. A report emanating from the office of Rudolf Hess, Hitler's deputy, indicated that Tuka was a sort of lone wolf considered by the Tiso group as a disagreeable intruder.[83] The German consul in Bratislava, Druffell, expressed the opinion that Tuka was unable to form an adequate power-apparatus (*Machtapparat*) to carry out the total separation of Slovakia from Prague and that he had not many real supporters.[84]

The assessment of leading Slovak personalities given by Keppler's assistant, Edmund Veesenmayer, was probably decisive. This economist was sent in February by the German Foreign Ministry to Slovakia in order to study the political situation. Although he thought well of Tuka and Ďurčanský, he proposed that Tiso, "a modest, sound and quiet man," should assume the leadership of Slovakia. He submitted his findings to Keppler, who gave them in turn to Ribbentrop.[85]

In Slovakia Veesenmayer entertained contacts with the separatist circles and tried to cow them by inaccurate contentions that Hungary was preparing to occupy Slovakia by mid-March. The only way to avoid it, he declared, was to proclaim Slovak independence.[86]

* * *

East of Slovakia, in Carpatho-Ukraine, the situation was equally unsettled. Several serious incidents occurred at the beginning of January at the border with Hungary. During the night of January 5–6, fire was exchanged at the demarcation line near Mukačevo. Another incident took place south of Užhorod when the Hungarian irregulars attacked a Czechoslovak patrol.[87] The origin of the Mukačevo incident was rather obscure. It was apparently caused not only by the Hungarians, but the Ukrainian irregulars seemed to have had in it their share, too. The Czechoslovak note of January 17 spoke rather cryptically of "local situation" as being at the origin of the incident.[88] There were mutual protests and on January 12 talks began at Mukačevo to settle the incidents. Hungary accepted the Czechoslovak proposal to prohibit armed civil persons from approaching the demarcation line.[89]

In January and February Germany was still persevering in her negative attitude towards Hungary's plans. Ribbentrop told Csáky on January 16 that Germany opposed any isolated Hungarian action, and according to Hitler it was disloyal of Hungary to oppose the Vienna Award.[90] Hungary was restrained even by her loyal supporter, Italy. Foreign Minister Ciano described the Hungarian attempts to sabotage the Award as "a silly policy" and he exhorted Budapest to be more correct and to abstain from provoking incidents. Mussolini himself seemed to be irritated by Hungarian actions.[91]

Warsaw regarded Carpatho-Ukraine as a center of anti-Polish activities and feared that a wide autonomy of that region could foster similar movements among the large Ukrainian minority of eastern

Galicia. The Polish minister in Prague protested unceasingly against the Ukrainian propaganda emanating from Chust.[92]

The January incidents strengthened the conviction of the Czechoslovak government that it should take energetic measures to maintain its authority in Chust and forestall complications which could be created by radical Ukrainian nationalists.[93] Prague therefore abandoned its previous reserve and appointed, on January 16, the third minister in the Carpatho-Ukrainian government, General Lev Prchala, a Czech well acquainted with conditions in the eastern part of the state.[94] The Chust government refused, however, to accept him. The political disarray continued. Chust was teeming with foreign agents and, as an American observer remarked, was "reeking with intrigue."[95] The economic life of the province was crippled. In mid-February Révay reported to the press in Prague that the requirements for the coming year were estimated at 310,488,909 crowns, the revenues only at 66,604,224 crowns.[96]

The principal adversary of General Prchala was the radical Unkrainian nationalist, Minister Julian Révay. Not discouraged by the opposition of the Chust government, Prague demoted Révay on March 6, on the very eve of the final crisis. He ws succeeded by the moderate Stefan Kločurak (Minister of Economics). Prchala was assigned the portfolios of Transportation, Finance and moreover with that of the Interior, responsible for the maintenance of law and order.[97] However, no time remained to give him the occasion to influence the reshuffled government.

CHAPTER IV
THE END OF CZECHOSLOVAKIA

Prague's Last Attempts to Appease Berlin—Germany Refuses the Guarantees

The unsatisfactory result of Chvalkovský's journey to Berlin in January indicated precisely the atmosphere of painful uncertainty felt in Czechoslovakia during the few weeks before the end of the state. Settlement of the territorial problems had not brought any relaxation, and Czechoslovakia had to grapple with several serious political issues, each of which was practically menacing her existence. Hitler's remarks about Czechoslovakia in his Reichstag speech of January 30 were unable—because of their laconism—to dispel the apprehensions.[1]

The decline of parliamentary democracy in Czechoslovakia proceeded only at a slow pace and under foreign pressure. Nevertheless after Chvalkovský's return from Berlin, the tempo had to be stepped up. Several steps were taken to meet the criticism expressed by Berlin. Above all the remaining supporters of Beneš, the *Beneš-Anhänger* who inspired such hatred and distrust in the German leaders were to be removed. So the daily *Národní Osvobození*, organ of the former legionnaries from the First World War, suspected of "benešism", had to cease publication. In the last days of February, the municipal council of Prague, known as a citadel of the Beneš supporters, was dissolved by decree and the mayor, Petr Zenkl, one of the pillars of the preceding regime, was removed from office. Even before Chvalkovský's visit to Berlin severe measures were taken against the communists. By a decree of the Supreme Administrative Court all communist parliamentarians—25 deputies and 15 senators—were deprived of their seats on December 28, when their party was suppressed.[2]

In spite of its reluctance to treat the Jews in the same radical way as Germany,[3] Prague had to take several measures to at least partially appease Berlin. A decree was published on Feburary 2 about the control of citizenship acquired after November 1, 1918. Another decree regulated the residence of refugees in Czechoslovakia, especially those of German origin. In principle, they were threatened by expulsion. Each case was, however, to be examined separately by the authorities. As to the German emigré press, published for the most part in Paris, its importation and distribution were prohibited even before Chvalkovský's trip to Berlin. The Czechoslovak press was ordered to suppress any criticism of Germany. The law on the protection of the Republic was modified: it was prohibited to slander foreign heads of state and their representatives.[4]

Immediately after Chvalkovský's return, the government authorized the activities of the German National-Socialist Party.[5] Until then the swastika was permitted only in private premises. Now it could be hoisted even in public, simultaneously with the official Czechoslovak flag. The first time the swastika flags were to be seen in Prague in greater numbers was on January 30, the anniversary of the beginning of Hitler's regime.

Under the chairmanship of Minister of Justice, Jaroslav Krejčí, a special commission was set up to deal with the demands of the German minority. It proved, however, quite ineffective. The Germans ignored it and deputy Kundt behaved in Prague like the official protector of the remaining Germans. His statements were symptomatic of the changing situation. On February 4, 1939, he delivered a lecture in the Academy for German Law in Berlin in which he denounced the Czechs for their alleged mistreatment of the German minority and spoke of Czechoslovakia as of a semi-independent state. He further stated that he would soon submit to Beran his proposals concerning the minority problems and added threateningly that "the Czechs would be amazed."[6]

He presented them orally to Beran on February 23. They were based on a proposal elaborated by his, Kundt's, legal advisor, Dr. Herbert Kier, and would have made the German minority in Czechoslovakia virtually a state within the state. The German National Socialist Party was to be the sole representative of the German population. The areas inhabited by the Germans were to be clearly delimitated and the German minority was to be represented in the government by a special officer with the status of a minister.[7]

The Czechoslovak premier agreed to discuss Kundt's demands and to co-opt him or a personality designated by him as minister for the German minority. At the same time Kundt compiled a report complaining about the conditions of remaining Germans, based on the exaggerated reports of his *Arbeitsämter* and in a letter to Hitler he declared that the situation was so bad that it required "speedy and sweeping decisions."[8]

Just at this juncture he was recalled to Berlin from where he returned only with the German occupying army.[9] His mission in Czechoslovakia had become superfluous, for Hitler had other plans than merely to integrate the German minority into the framework of the rump-state. In

Berlin Kundt was received by Hitler only once—for just about five minutes.[10]

The Germans continued to view the Czechs with distrust. The German chargé d'affaires raised doubts as to whether the measures undertaken under the pressure of Germany after Chvalkovský's return from Berlin would have any practical effect. Germany was watching closely for any signs which would indicate resistance to her policy. If persons who had incurred Germany's displeasure were appointed to official posts, the German legation in Prague intervened without delay. The Czechoslovak diplomats abroad who were critical of the Munich Agreement were denounced.[11]

Berlin naturally followed closely the Czechoslovak press and attempted to influence it. The chief initiator in this respect was the German Press Attaché (*Pressebeirat*) in Prague, Karl von Gregory. He systematically goaded the leading Czech press officer, Zdeněk Schmoranz, chief of the Press Division of the Prime Minister's Office, to streamline the press according to the German demands and did not spare his objections to articles which he considered unfavorable to German political line and philosophy. As soon as October 13 he suggested the dismissal of Jan Hájek, chief of the Press Division of the Foreign Ministry, one of the pillars of the Beneš policy in the field of journalism, a man whom he described as "a rabid hater of the Germans" (*wütender Deutschenhasser*). He was offended when the Prague authorities did not take steps against foreign newspapermen reporting impartially about the plight of the country (e.g. against the American journalist G.E.R. Gedye). Finally, the German legation turned directly to Chvalkovský, urging him to settle the matter according to the German wishes. The measures proposed concerned the organization of the press, prohibition of papers in German language published without the German official authorization as well as the distribution of German books and newspapers criticizing Germany, and cleaning up among the representatives of the foreign press in Czechoslovakia. The organization of foreign press correspondents in Prague (*Association de la Presse Etrangère*) was to be purged of its anti-German writers and in the future no foreign journalists were to be admitted into it without the consent of the German legation.[12]

"When one realizes on the spot the terrible complexity of a situation at times tragic and always delicate, when one sees what painful problems the Czech leaders have to solve almost every day, what painful situations they are often facing, under what pressures, under what threats, after what threatening interventions they are sometimes—death in their soul—forced to act, one certainly does not feel he has the right to throw a stone at them, one is not in the mood for criticizing them, one must feel for their courageous efforts nothing but total sympathy . . . " in these words a French observer summed up the situation in Prague at the beginning of 1939.[13]

Almost identical terms were used by the minister of Czechoslovakia in Moscow Fierlinger when he spoke at the beginning of February with Assistant Commissar of Foreign Affairs, Vladimir Petrovich Potemkin. He refused the criticism of the neutralist policy of his country which was voiced in Moscow, and declared: "We don't need any reprimand, but encouragement and comprehension of our difficult situation." And he quoted the words of Chvalkovský: "If a great power wants us to pursue a different policy, let it tell us that it is willing to give us military help in the case when Germany would be planning to occupy Prague." Fierlinger repeated the same arguments to Litvinov on February 5.[14]

The Czechoslovak concessions to Germany were not limited to political issues. They extended equally to the field of economics. In Berlin in January, Chvalkovský was asked to cede to the Reich a part of the gold reserves of his country. On February 18, Göring, as commissar for the Four-Year Plan, urged Ribbentrop to press for the delivery of gold as quickly as possible because the situation of Germany in the field of foreign exchange was becoming more difficult every day.

The negotiations between the *Reichsbank* and the Czechoslovak National Bank took place in Berlin from February 26 to March 4. The Czechoslovak Bank had to deliver immediately the sum of 481 million crowns, of which 465.8 million was to be in gold, and 15.2 million in foreign exchange. The transfer took place on March 9 and 10th.[15]

There were concessions in the military sphere, too. After hasty talks, an agreement was signed on January 25 authorizing the passage of German troops by railroad through Czechoslovakia.[16] Toward the end of February it was decided, at German request, that soldiers of Sudeten German origin would be sent home and were not to be drafted again.[17] At the beginning of the same month the government announced a reduction in the number of officers and non-commissioned officers. They were to be transferred as far as possible into the civil service, for instance, as secretaries in the municipal or district administrative bodies. By a decree of the Ministry of National Defense, the deadline for demobilization was February 28. The class of 1936, which should have remained in service until the end of April, was released. General Ludvík Krejčí, chief of the General Staff, was dismissed. Prague informed Germany that the Czechoslovak army would be cut down from 24 divisions to approximately 14.[18] The defense budget, however, remained high in order to cover the expenses of the two mobilizations undertaken in 1938.

Meanwhile rumors about the upcoming action against Czechoslovakia were spreading in the Nazi inner circles. They spilled over to the diplomatic community in Berlin, though it was not easy even for seasoned diplomats to distinguish factual information from empty gossip. On the whole, it seems that by February there was little left of the secrecy which Hitler had ordered in connection with his plans concerning Slovakia. People in Hitler's circle were talking of a "dislocation" (*Auflösung*) of Czechoslovakia, and Ribbentrop declared at the same time that "there would be again trouble" if the Czechs did not realize that they had to respect German wishes.[19] On February 13, Weizsäcker wrote in his private notes that Czechoslovakia would be dealt a death blow within about four weeks.[20] Toward the end of the month, Herbert von Dirksen, the German ambassador to London, learned in Berlin that Hitler was planning a march into Czechoslovakia.[21] Henlein's deputy, K.H. Frank, heard similar rumors "time and again" in February.[22]

On the Czech side, Beran and Chvalkovský attempted to explain to their countrymen the situation and at the same time to appease Berlin in reaffirming their adherence to a close cooperation with the Reich. At a meeting of the parliamentary club of the Party of National Unity on January 25, Prime Minister Beran declared that it would be catastrophic to believe that every danger had been dispelled. In Brno, on January 29, he stressed friendship with Germany, and announced the reorganization and limitation of the armed forces.[23] On February 22, Chvalkovský declared: "We cannot play with the destiny, otherwise Munich would be a prologue to a new catastrophy. We would not survive a new crisis provoked by our own errors. The state is not yet past the danger."[24]

* * *

At the beginning of 1939 the Czechoslovak foreign policy—or what remained of it—had almost no options. To hope for any change of the international situation seemed at that moment but wishful thinking. Nevertheless even the leading circles were not giving up all hope. Beran himself—though convinced that Britain would keep pursuing her appeasement policy—declared in intimate company that it was necessary to wait for a changed situation. The leading economist, president of the biggest Czechoslovak bank, the *Živnostenská banka*, Jaroslav Preiss, was expecting an early outbreak of the war and was endeavoring not to trouble relations with the western powers.[25] Similar views about an approaching armed conflict were expressed by former President Beneš in a message addressed indirectly to Chvalkovský after his return from Berlin.[26]

For the time being these conjectures apparently had only academic value. Chvalkovský returned to Prague convinced by Hitler's words that no power in the world would send one single soldier to save Czechoslovakia. Nevertheless, in the midst of everyday problems arising from relations with the Reich, he was not forgetting the principal goal of his endeavors, the international guarantees.

When the answer to the Franco-British note of Feburary 8 was long in coming, he conceived the idea of neutrality as suggested by Mussolini in the course of the visit of the British ministers. On February 17, in discussing the reorganization of the Czechoslovak army with the counsellor of the German legation, Schleinitz, he declared that Czechoslovakia was thus giving up every means of defending herself. Therefore, the guarantee of her frontiers was all the more important. If she had the prospect of being recognized as a neutral state, she would abandon her whole treaty system. In that case, Chvalkovský continued, he could denounce the treaty with France. He could then consider as nonexistent the pact with Soviet Russia, and Czechoslovakia could abandon her obligations toward the League of Nations.[27]

On February 18, Chvalkovský asked the British chargé d'affaires, J.M. Troutbeck, whether Czechoslovakia could not make a declaration of neutrality "somewhat on the Belgian model of two years ago," and he requested that he sound out the opinion in London. He mentioned the same problem to the French and Italian envoys.[28] On February 22, Prague handed to the four signatories of the Munich Agreement an aide-memoire recalling their promise of guarantees. To facilitate its fulfillment, Czechoslovakia stated that she was ready to make a solemn declaration concerning particularly the engagement of a strict neutrality and non-interference in possible disputes of the great powers.[29]

This initiative of Prague was not to the liking of Berlin. The audacity with which the feeble neighbor appealed to the other powers raised its indignation. Although Czechoslovakia informed Berlin first, her chargé d'affaires, Ladislav Szathmáry, was received by Weizsšacker on February 22 in a rather unfriendly way: Whether the Czechoslovak demarche in Berlin took place half an hour sooner or later, declared the German diplomat, seemed unimportant. What really counted was the fact that Czechoslovakia had approached all four Munich powers simultaneously without a preliminary consultation with Berlin. As for the problem itself, the guarantees, Weizsäcker reserved his reply.[30]

On February 28, Mastný himself visited the Wilhelmstrasse to explore the situation. He complained to Weizsäcker of the vicious circle in which Czechoslovakia found herself: She could not be consolidated internally in the absence of a frontier guarantee, and she could not receive a frontier guarantee, because she was not internally consolidated. Weizsäcker manifested the same vagueness as a few days earlier in his conversation with Szathmáry, and postponed a concrete answer to the question of the guarantees until later.[31]

This negative attitude of Berlin was, however, not the only disquieting symptom. On Febrary 11, Ribbentrop declared that Germany was not interested in a speedy conclusion of the work of the German-Czechoslovak delimitation committee.[32] The Czechoslovak representatives, though naturally ignoring these instructions of the German minister, felt immediately the lack of good will and the wish to prolong the talks.[33]

Under these circumstances the Prague government wished to get more detailed information than was possible through normal diplomatic channels. Among other things it wanted to know to what degree it could deal with Kundt. Out of personal ambition Kundt was at that time attempting to concentrate in his hands all negotiations concerning the extant minority problems and was by-passing the official intergovernmental committee set up by the agreement of November 20.[34] Besides this there were several problems of foreign policy which Prague wished to clarify. Accordingly two emissaries were sent to Berlin: an unofficial one, the agrarian journalist, Vladimír Krychtálek, who had already paid a visit to Berlin in November, and an official one, Chvalkovský's chief of cabinet, Dr. Hubert Masařík. With Mastný having reached the age of retirement and about to leave his post, Chvalkovský wished to obtain direct information through a man of his trust. Masařík intended to use this end his friendly relations with the chief of the section for Austria (at that moment in liquidation) and Czechoslovakia in the German foreign ministry, Counsellor of Legation, Günther Altenburg, whom he met several years ago in Sofia.[35]

With detailed instructions on most of the controversial issues and authorized to make large concessions, Masařík called on Altenburg on March 1. He recapitulated the problems mentioned by Chvalkovský in Berlin in January and declared that the Czechoslovak foreign minister was at pains to deal with the points then discussed with Ribbentrop. In the majority of them, Chvalkovský—according to Masařík—had succeeded. Masařík stressed the instructions issued to the press, the aryanization efforts and the dismissal of the followers of Beneš from the administration. As to disarmament, he stated that the large number of officers could not be discharged as quickly as the troops were demobilized. He also mentioned the moves taken to satisfy the demands of the German minority.

The principal aim of Masařík's visit was the question of the guarantees. He tried, therefore, to explain the origins of the Czechoslovak memorandum of February 22 and referred to Hitler's recommendation to Chvalkovský that Czechoslovakia should no longer play great power politics, but confine herself to her own affairs. "The Czechoslovak government," Masařík declared, "was grateful for every piece of advice from the German government's side as to how this aim of neutralizing Czechoslovakia could be further promoted."

Then the Czech visitor passed to the problem of the unsettled eastern part of the country. He explained the difficulties created by the resistance of Chust to the central government. He also complained of the Hungarian and Polish agitation against Carpatho-Ukraine and stated that Prague considered the Vienna Award as binding. He kept silent on the German interference in Slovakia saying only that "the Slovak transmissions from the Vienna broadcasting station were found to have a disturbing effect."[36]

In conclusion, Masařík enumerated the concessions which Czechoslovakia was ready to make to achieve friendly relations with Germany. Prague would like to be informed about the German wishes regarding the German minority. All requests would be given the utmost consideration. The Czechoslovak government was ready to admit a German minister, to be nominated by Berlin, into the cabinet. This minister, Kundt, or someone else, would be a trustee of Germany in the cabinet. His presence would insure that the cabinet would not make any decisions which were not compatible with friendly relations between Berlin and Prague. The reorganization and reduction of the Czechoslovak army was to be carried out in accordance with Berlin's wishes. To control this, the number of German military attachés in Prague could be increased. According to Masařík, all these were "suggestions" and any German request "would be gratefully received."

The proposals did not meet, however, with the expected reception. Altenburg listened to them passively, without hiding his skepticism about the treatment of the German minority or the memorandum presented by Prague to the four major powers.[37] When Masařík called on him again on March 2, to ask what answer he could take back to Chvalkovský, Altenburg answered evasively that Germany was far from satisfied with the attitude of the Czechs.[38] The spirit of Beneš persisted. The situation of the German minority was worse than at the height of the Sudeten crisis. Masařík replied that his task was to express Prague's readiness to enter into all discussions and give all guarantees. He added that the consolidation of the state was all the more difficult because the Slovaks were relying on German assistance. When he asked whether Chvalkovský could soon make another journey to Berlin, the answer was yes, later, when the consolidation had progressed.[39]

Similarly sterile was the second journey to Germany made by Beran's emissary Krychtálek. He was to see Kundt who was at that time in Berlin, and discuss with him the German demands. Also he had to find out the German attitude to several problems of foreign policy: Should Czechoslovakia wait or give up the British and French guarantee of her borders? Would Germany assume then the guarantee alone? Could Czechoslovakia conclude a treaty with Poland about coal deliveries? How far could the Prague government go in its friendly relations with Italy? What attitude should it adopt to Yugoslavia?

Krychtálek attempted without success to be received by Ribbentrop. He was told that it was unthinkable inasmuch as Czechoslovakia had tried to the get promised guarantee by by-passing Berlin. Ribbentrop, who saw Krychtálek by chance in the lobby of the ministry, only dropped a disparaging remark: "Is this the newspaperman from Prague? Beran should hurry up. Let them there not take our opinions lightly."[40]

Ribbentrop marked Altenburg's memorandum on Masařík's visit for the attention of Hitler. On March 5, however, Hitler's aide, Walter Hewell, added a marginal note: "Führer not interested."[41] For at that time, Hitler was preparing the final blow. In the first place he refused any international guarantee. A note dated February 28 was handed on to the British and French ambassadors on March 2, as the answer to the demarche of February 8. As a pretext for a new postponement of the guarantees Hitler used the Polish and Hungarian demands for a common frontier, the same demands which he had turned down three months ago.

The note, the essential part of which was drafted by Hitler himself,[42] stated that already during the Munich conference Germany made it clear in unequivocal terms that it could consider a guarantee of Czechoslovakia only if the other neighbors of that state would also be prepared to assume similar obligations. However, between Hungary and Poland on the one hand, and Czechoslovakia on the other, a difference of interpretation existed as to the accuracy of the demarcation of the frontier line now agreed upon. According to the German government, the undeniable danger still existed that "guarantees prematurely given would lead not to a reasonable solution of the internal problems of Czechoslovakia, but rather to a stiffening of antagonisms, and might thereby contribute toward inciting fresh conflicts." The guarantees given by the western powers could be rather "one more factor toward the stiffening of irrational tendencies, as was the case in the past." After all, the general development in this European area fell first and foremost within the sphere of the most important interests of the German Reich, not only from the historical point of view, but also from the point of view of geography and, above all, economy. Hence, the German government believed that it was imperative to await first a clarification of the internal development of Czechoslovakia, and the improvement of her relations with the surrounding states.

The note refuted not only the French and British move, but also the Czechoslovak memorandum of February 22. On March 3, Weizsäcker summoned Mastný to inform him of the German answer. Mastný—according to the German minutes—was "obviously uneasy" during the whole conversation and objected that to his knowledge there was no mention at the Munich conference of a guarantee by the other neighbor states of Czechoslovakia. "A guarantee given today would be no premature promise," said Mastný. "On the contrary, precisely through a guarantee the present state of suspense would be terminated."[43]

In spite of the negative attitude of Germany the Czechoslovak diplomats in Berlin tried once more to sound out the Wilhelmstrasse. On March 9, counsellor of legation, Miroslav Schubert, called on Altenburg. His conversation with the German diplomat somewhat dispelled his worst apprehensions. Schubert mentioned at first the campaign of the German press against Czechoslovakia which started at the beginning of March, and remarked that Berlin used that method every time when it wanted to prepare the ground for an immediate action, as in the case of Austria and the Sudeten. Prague could not understand the present campaign and was afraid that it would confuse the relations between the two states. Czechoslovakia, Schubert continued, fulfilled all the German demands and was ready to proceed in the same way in the future, but she must know the real desires of Germany. To support his words, Schubert enumerated nine cases where the authorities of the Sudeten territory announced an imminent occupation of Czechoslovakia. Altenburg expressed his indignation and said that these cases would be closely investigated. Schubert then drew the attention of the German diplomat to rumors circulating in Berlin about a nearing aggression on Czechoslovakia and the concentration of the German forces near the frontier. Altenburg refuted and ridiculed them declaring that he could give his official denial. He did not, however answer, the question of what the demands of Berlin were.[44]

The disquieting rumors continued to spread dispelling the hopes which might have arisen from this conversation with Altenburg. On March 8 the liaison officer of the French Secret Service in Prague learned from his office that Germany was preparing to occupy Czechoslovakia in the very near future.[45] On March 10, the first secretary of the French embassy in Berlin, M. Hardion, communicated to Schubert, probably on the basis of the same information, reports about the prepared assault on Czechoslovakia.[46]

Independent Slovakia

The Slovak question—previously only a problem of domestic politics—acquired in March an international character, dangerous to the existence of the state. March began in Prague with a detailed discussion of the Slovak problems. On March 1, Deputy Slovak Prime Minister Sidor and Minister of Finance Teplanský arrived in the capital to discuss them with Beran and other ministers of the central government. In the afternoon the ministers of the central government who were entrusted with the Slovak problems met with the Slovak representatives. On the agenda was the Slovak contribution to the federal budget. The Slovaks requested that their share be lowered from 17 to 12 per cent. Another item was authority of the Slovak delegates in the central ministries, which the Slovaks wished to be considerably broadened. Appointment of more Slovak officers in the army was a further Slovak desideratum.[47]

The meeting quickly changed to a polemic discussion of Czech-Slovak relations. Prime Minister Beran criticized the recent declarations of the Slovak leaders, especially the government declaration of Tiso and the speeches of Mach and Murgaš about Slovak independence and urged the Slovak government to assume a clear and firm attitude. However, the chief Slovak speaker, minister Sidor, refused to make any basic declaration of loyalty as demanded by Beran. Chvalkovský stated that the agitation in Slovakia was making the international guarantee of the state illusory.[48]

At the same moment another Slovak delegation was in Berlin, more numerous than that negotiating in Prague. It was sent there by Tiso without the knowledge of the central government and stayed in Germany from February 25 to March 3.[49] It was composed of Minister of Industry and Commerce Pružinský, Minister of Transportation Ďurčanský, and deputies Peter Zaťko and Štefan Polyak. The official mission of the delegation was to deal with economic questions, political problems, however, were in the forefront. The Slovaks were told by the Germans that Germany wanted to assist Slovakia in the economic field, but on the condition of a total separation from the common state, for otherwise the assistance would undirectly profit the Czechs.

Ďurčanský at that time, according to his own account, utilized every occasion when he met German personalities to prepare the declaration of independence. Together with other delegates he met Göring on February 28 and used the meeting "to clear up the situation." On March 1, he was received privately by Ribbentrop. The German minister assured him that Germany would be ready to guarantee the Slovak frontiers against any outside aggression if Slovakia declared her independence at a suitable moment.[50]

This visit to Berlin made the situation still more tense and the central government as a matter of caution reinforced the garrisons in Slovakia.[51] Nevertheless, in the course of the later discussions of the Slovak cabinet, the cautious trend seemed to have prevailed. There were two meetings. In the first one, on March 4, the results of the talks in Prague and Berlin were deliberated. Sidor and Teplanský expressed the opinion that "the breaking of the bread" was approaching and that a clear decision was necessary. Pružinský and Ďurčanský reported on their visit to Germany and their talks with Göring.[52] The discussion continued on the 6th. This time even the members of the presidium of the Diet were present. It was unanimously decided to achieve independence in an evolutionary way and not to proclaim it immediately. The negotiations with the central government were to continue and the members of the Slovak government were still to go to Prague in the course of the week.[53] The Slovak communiqué of March 6 stated that the Slovak government regarded the political and constitutional status of the province of Slovakia as "settled by the law concerning the autonomy of Slovakia."[54]

Prague outwardly welcomed the Slovak statement and the press service of the central government published an optimistic communiqué about the Slovak decision. However, in reality the government circles did not trust the Slovak declaration entirely and were convinced that it was but a cloak veiling irredentist activities.[55] The leading paper of the former Agrarian party, *Venkov,* while assessing the Slovak statement as a positive step, took at the same time issue with the separatist ideas propagated by Tuka and did not hesitate to declare that the Slovak people should expel such individuals.[56] The Slovak communiqué was not published by a single Slovak paper with one exception, that of *Národnie Noviny* which was opposed to the separation.[57] On March 7, *Slovák* pointed out that Slovakia wanted "to maintain a free hand" in building her future and another paper, *Slovenská Politika,* wrote in a similar tone.[58]

The two meetings of the Slovak cabinet only postponed the final decision. The moderates apparently mistrusted the Germanophile leanings of the radicals and were realizing the German danger. Even the Germans were aware of this mood and the German consul in Bratislava Druffel confirmed on March 10 that in Tiso's entourage the fear was that the Germans, once they had been invited, would not leave.[59]

In their dilemma the moderates turned to Poland and Tiso sent deputy Pavol Čarnogurský to Warsaw to sound out the Polish attitude. He was received twice (on March 5 and 9) by Polish Deputy Foreign Minister,

Mieczyslaw Arciszewski. He declared to him that Slovakia did not want to secede from Prague as long as the conditions agreed upon in Žilina on October 6 existed. If, however, the further existence of Czechoslovakia proved impossible, the Slovak government was asking for Polish consent to a declaration of independence, and for aid and international protection. Slovakia was opposed to any form of incorporation into Hungary. To this Arciszewski replied that Poland would respect the Slovak decision to stay in a common state with the Czechs. If Slovakia were to form an independent state, Poland promised her assistance and would recommend that Budapest recognize Slovak independence.

These statements of the Polish diplomat sounded promising especially as far as the danger of Hungarian occupation was concerned. The only flaw was that they did not mention one crucial point, that of the Polish attitude to a possible German action against the integrity of the Czechoslovak state. At that moment Poland evidently did not consider the integrity of Czechoslovakia to also be a matter of her own security.[60] It seems that she was still preoccupied mainly with the Carpatho-Ukrainian question. According to German ambassador Moltke she did not desire to incorporate Slovakia into the Polish state, but was averse to an independent Slovakia under German influence. Beck's instructions to Papée, the Polish envoy in Prague, confirm this opinion of the German diplomat.[61]

The vacillation of moderate Slovak elements ran against the German projects and Berlin therefore increased its pressure on Bratislava. In the evening of March 7, Arthur Seyss-Inquart, the governor of Austria, accompanied by his aid Franz J. Hammerschmied, arrived in Bratislava and at 6:00 P.M. met Sidor. In the presence of Tiso he discussed at length the possibilities of an independent Slovak state. He pronounced himself against the "evolutionary" thesis and declared that the aim would be reached neither by a slow progression nor by jerky leaps. "It was not enough to run, one had to jump as well." That was the only way to reach the goal.[62] Tiso was, however, not entirely inaccessible to the German overtures: At the end of the conversation it was decided that he would meet Seyss-Inquart the next day at Bruck a.d. Leitha, on the other bank of the Danube, to learn whether he could be received by Hitler in Berlin to discuss the declaration of independence.[62]

Sidor was concealing these Slovak contacts with the Germans. He did not say a word in Prague about the German threats that the existence of Czechoslovakia would shortly come to an end, and he did not say a word about the Slovak contacts with Warsaw. However, the Prague government learned about the Slovak dealings with the German emissaries from other sources and its mistrust of Bratislava increased.

Beran's confidence in Tiso was shattered, the hopes raised by the visit of President Hácha to Slovakia fainted away. A decision seemed urgent. Beran declared himself for the immediate dismissal of the Tiso governemnt as recommended by General Eliáš in February. However, he attempted for the last time a peaceful solution and invited Tiso and the Slovak ministers to Prague. It was not difficult to predict that Tiso, who was even avoiding telephone conversations with Beran, would not come. Indeed, in the evening of march 8 only Sidor and Teplanský arrived.

On March 9, at 4 P.M., the cabinet meeting of the common government, the last one in the united state, was opened. Beran criticized Tiso's absence and reproached him that he had not come to Prague, yet he had time to receive Seyss-Inquart and other German emissaries. According to Beran, Tiso had broken his oath of deputy and could not fulfill the duties of the Slovak Prime Minister any more.

The session became dramatic when Teplanský spoke about the report of Ďurčanský and Pružinský to the Slovak cabinet about their journey to Berlin. He stated that the Slovak ministers did not deal only with economic problems in Berlin, but were also asking Marshal Göring for assistance to separate Slovakia from the Republic and proclaim an independent Slovak state. "A great wave of emotion spread in the Council of Ministers. Someone shouted that it was high treason," says Ladislav Feierabend, witness of the scene, in his memoirs.[63]

In spite of the alarming news from Bratislava, Prague still deluded itself that Germany had no direct interest in the relations between the central government and Tiso. Recent Czech action in Carpatho-Ukraine, a region where Germany was evidently interested, had encountered no protests from Berlin. This may have emboldened Prague to act in a similar way in Bratislava. Chvalkovský was in those critical days in continuous contact with the German legation. The attitude of Berlin was decisive, for Prague dared not and could not dare to act counter Berlin's wishes.

On March 7, Chvalkovský stated to German chargé d'affaires Hencke how anxious he was to know Germany's concrete wishes on the policy to be pursued by Prague in Carpatho-Ukraine and Slovakia. The reply was evasive. Hencke merely reminded Chvalkovský of his (Chvalkovský's) own words that the guiding principle for Czechoslovakia in this matter was the Vienna Award.[64]

In the course of the cabinet meeting on March 9, which had to decide the fate of the Tiso government, Chvalkovský summoned Hencke at 5:15 P.M. and tried again to get some private information about the issue. Hencke continued to be vague. He declared to Chvalkovský that he knew nothing of any political plans of the Reich government concerning

Slovakia. Chvalkovský nevertheless, asked the German diplomat to find out from Berlin "as quickly as possible but tactfully" whether, during the conversations with the Slovak ministers, the separation of Slovakia had actually been mentioned as a condition for economic help and whether Germany wanted events to take this turn. "If Berlin wants an independent Slovakia, then Prague will somehow reconcile itself to this solution," declared Chvalkovský. "As foreign minister of the central government, he did not want to senselessly pursue a policy which was contrary to Berlin's wishes." He requested a quick answer, possibly by telephone from Berlin. Hencke sent his report only as a "letter telegram." On March 12, in Berlin, Altenburg added to it a marginal remark: "On the oral instructions of the RAM (*Reichsminister* of Foreign Affairs) no reply is to be given."[65]

Late in the evening of March 9, Hácha signed a document dated the 10th which demoted the Slovak government. The ministers Tiso, Ďurčanský, Pružinský and Vančo were deposed. The news was announced on the radio at 7 A.M., March 10, in a proclamation outwardly optimistic though with a hidden concern about the German reaction. It assured that not a hair would be changed in the autonomous status of Slovakia whose freedom could be maintained only in the common Czecho-Slovak Republic. The proclamation invoked the great powers which initiated the decisions of Munich and Vienna as witnesses to the agreement between the Czech and the Slovaks and declared: "Whoever tells you that the German Reich wants to detach Slovakia from the Czecho-Slovak state is a faithless adventurer." Another declaration, in the Czech language, openly criticized Tuka and Mach and reproached Tiso with weakness and indecision. Teplanský spoke in a similar vein on the Bratislava radio shortly after noon: "We cannot let foolishness and helplessness endanger the dearly bought freedom."[66]

The Slovak Minister of Education, Josef Sivák, was appointed Prime Minister and entrusted temporarily with all ressorts except finance. This ministry remained in the hands of its former incumbent, Pavel Teplanský. Sivák was at the moment on his way to Rome with Minister of Agriculture Feierabend where they were to represent Czechoslovakia at the coronation of the new Pope. When he learned of his appointment Sivák declined to accept it.[67] In his absence Teplanský was to act as his deputy. Sidor, as a member of the central government, was not affected by the measures of March 9 and continued to figure as State Minister for Slovakia and Deputy Prime Minister of the central government.

The sympathies of foreign diplomats in Prague were generally on the side of the central government. Even Hencke had to admit this. The Italian minister, Francesco Fransoni, declared to him on the 10th that the

Czechs were right, that the Slovaks had committed high treason and Ďurčanský and Pružinský had proved their disloyalty. Furthermore, the Hungarian minister, János Wettstein, remarked to Hencke on the 11th: "But you have administered strong doses to the Slovaks."[68]

The Germans remained silent. When Chvalkovský explained the Czech action to Hencke on the 10th, he repeated his standpoint: If Germany wished the separation of Slovakia, she should say it openly to him. Again Hencke remained noncommittal and only feigned to be surprised that shortly after Prague's optimistic words the government took such radical steps in Slovakia.[69]

Friday, March 10, was a stormy day for Bratislava. Police reinforcements arrived in the city late the preceding night and at dawn troops and Czechoslovak gendarmes had in their power public buildings all over Slovakia. The ministers Eliáš, Kalfus and Teplanský were directing the operation. The military commander was the Czech general, Hugo Vojta. The Czech forces were controlling the highways leading to Bratislava and armored vehicles were ready in the barracks. At 11 A.M. martial law was declared in Bratislava, Piešťany and Banská Bystrica. Tuka, Mach and Černák were detained and interned in Moravia.

Tiso learned about his demotion during the night and received the respective decree of President Hácha in the morning. The radical separatists did not acknowledge the Czech measures, and in a statement for the German press they declared them unconstitutional and in violation of the law on autonomy.[70] Ďurčanský fled to Vienna. Even before he had reached the city he sent Hitler a telegram in which he protested against the Czech action. In a speech delivered on Vienna radio in the evening of the same day he declared himself the "legitimate representative of the Slovak people."[71]

The appointment of Sivák was but a temporary measure and Prague and Bratislava had to negotiate about filling the gap created by Tiso's demotion. It was impossible to re-appoint Tiso. The only acceptable man seamed to be Sidor and Prague eventually resigned itself to appointing this rather vacillating and unpredictable candidate. The government list was ready in the evening of the 10th. Sidor apparently realized the advantages of the larger frame of the Czechoslovak state and was shrinking from the plans for an independent Slovakia to materialize in the near future. He was not averse to the Prague offer and made a list of the conditions on which he was ready to accept the office, among others cancellation of the Czech military measures in Slovakia, release of persons arrested in the course of the Czech action, and appointment of a Slovak officer to the head of the Slovak military command post in Bratislava.[72]

The next day, March 11, the presidium of the Slovak diet submitted the proposed list to President Hácha in Prague and at 10:50 P.M. the Prague radio announced the formation of the new Slovak government headed by Sidor.[73]

While the negotiations were still proceeding the Czechs began to retreat in Bratislava. Beran conceded to Sidor that the Czech commander could not issue any order without Sidor's previous consent, and thus the Czech commander was practically made dependent on the Slovak Prime Minister.[74] In Bratislava, the previous military measures were progressively eased and the patrol disappeared. The Czech gendarmes left the government headquarters on Saturday evening. The administrative power was returned to the civil authorities and to the Slovak gendarmery. The session of the Slovak Diet, which ws originally to take place on March 14, was postponed until the 28th.

In the course of March 11 Ďurčanský sent his emissary twice to Bratislava to persuade Sidor to declare independence. Sidor was reserved and persevered in this attitude even in the evening of the same day when he was visited by two German emissaries, one of them the newspaperman and member of the German *Sicherheitsdienst*, Lorenz Carbus. The German visitors declared that the time had come to declare the independent Slovak state, and asked him to do so on the radio. Sidor hestiated but agreed that Slovak independence could be proclaimed by somebody other than him.[75]

Ďurčanský's activities moved still in another direction. In the late afternoon he drafted the declaration of the Slovak independence. The text was communicated to the official German news agency (DNB) which, however, prudently delayed its publication until further notice.[76] At about 10:00 P.M. Ďurčanský framed a telegram to Hitler announcing the declaration of independence and requesting a German guarantee of the Slovak frontiers.[77] Anticipating with certainty that Sidor would accede to his proposals, he handed the German representatives in Vienna the list of the proposed government of independent Slovakia headed by Tiso as President and Sidor as Prime Minister. He had evidently misjudged the situation in Bratislava. At the same time when he was sending his telegram to Hitler the news of Sidor's appointment arrived in Bratislava: Sidor was accepting the premiership from the hands of President Hácha and at midnight he confirmed it in a short broadcast speech.[78] Ďurčanský and his Austrian sponsors, Seyss-Inquart and the Austrian Gauleiter Josef Bürckel, were thus in a difficult imbroglio.

Even before the announcement of Sidor's appointment Berlin sensed that something had gone wrong. Hitler prohibited his local dignitaries in Vienna from continuing negotiations with the Slovaks and instead sent his roving ambassador, Wilhelm Keppler, to Bratislava to inform himself on the spot.[79] In the early hours of Sunday, March 12, between 2 and 3 A.M. a high level German delegation led by Keppler arrived in Bratislava to sound the ground. Keppler was accompanied by Arthur Seyss-Inquart, the governor of Austria, his assistant Dr. Franz J. Hammerschmied, and Josef Bürckel, the Austrian Gauleiter. The conversation with Sidor showed that he would not be opposed to the radical separatists, that one could not, however, count on his active participation. When Bürckel produced a copy of Ďurčanský's telegram to Hitler in which he, Sidor, paraded as Prime Minister, Sidor flatly denied any share in its preparation or knowledge of its existence. The Germans were deeply disappointed. Again, Sidor could not be gained for the radical cause. "The mood was like a wake beside the body of a dead man," was Sidor's description of the atmosphere of the closing moments of the meeting.[80]

In Vienna, in spite of everything, Ďurčanský was persisting in his radical separatist propaganda and condemned any arrangements with the Czechs: "Enough of indecision, enough of compromises! . . . Be patient and firm . . . Don't be afraid to fight, don't be afraid of any sacrifice," he exhorted his countrymen on the radio on March 12.[81] In Petržalka (Engerau), on the southern bank of the Danube, occupied by Germany since October, Bürckel was preparing, apparently on his own initiative, an action against Bratislava, with the help of a SS-detachment from Vienna. He gave up only on the explicit order of Hitler.[82]

Keppler, after his return to Vienna, considered the situation as spoiled. It seemed to him that Seyss-Inquart and Bürckel had been deceived by the Slovaks and he wanted to return to Berlin. But he was ordered to remain in Vienna, for he had to accompany "a Slovak personality" to Berlin.[83]

This personality was Tiso, whom the Germans were now approaching directly. They sent the chief of the organization of Slovak youth, Janko Dafčík, to Bánovce, the Tiso's parish where the deposed Slovak premier arrived on Saturday to be at a safer distance from the Czech operations in Slovakia. Dafčík came with a message from the German consulate urging Tiso to visit Hitler.[84] Tiso agreed and left for Bratislava.

On the following day, Monday, March 13, a conference of the Populist leaders was held at the party secretariat. Having previously consulted with Sidor, Tiso announced that he had been invited to visit Hitler, and asked if he was to accept the invitation. The discussion was short and the answer affirmative.[85] Toward noon Tiso left for Vienna from where, accompanied by Ďurčanský, he took a plane for Berlin.

He arrived at 5 P.M. and was received with honors reserved for a representative of a foreign power. After his arrival he had a talk with Ribbentrop who indicated that Germany would remain a mere spectator if Hungary invaded Slovakia unless Slovakia declared without delay her independence. "We cannot wage war against anyone just because he holds Slovak territory in his power," declared Ribbentrop. Tiso pointed out his government declaration of February 21 about the building of the Slovak state, adding, however, that the Slovaks would never initiate the liquidation of the Republic. Only if they should see that the situation was developing so that the separation would be more advantageous would they consider it their duty to secede from the common state. Ribbentrop pretended that he could not understand this hesitation and Tiso replied to his reproach by pointing out the insufficient training of the Slovak people.[86]

This conversation foreshadowed what Tiso was going to hear from Hitler. The Chancellor was brutally open in his words. The audience lasted a little more than half an hour, from 6:40 to 7:15 P.M. in the new chancellery. Tiso was accompanied by Ďurčanský; on the German side were Ribbentrop, State Minister Otto Meissner, State Secretary Keppler, the Generals Keitel and Brauchitsch and Press Chief Otto Dietrich. The conversation—like so many others—was a long monologue by Hitler to which Tiso could, however, add some remarks. Hitler's arguments followed the line he used in his talk with Tuka.

To begin with, Hitler criticized severely the attitude of the Czechs after Munich. According to him, during recent weeks the situation had become intolerable and the old "Beneš spirit" had come to life again. The Czechs continued to persecute the Germans whose situation was worse than before Munich. His second disappointment had been the attitude of Slovakia. At the beginning he thought erroneously that they wanted to return to Hungary. It was only during the crisis that he abandoned this idea, when for the first time he noticed that Slovakia wished independence. Now he had sent Keppler to Bratislava who learned that Sidor was against the separation. Had Hitler known this earlier he could have left matters as they were at the time instead of alienating his Hungarian friends. Germany had no interests southeast of the Carpathians. The question was whether Slovakia wished independence or not. "It is a question not of days but of hours." If Slovakia wished to become independent he would support and even guarantee her efforts. If she hesitated or refused to be separated from Prague he would leave her to her fate. "We have no need for the Slovaks; we shall not take their part unless they sufficiently prove that they want to live their independent lives to the fullest extent," declared Hitler. He further indicated that otherwise he would leave them to Hungary. Turning to Ribbentrop, the

Chancellor asked if he had anything further to add. Ribbentrop, too, emphasized that the decision was necessary in a matter of hours, not days. And to impress the visitors he handed Hitler a report about Hungarian troop movements on the Slovak frontier.

This harping on the Hungarian theme convinced Tiso that this was the heart of the matter. Hitler's hint that the Slovaks had to act with lightning speed (*blitzschnell*) left no doubt about the seriousness of the situation. Tiso thanked Hitler and assured him that he could rely on Slovakia. Cautiously he added that he could make no definitive statement at once, let alone make a decision.

In spite of this cautious statement Tiso had no doubts about what line to take: to declare independence without any delay. He wished to settle the whole thing in Bratislava, not Berlin. Accordingly he telephoned immediately from the Czechoslovak legation to Prague and Bratislava without, however, disclosing to anybody the results of the audience with Hitler. He only asked Hácha to summon the Slovak Diet for March 14.[87]

Prague agreed and Sidor announced the convocation of the Diet on the Bratislava radio, adding: "With the help of God our deputies will decide and from their decision will arise a better future for the Slovak people." Explosions of German bombs brought secretly to Bratislava some days earlier were to convince those who were still hesitating. The extremists placed infernal machines in different parts of Bratislava and their din was heard in the night preceding the session of the Diet. In the garden adjoining Sidor's villa the police discovered a TNT bomb weighing 13 kilograms and produced in Düsseldorf.[88]

In the meantime, the talks in Berlin continued, this time at the German Foreign Ministry, and did not end until nearly 2 A.M. Tiso resisted Ribbentrop's pressure to make the declaration of independence while still in Berlin and there was disagreement about the proper term which would define the relationship between Germany and Slovakia. The Germans spoke of "protection" (*Schutz*), whereas the Slovaks preferred the term of "guarantee." A telegram was drafted by Tiso and Keppler using both terms, but in the end it was not used.[89]

Tiso returned to Bratislava in the morning of March 11 and at the meeting of the cabinet reported on his talks with Hitler. The cabinet decided to proclaim independence and drafted an appropriate government declaration.

At 10:57 A.M. Vice Premier Mederly opened the session of the Diet. At 11:10 the session was declared secret and the corridors were occupied by the members of the Hlinka Guards and the Slovak soldiers commanded by the Slovak officers. Sidor took the floor the first. He explained how he was appointed Prime Minister and remarking that he had not yet been sworn in, he announced his resignation.

Then Tiso apoke about his journey to Berlin. After him the speaker of the Diet, Martin Sokol, put the crucial question to the deputies: "Are you or are you not for Slovak independence?" To assure success, secret balloting was given up and the procedure was chosen which not only seemed more solemn, but also more reliable: The deputies voted seated or standing. The answer was unanimous and at 12:07 P.M. all deputies stood up as one man. The speaker stated that the independent Slovak state was proclaimed and the deputies sang the Slovak anthem.[90] The session was adjourned to prepare the bill proclaiming independence and to discuss the composition of the new government.

The declaration of independence read by Tiso reproached the government of Prague for the violation of the constitutional law and emphasized that the Slovak Diet expressed its confidence to the Tiso government. The relations between the Czech and Slovak nation had lost all their legal basis,for the Prague government instituted a Czech dictatorship over the Slovaks. "The time has come to take into our hands the fate of our people if we want to avoid a political death. If we want to assure the future of our people, we must terminate the common political life with the Czech people. For that reason we have decided to claim for our Slovak people the absolute right of self-determiniation."[91]

The Diet was then called upon to pass the law about independence. Of its five short paragraphs, the first declared the "Slovak land" an independent and sovereign state. The second paragraph stated that until the publication of the constitution the executive power would be in the hands of a government appointed by the praesidium of the Diet.

Josef Tiso remained Prime Minister. His Deputy and Minister without portfolio was Vojtěch Tuka. Sidor became Minister of the Interior. Other members of the government were: Ďurčanský (Foreign Affairs), Gejza Fritz (Justice), Sivák (Education), Pružinský (Finances), Gejza Medrický (Economy), Julius Stano (Transportation), and Lieutenant-Colonel Ferdinand Čatloš (National Defence).[92]

The world learned of the proclamation of independence at 12:25 P.M. from the Bratislava radio. Moreover, the new Foreign Minister, Ďurčanský, sent to all powers a note announcing the creation of an independent Slovak state and asking for recognition. To Hitler was addressed a telegram expressing the Slovak gratitude. One of the first states to recognize independent Slovakia was Poland, who on the following day announced her decision to install a legation in Bratislava.[93]

On March 15, Tiso sent Hitler a brief telegram announcing that the Slovak state was placing itself under his protection and asking him to assume it. Hitler's answers was equally short. Disagreements which were revealed in the talks in Berlin two days ago may explain the laconism of this exchange.[94]

The victory of the Slovak separatists was not without discordant notes. The friendly hand which they imagined to find in Germany became oppressive at the very beginning of the independence. Early in the morning of March 15, at 5:20 A.M., the German consul in Bratislava notified the new Slovak Foreign Minister Ďurčanský that the German troops would cross the Slovak frontier and advance to the line Nové Mesto—eastern escarpment of the Little Carpathians—the valley of the Váh. Ďurčanský expressed surprise since the measure had not been provided for in the conversations between Tiso and Seyss-Inquart. However, he promised to do his utmost to have it carried out without friction. German troops began to march at 6:00 A.M. of March 15, and by midday they reached Malacky, 35 kilometres north-west of Bratislava and Trenčín by the evening. They occupied not only the region specified by Druffel, but further north-east penetrated even into the valley of the upper Nitra and in several places they confiscated war material. On March 16 Ďurčanský had to ask Ribbentrop to forbid the military authorities to take such action "at the moment of joy and thankfulness."[95]

The actual negotiations about the future German-Slovak relationship took place in Vienna on March 17 and 18. Slovakia was represented by Tiso, Tuka and Ďurčanský, Germany by Keppler and Ribbentrop's legal advisor, Dr. Friedrich Gaus. On the second day even Hitler took part in the discussions. The Slovaks, primarily Ďurčanský, opposed the Wehrmacht's insistence on building fortifications in western Slovakia, along the Little Carpathians. Only Tuka was in agreement with the German demands from the start. Finally the Treaty of Protection was signed in Vienna on March 18. After its signature by Tiso it was signed in Berlin by Ribbentrop on March 23 with a confidential protocol on economic and financial cooperation. The treaty gave Germany the right to set up military bases in western Slovakia in the region of the river Váh, in a zone, bounded on the west by the frontier of the Slovak state and on the east by the general line of the eastern edges of the Little Carpathians, the White Carpathians and the Javorník Mountains and to man these installations with such forces as the German Wehrmacht would consider necessary. It further stipulated that Slovakia in organizing her army and conducting her foreign policy must always proceed "in close consultation with Germany."[96] It gave the Slovaks not only protection against her neighbors, but brought them also a vassalage which rendered illusory the right of self-determination invoked only a few days earlier.

Occupation of Carpatho-Ukraine

After the separation of Slovakia, Carpatho-Ukraine lost all connection with the Czech lands. In this confused situation, the Chust government attempted to accede to complete independence under the German protection. The attempt was, however, crushed immediately by Hungary.

In the first days of March there were no indications yet that the situation would change. Germany was still supporting the status quo and opposing the common Polish-Hungarian frontier. On March 6 Hungary presented a new idea. General secretary of the Hungarian Foreign Ministry, János Vörnle, appeared in Prague and proposed to buy Carpatho-Ukraine from Czechoslovakia, apparently in the hope that the German opposition to an armed Hungarian action could be circumvented in this way. He met with a cautious reaction from Chvalkovský; and the German chargé d'affaires, Hencke, whom he saw immediately after his talk with the Czechoslovak minister showed but "little understanding."[97]

As late as March 10 Berlin manifested no inclination to yield to Hungarian wishes.[98] Then on Sunday, March 12, the situation suddenly changed. Hitler was inviting Tiso to Berlin and preparing his moves against Prague. In this context he abandoned Carpatho-Ukraine, one of the irons he had been keeping in the fire. His die was cast. He sent for the Hungarian minister Sztójay and informed him that he had withdrawn his "restraining hand." At the same time he admonished Hungary to limit herself only to Carpatho-Ukraine and not to attack Slovakia the fate of which could be discussed later. Sztójay then left immediately by plane for Budapest.[99] There, in the morning of Monday, March 13, German minister Erdmannsdorff, accompanied by Dr. Altenburg from the German Foreign Ministry, called on Regent Horthy, Prime Minister Teleki and Chief of the General Staff, General Henrik Werth, to repeat Hitler's message. The Hungarians received the German suggestion with enthusiasm, they were, however, at the same time aware of their military weakness. General Werth promised that he would strike within a week at the latest. "It would be too late," objected the Germans.[100] Even Horthy, in the letter of thanks he wrote to Hitler the same day, pointed out the military difficulties of his country (fresh recruits only five weeks with their units etc.). However, he reassured the Germans that Hungary was laying her plans: "On Thursday, the 16th of this month, a frontier incident will take place, to be followed on Saturday by the big thrust," Horthy promised.[101] Eventually Hungary, in spite of her initial vacillation, synchronized her actions with those of Germany.

Italy was informed of this only later. Ribbentrop announced the German decision to Attolico in the evening of March 13, when he indicated to him the German intention concerning the Czech lands and Slovakia.[102] The following morning Attolico received the confirmation from Weizsäcker. The Italian ambassador listened calmly, remarking only that people in Rome would probably wonder why Germany had given the Hungarians a free hand without first getting in touch with Rome.[103] Ciano was indeed offended and complained in his diary: "The Axis is functioning only to the advantage of one partner who has the upper hand and acts on his own initiative without any regards for us." Mussolini, on the other hand, appeared unconcerned. Consoling himself with the advantage of a common Polish-Hungarian frontier, he ordered Ciano to recommend that the Hungarian government proceed with vigor.[104]

Hungary started her diplomatic as well as military action on March 14. At 3 P.M. a respresentative of the Foreign Ministry handed over to the Czechoslovak minister in Budapest a 12-hour ultimatum requiring Czechoslovakia to begin evacuation of Carpatho-Ukraine within 24 hours. The Czechs should at once liberate persons of Hungarian nationality, cease to persecute persons of Hungarian origin and should issue weapons to the Hungarian defense organizations. Prague accepted the ultimatum at 8 P.M. but refused to allow the formation of defense organizations.[105]

Under these circumstances the fate of Carpatho-Ukraine was sealed and the political moves of the Chust government were doomed to complete failure. In the early morning of March 14, at 1:30 A.M., even before the declaration of the Slovak independence and before President Hácha left for Berlin, Vološyn, foreboding things to come, sent a deputation to the German consul in Chust which delivered him a telegram with a request for transmission to Ribbentrop. The telegram asked the German minister "to take cognizance of our independence under the protection of the German Reich."[106]

This was the first of several messages in which the Carpatho-Ukrainian government, in the course of the three days, March 14 to 16, tried to influence Germany and tilt her in the favor of Carpatho-Ukrainian independence and against Hungary. All was in vain. In response to Vološyn's telegram Ribbentrop ordered his subordinates to take no steps in the direction requested by Chust (*nichts zu veranlassen*).[107]

The same day (March 14) at 3 P.M., the Diet, meeting at Chust, proclaimed independence. Vološyn became President, Julian Révay was appointed Prime Minister and Minister of Foreign Affairs.[108] After the proclamation of independence Vološyn sent a telegram to the Prague government thanking the Czech people and their government for twenty years of common existence.[109]

However, disillusionment was not long in coming. Two hours later Weizsäcker bluntly declared that Germany did not accept the offer of a protectorate and advised the Carpatho-Ukrainian government to offer no resistance to Hungarian troops.[110] Vološyn therefore turned to Budapest and asked it in the evening for acknowledgment of independence offering in return permanent friendship and close cooperation. Budapest, however, sent Chust an ultimatum expiring at 8 P.M. on March 15 and asked Vološyn to transfer the governmental power to the commander of the Hungarian troops.[111] Chust answered that it was sending three representatives to Budapest. The Hungarians replied that they would receive them, but that they could not halt the military operation.[112]

The Hungarian army began the operations early in the morning of March 14 and attacked from the region between Mukačevo and Svalava. It was unable to start action along the whole frontier and only the next day became active also in the eastern sector, in the direction of Chust. The Carpatho-Ukrainian government then entrusted the Czech general, Oleg Svátek, with the defense. The Czechoslovak units lead until midday of March 15 a staunch defensive action, then, as a result of the changed political situation, they started fighting in retreat in the direction of Slovakia and Rumania. In the morning of the 16th, they withdrew from Chust. Vološyn, after their withdrawal, left Chust for Velký Bočkov and crossed the border of Rumania. The Hungarian troops entered Chust at 4:50 P.M. The last resistance was offered by a unit consisting of the Ukrainian high school students who succumbed with great losses after a 90 minutes fight. On March 16, the Hungarian units reached the Polish frontier near the Polish railroad station of Bezkid where the meeting with the Polish troops was celebrated.[113]

These changes near her frontiers and the success of Hungary alarmed Rumania. Although in the fall she was categorically opposed to the separation of Carpatho-Ukraine from Czechoslovakia, she manifested a greater moderation in the spring of 1939. On his visit to Warsaw in the first days of March, Foreign Minister Grigoire Gafencu indicated to Beck that he agreed with Poland on Carpatho-Ukraine and that he preferred to see the Hungarians there as opposed to anyone else.[114]

Rumania asked first for the cession of a bordering zone inhabited by Rumanians. Then she limited her demands asking for the railroad line Lona-Jasina (Körösmözö) and 15 villages with Rumanian population north of Sighetul Marmaţiei. To support her demands she mobilized three classes.[115] Finally she put up with the new situation and maintained neutrality. When Vološyn asked on March 16 for the attachment of his country to Rumania, Bucharest refused and let him know that in Rumania he was considered a mere political refugee without any political status.[116]

The common Polish-Hungarian frontier thus became a reality, however under totally changed conditions on the Central-European scene. Hungary increased her territory by 4,281 sq. miles (11,085 sq. kilometers) and her population by 552,142 inhabitants (census 1930). Until July 1939 former Carpatho-Ukraine was under military administration. Then a temporary status was introduced which lasted, however, through the whole of the Hungarian occupation. The region got a new name: Subcarpathian Territory and was administered by a Commissar of the Regent. The Commissar was always a Hungarian. One of them was Miklós Kozma, the man who organized the Hungarian subversive activities undertaken there by Hungary after Munich. Instead of regular elections the Budapest Parliament co-opted several representatives from the new province, half of them Magyars. This parliamentary delegation was headed by Andrej Bródy, the same man whom the Prague government had arrested in the fall of 1938 for his contacts with Hungary.[117]

After the Second World War the territory returned for a brief time to Czechoslovakia. On June 29, 1945, Czechoslovakia was forced to abandon it to the Soviet Union by a treaty which incorporated it as "Transcarpathian Region" to the Ukrainian SSR.

Hácha's Journey to Berlin—The Protectorate of Bohemia-Moravia

Hitler's planned actions against the Czech lands depended on the successful outcome of the separatist campaign in Slovakia. The events in the eastern part of Czechoslovakia were closely connected with the political and military steps he was preparing against Prague. As on other occasions, he apparently acted on the spur of the moment adroitly exploiting a favorable conjuncture. He made his decision rapidly and without long preparations. To believe Göring's Nuremberg testimony, Hitler sent him a letter at the beginning of March, when the Marshal was in Italy for a cure, and informed him that he was determined to eliminate Czechoslovakia "as a source of danger right in the center of Germany." Recalled by Hitler, he returned to Berlin in the morning of the 14th of March.[118] Even Ribbentrop was absent having gone to Kiel where his wife underwent an operation. He too had to return quickly.[119]

The Czech action in Slovakia gave Hitler a welcome pretext to accelerate his moves. The decisive day was March 10. Prague had just demoted the Tiso government and in Bratislava General Vojta was attempting to master the confused situation. The demoted minister

Ďurčanský had fled to Vienna to continue his endeavors for separation. Under these circumstances Hitler decided to act. In Berlin, at 4:57 P.M. of that day, marching orders for the German army were issued. The lines of departure for the *Einmarsch* were to be reached in the evening of the 12th at the latest. The action itself was to start on March 15. Hitler reserved for himself the hours of the crossing of the border.[120] According to the directive of December 17,[121] the operation was prepared only with the peacetime army, without reinforcement by mobilization. Even here there was some improvisation. However Berlin, not fearing any military steps by the western signatories of the Munich Agreement, readily took this risk.[122]

Hitler did not confine himself to issuing the marching orders. In addition he ordered the Supreme Command of the Armed Forces to draft an ultimatum to Czechoslovakia demanding the capitulation of the army. The draft enumerating seven points aimed at paralyzing any Czech armed resistance was ready on March 11.[123] Besides this, the Supreme Command prepared two leaflets to be thrown from the air over Bohemia and Moravia, one addressed to all inhabitants of the area, the second aimed only at its German population. The first leaflet alluded to alleged acts of Czech terrorism and proclaimed that the German troops were entering Bohemia and Moravia to restore law and order. "Any resistance will be crushed with lightening speed," threatened the proclamation. The second leaflet asked local Germans to cooperate with the invading German army.[124]

Similarly the German Foreign Ministry was preparing the ground. On Ribbentrop's order a telegram addressed to "the Government of Prague" was drafted which also referred to alleged Czech terrorism. It spoke of "cries of help by Germans" and announced that the German government had to take steps necessary to halt "the unbearable situation" there. The telegram asked the Czech government to send immediately a plenipotentiary to Berlin to discuss further measures.[125] Another version of the telegram, dated March 14, probably drawn up while negotiations about Hácha's visit to Berlin were not yet terminated did not ask for a plenipotentiary any more, but instead repeated the seven points of the ultimatum proposed by the German Army.[126]

These German moves did not escape the attention of foreign observers. The French embassy spoke of military preparations in certain German garrisons, especially those of the Berlin region, on March 11th and 12th.[127] On March 12, the British embassy relayed to London a piece of information from Munich according to which a state of emergency had been declared for the Munich garrison. On March 14, the British Assistant Military Attaché in Berlin related—though he was unable to confirm—the movement of troops from Dresden to Breslau on Sunday night.[128] According to American sources, rumors of German movements began to reach Berlin on Monday, March 13, and on Tuesday had been definitely confirmed. Troop movements between Dresden and Breslau and between Munich and Vienna were reported. On March 14, the American consul in Breslau reported "extensive troop movements during the last 48 hours in direction of Moravia." The American legation in Prague had similar information.[129]

In the same way the news of the prepared ultimatum spread among the Berlin diplomats. According to Henderson, it was wired to the German legation in Prague sometime Saturday, but probably was revoked before it could have been delivered.[130] The French ambassador Coulondre had yet another version: He learned from a German source that the ultimatum was to be handed over to the Prague government on Monday, the 13th.[131]

The Czechoslovak Intelligence Service had the first notion of the forthcoming occupation on March 11. On that day its German agent, Paul Thümmel, reported that the German army would march into Bohemia and Moravia on the 15th. The head of the Service, Colonel František Moravec, and the deputy chief of Staff, General Bohuslav Fiala, then went without delay to the office of the Prime Minister to inform the government. The cabinet was just in session, however Beran received them in the presence of three other ministers, among them Chvalkovský. The Foreign Minister, remembering the hazy background of the May mobilization of 1938, discounted their news as alarming and false. Peremptorily he warned Moravec against the dissemination of "false information."[132]

Simultaneously the German press resumed the violent attacks on Czechoslovakia. In the evening of March 12, the Ministry of Propaganda ordered that on the following day the entire first page of the newspapers should be devoted to news from Czechoslovakia. Stories about alleged Czech terrorism were furnished by the official German News Agency, *Deutsches Nachrichten-Büro* (DNB) and the papers could not do their own research.[133] "What was desired was the biggest possible splash, the largest letters, headlines over the entire page couched in the sharpest tone," such were the directives.[134] Accordingly, on the following day the propaganda campaign started at full blast.

Berlin also tried to foment troubles in Bohemia and Moravia which could serve as a pretext for intervention. From the beginning of the Slovak crisis there had been signs of agitation among the German minority. On Sunday the 12th, the Germans of Czechoslovakia were celebrating the Day of the Heroes honoring the German soldiers fallen during the First World War. Berlin intended to use this occasion to provoke trouble and the *Volksdeutsche Mittelstelle* ordered the head of the Nazi student organization in Prague, Rudolf Meckel, to "start actions immediately."[135] It was not an easy task, for the Czechoslovak authorities were endeavoring to avoid incidents and ignore the German provocations. "It was very difficult to rouse feelings among the Czechs," Meckel reported on March 13.[136] In similar vein were the reports of the German legation in the following days speaking about "a reserved attitude of the Czechs" and the "general calm situation."[137] The provocations were especially intensive at Brno, but even there the Czech side maintained a marked reserve.[138]

In Prague at this time Chvalkovský was conceiving the idea of a journey to Berlin. On the 13th at noon, he had another vain conversation with Hencke. The German diplomat only declared that the blame for the events lay with Prague, which had not succeeded in a basic change of political line.[139] However, even now Chvalkovský persisted in underestimating the military intelligence reports. At the cabinet session in the afternoon Minister of National Defence Syrový produced a map showing the deployment of German troops along the Czechoslovak borders. Chvalkovský objected that the soldiers were exaggerating in the same way like in May of the preceding year. Yet he had a feeling as if he were "in the fog" and in this state of mind originated the idea of a journey to Berlin. He called Mastný in Berlin and asked him to arrange an audience with Hitler for the following day, March 14. Shortly afterwards, this original plan was enlarged to include even the President. The plan of President Hácha making a journey to Berlin was born during the short drive of ministers Chvalkovský and Havelka from the office of the Prime Minister to the audience with Hácha.[140] The President agreed to the suggestion that he should go accompanied by his Foreign Minster to Berlin to discuss with Hitler the pending problems.

The suggestion was in line with Hácha's opinions. In the course of the September crisis, he suggested direct contacts between the political leaders and was convinced that important problems like the Sudeten issue could best be solved by personal talks.[141] Accordingly, in March he accepted the suggestion of his advisors. The visit was to elucidate the situation in Slovakia, to put the blame for the violation of the constitution on Tiso and to find out why the Reich was interfering in Czechoslovak affairs.[142]

With Hácha's consent, Chvalkovský asked Hencke in the evening of the 13th to arrange the reception for the President in Berlin. Hencke promised to go to the President within twenty minutes, and immediately afterwards consulted Berlin.[143] Ribbentrop prohibited him from visiting

Hácha and instructed him to accept only written communication from the President. Chvalkovský, who was already in the President's office, was taken aback by this refusal and pointed out the painful situation created by the fact that the President was expecting Hencke. The German diplomat, however, persisted in his refusal and only repeated that the President had to send his communication in writing to the legation.[144] According to Ribbentrop, Hitler wished to conduct the negotiations with Prague himself and did not wish anybody else, even the legation, to interfere in any way.[145] Hencke then retreated to his private residence.[146]

On the following morning, at 10:30 A.M., Chvalkovský, in accordance with what he had heard from Hencke the preceding evening, sent a letter to the German legation inquiring whether through Hencke's good offices "His Excellency The Reich Chancellor would grant President Dr. Emil Hácha the opportunity of a personal interview."[147] The German diplomats were absent and the messenger had to return. The isolation of Hencke was, however, not hermetic. Chvalkovský sent the letter again, this time to Hencke's private residence.[148]

Berlin was evidently waiting for the decision of the Slovak Diet assembled at that very moment to declare independence. Hitler did not want to negotiate with Prague before the Slovak question was settled in accordance with German wishes.[149] Presuming that the Slovak diet would vote sometime before 2 P.M., Weizsäcker shortly before noon instructed Hencke to see Chvalkovský at 2 P.M. to notify him that Hitler was ready to receive Hácha in the evening.[150] This time was kept and at 2:45 P.M. Hencke reported that Hácha would arrive. Because of the President's heart condition and of unfavorable weather, Hácha would not travel by air, but by train.[151]

In the meantime rumors of the German intentions were acquiring a more concrete form. According to a French news correspondent, a German personality declared in the evening of March 13 that the fate of Bohemia and Moravia was settled. "What Germany wishes, is a pure and simple annexation of these provinces." Next morning the statements from the German quarters indicated that grave events could be expected for the situation had become "untenable."[152] The Czech newspaperman, Ludvík Jehl, correspondent of the Prague semi-official news agency *Centropress* learned these rumors toward noon of March 14 and telephoned them from Berlin to Prague at about 1 P.M. The Press Chief, Zdeněk Schmoranz, transmitted the news immediately to Minister of Justice, Jaroslav Krejčí, and Prime Minister Beran.[153] At the same time, Mastný reported from Berlin a piece of information received from the French embassy. He communicated "with every reserve: The French embassy has fears which it reported also to Paris that Germany was planning the occupation of the Czech lands for the following day i.e. March 15, at first by the *SS–Verfügungsgruppe* and in the case of resistance by the army."[154]

In Prague, even at this juncture, these warnings were received with mistrust. Chvalkovský underestimated the reports and Minister of National Defense, Syrový, thought that Prague could be reassured because it was fulfilling all German demands.[155]

The presidential train left Prague at 4 P.M. Besides Chvalkovský, the President was accompanied by two members of his personal staff, Josef Kliment and Břetislav Morávek, and by his daughter, Mrs. Milada Rádlová. Hácha made no public statement before his departure. The government, however, tendered its resignation to forestall any political complications which could have compromised the President's mission.[156]

Even after Hácha's departure there was still some glimmer of hope in Prague. When in the evening of the same day minister Feierabend reported to Beran from Rome the alarming news about Czechoslovakia published in the Italian press, the Prime Minister replied: "The situation here of course is not rosy," and added that at the meeting of Hácha with Hitler the future of the Czech lands would probably be settled. "We shall be the same tiny state like Slovakia," declared Beran.[157] According to the Second Secretary of the American legation, George F. Kennan, it was generally thought as late as Tuesday, March 14, that "the mutilated remnants of Bohemia and Moravia would be left to preserve the fiction of independent Czechoslovakia and serve as a source of foreign exchange and raw materials to Germany."[158]

In the afternoon of March 14, the disintegration of the state was accelerating. The President had not yet left, when Prague received the Hungarian ultimatum demanding evacuation of Carpatho-Ukraine. While the special train with President Hácha was still proceeding to the north, several motorized units of the German army and a part of the *SS–Leibstandarte Adolf Hitler* penetrated Czechoslovak territory in the neighborhood of Moravská Ostrava at 6:10 P.M. At 7:25, they occupied police headquarters, the town hall and the railroad station of Moravská Ostrava.[159] From there they advanced in the direction of the twin town of Frýdek-Místek where they met with a short resistance of the 8th Czechoslovak regiment of Silesia.[160] In order to carry out this surprise action the *Leibstandarte* had been ordered to reach its line of departure as early as March 11, not on the 12th like the other formations.[161] Beran telephoned the news immediately to Mastný in Berlin to report it to Hácha on his arrival. Mastný thought that the movement in question was a simple transfer of German troops.[162] In reality, the Germans were securing a region of prime importance for their railroad communications and their heavy industry, for they had not forgotten the haste with which the Poles had occupied Bohumín in October.[163]

In the meantime Berlin was awaiting Hácha's arrival. The President's visit did not, however, bring about any changes in Hitler's plans. The Führer persisted in his decision to occupy the Czech lands and very probably was only deliberating the tactics to be used in his forthcoming meeting with Hácha. When Ribbentrop, after his return to Berlin, asked Hitler shortly before the arrival of the Czechs whether he should prepare a state treaty (*Staatsvertrag*) Hitler replied that he wanted "to go much further."[164]

Hácha's train arrived in Berlin at 10:40 P.M. At the Anhalt station the delegation was greeted by Minister of State Meissner and was then taken to the *Adlon* Hotel on the avenue *Unter den Linden* where Hácha was kept waiting for about two hours. At 11:20 P.M., Chvalkovský was received by Ribbentrop, who then visited Hácha in the hotel. Chvalkovský would have liked to postpone the conversation until the next morning, but Ribbentrop insisted that Hácha see Hitler immediately. The conversaton, he promised, would be brief. Above all, the President should express his confidence in the Führer.[165] After this talk—to believe Ribbentrop—Hitler instructed him to draw up the draft of an agreement. Evidently it was the declaration forced later upon Hácha, the crucial part of which was just the expression of confidence in Hitler.[166]

At 1:10 A.M., on March 15, Hácha, accompanied by Chvalkovský, visited the Reich Chancellery. They were received by Hitler, surrounded by Field Marshal Göring, General Keitel, State Secretary Weizsäcker, and Press Chief Dietrich. A record of the conversation was made by Counsellor of Legation Walter Hewel. After his return to Prague Hácha wrote his own report.[167]

The President was coming without precise knowledge of Hitler's intentions. Owing to the distrust of Beran and Chvalkovský of the persistent rumors and signals of an imminent German action, he still had on his mind above all the Slovak problem and its constitutional aspects, an issue which at that moment had already lost almost all its significance. On his way to his suite, he learned in the corridor of the hotel of the German occupation of Moravská Ostrava without apparently paying much attention to this incident.[168] Thus his introductory statement was at a strange dissonance with the real situation, and the Führer quickly pushed aside this academic dissertation.

First Hácha presented himself: a judge aloof from politics. He had accepted the office of the President only as a national and civic duty. With the representatives of the former regime, he entertained only strictly official relations, never intimate. "Then I passed to the Slovak problem in which I saw the essential reason of my journey," narrates Hácha in his report. He declined the Slovak reproaches that his measures were unconstitutional. "I have been too long a jurist and a judge to commit an unconstitutional act," he added. From the Slovak question he passed to the Czech-German relations and to the fate of his people. He expressed the conviction that the destiny of the Czech people was in the Führer's hands.

All these explications made Hitler impatient. He felt, he said later, as if he were "sitting on burning coals,"[169] for he had decided to take action regardless of the results of his conversation with Hácha.[170] He replied with a long anti-Czech philippic. He reproached Czechoslovak foreign policy for its anti-German attitude; for instance during the occupation of the Rhineland when Prague was ready for a military action on the French side, or during the Abyssinian conflict, and, naturally, during the May crisis of 1938. The "Beneš spirit" had not disappeared. Hitler once more reproached Czechoslovakia that her army was too large for her new international position.[171] He had given an order to the German troops to invade Czechoslovakia and incorporate her into the German Reich. He wished to grant Czechoslovakia the fullest measure of autonomy, more than she had ever enjoyed in Austrian days. He no longer had any confidence in the Czechoslovak government. Germany's attitude would be decided "tomorrow and the day after" and depended on the attitude of the Czech people and army toward the German troops. He believed in the honesty and sincerity of Hácha and Chvalkovský, but he had doubts as to whether the Prague government had a chance to prevail upon the population as a whole. The German army had already marched and in a place where resistance was offered, resistance had been ruthlessly broken.

The German army was to enter Bohemia and Moravia at six in the morning from all sides, and the German air force was to occupy the Czech airfields. According to Hitler there were two possibilities: if the German entry developed into fighting, resistance would be broken by brute force with all available means; or the entry would take place satisfactorily, in which case it would be easy to grant Czechoslovakia autonomy and a certain measure of national liberty. "The hours were passing," threatened Hitler. At 6 o'clock the troops would march in. He was almost ashamed to say it, but before every Czech batallion there was a German division. The German military action, Hitler continued, was launched on a grand scale.

Hácha defended himself: He and Chvalkovský had hoped to settle the relations between the two states in a friendly way, but they were confronted with a fait accompli. Naturally he understood that any resistance was useless. Hitler then proposed to Hácha that he consult with his advisors and get in touch with his Prague offices. The military machine now already in motion could not be stopped. At this moment Hácha asked if the whole reason for the invasion was to disarm the Czech army. This could perhaps be done in some other way, and he suggested a gradual limitation of the army and a gradual delivery of its weapons.[172] Hitler replied that his decision was irrevocable. He saw no other possibility of disarmament. And he turned to his collaborators and asked whether they shared his view. They confirmed Hitler's point: "The only possibility of disarming the Czech army was by the German army."

Declaring that this was the most difficult task of his life, Hácha, accompanied by Chvalkovský, withdrew to examine the ultimatum submitted to them by the Germans. It had seven points as drafted by the German High Command on March 11:

1. The armed forces and police troops will remain in their barracks and will lay down arms.
2. All military, transport and private aircraft will be grounded and military aircraft will be parked on peacetime airfields.
3. All antiaircraft guns and antiaircraft machine guns will be withdrawn from their emplacements and stored in the barracks.
4. No alterations will be carried out on airfields or their installations.
5. No interruption to public life will take place.
6. There will be no disturbance of economic life.
7. Complete reserve will be maintained in public expression of opinion, whether in the press, theater, on the radio or at public functions in general. Troops which would make any preparations to resist would at once be attacked and wiped out. Military aircraft which would leave their landing grounds would be attacked and shot down. Airfields taking defense measures would be bombed.[173]

Chvalkovský telephoned to Beran's Prague residence at 2:15 A.M., announcing the imminent German invasion and the contents of the agreement proposed by the Germans. Hácha talked to General Syrový and asked him to forestall any attempt to resist. When Syrový drew his attention to the short delay that he had at his disposal, Hácha, in spite of this, insisted on his instructions. To Beran, Hácha said: "I announce to you a terrible thing. The Czechoslovak Republic will be occupied."[174]

When the conversations in Berlin were resumed, the military situation was once more discussed. Göring declared to Hácha that in the case of organized resistance by the Czechoslovak army he would order his aircraft to demolish Prague. Hácha in his report quotes in German what Göring (almost verbatim) had told him:

> "I have a difficult duty. I would be extremely sorry if I had to destroy that beautiful city. But I would have to do it so that the English and the French know that my air force can do a hundred per cent job. For they do not want to believe it to this very day and I would like to demonstrate it.[175]

Having discussed the disarmament convention, Hácha received from Ribbentrop a draft of a declaration stating that he was placing the fate of the Czech people and country in the hands of Hitler. Hewel's minutes pass over this stage of the Berlin conversations. Neither are we informed about the exact time of this episode. Chvalkovský at this moment telephoned Prague from an adjoining room. According to his statement to the author, Chvalkovský then rejoined the President. Hácha showed him the document. At first Chvalkovský thought that it was a simple communiqué for the press, but reading the paper attentively he saw immediately that it was a new stage of German pressure.

The declaration stated that the Czechs were received in Berlin "at their request" and affirmed that Hácha had declared that he confidently placed the fate of the Czech people and country in the hands of the Führer of the German Reich. "The Führer accepted this declaration and expressed his intention of taking the Czech people under the protection of the German Reich and of guaranteeing them an autonomous development of their ethnic life as suited to their character."[176]

This meant an escalation of the German demands, an escalation which went beyond the capitulation convention. Hácha then called Prague again and read the text of the declaration. Beran asked him to talk once more with Hitler. Hácha, however, though reluctantly, then added his signature. With the hope of weakening the bearing of the document, he demanded cancellation of the words "in the name of the government" which were in the draft. The Germans, sure of their success, agreed. Hácha pointed out also that he did not say that he was "placing" (*legt*) the fate of his people in the hands of the Führer, but that the fate "rested" (*liegt*) in his hands. The Germans, however, did not take this nuance into consideration, and the original text was maintained.[177] The document was signed on the 15th of March, at 3:55 A.M. Then, for the third time, Hácha telephoned Prague: "All discussion is henceforth vain. I signed the declaration, without authorization, I know. But in the present situation I tried to save at least our people."[178] Before signing an idea came to him to resign. He rejected it, convinced that he had to save what could be saved.[179]

Thus ended the talks at the Reich Chancellery. As Meissner was taking leave of Chvalkovský, he asked him whether he was satisfied. "Our people will curse us and still we have saved their existence. We have preserved them from a horrible massacre," was the reply.[180]

After their return to the Hotel Adlon from the Chancellery around 5 A.M., the Czechs discussed in detail the events of the night. Hácha listened in silence while Chvalkovský affirmed that from the constitutional point of view the signed declaration was of no value. Minister Mastný, who had not been admitted to the negotiations with Hitler, pointed out the dangers of the German propaganda and expressed the opinion that the Germans would implement the agreement according to their own interpretation.[181]

At about 3 A.M., March 15, while Hácha was still in the Reich Chancellery, Keitel received from Hitler the final marching orders to start the action at 6 A.M.[182] During the night Hitler issued a proclamation to the German people, probably prepared before his talk with Hácha. He justified his intervention by the alleged Czech terrorism against the German population. This terrorism had forced him to send the German troops to Bohemia and Moravia to "disarm the terrorist bands and the Czech forces which were protecting them." A similar proclamation was issued to the army, ordering it to break, by all possible means, any resistance. The voice of Goebbels, after 5 o'clock in the morning, scanning all the texts drafted in the course of the night left no doubts about the will of the Reich to proceed with brutal energy.[183]

An era was closed, a new one was beginning. Prague was awaiting the coming events. The Prague radio service started announcing the German *Einmarsch* at 4:00 A.M. The announcement by the Ministry of National Defense was repeated over the air every five minutes. It was an order to all formations of the Czechoslovak army not to resist the German advance, warning that in the case of the slightest resistance the German army would interfere with utter brutality.[184] The editor-in-chief of the Czechoslovak Press Agency, Arnošt Bareš, informed the legations and the representatives of the foreign press about things to come. The General Staff and the Foreign Ministry were burning their secret documents.[185] The news of the upcoming occupation was slowly spreading. "The city under our windows looked no different than it had any other night. The only difference was the lights being gradually switched on: at the neighbors, downstairs, upstairs, in the entire street. We were standing at the window and saying to ourselves: 'They know it already.'" In these words Milena Jesenská, a friend of the late Franz Kafka, described her impression of the grim night.[186]

The occupation was carried out by two army groups: the Third advancing from the region of Dresden to Bohemia and headed by General Johannes Blaskowitz, and the Fifth, commanded by General Wilhelm List and marching from Vienna into Moravia.[187] The first German soldiers appeared in the Prague castle at 9:15 A.M. The German advance units penetrated into the streets of the inner city at 10:30 A.M. The German soldiers occupied all important buildings and offices, especially the police headquarters, the main post office building, the telephone exchange, etc.[188] The head of the Czechoslovak military intelligence, Colonel Moravec, with ten members of his staff escaped with British help on a Dutch plane the preceding day carrying away the most important of their files and lists of agents. Other material had been destroyed before their departure.[189]

Because of unfavorable weather only a few German propaganda flights were undertaken on the day of the *Einmarsch*. There were some reconnaissance flights and also several emergency landings caused by the weather. Only in the afternoon of the following day several flights were undertaken over Prague and Brno, but even then the clouds forced three wings to return.[190]

In Berlin, the train with Hácha left at 11:16 A.M., March 15. The President's suite was increased by a representative of the German Protocol Department and a German officer.[191] Under the pretext that the tracks were covered with snow the train halted frequently and arrived at the border at Terezín after 6:00 P.M. Unaware of Hitler's further intentions the Czechs were still hoping that the German occupation was a temporary measure and that the relative independence of their country would be restored. Hácha was greeted in Terezín by minister Havelka. He embraced him saying: "Do not worry, we shall have an independent state." According to Chvalkovský, the signature in Berlin did not concern the independence of the country. Further negotiations were to be held in Prague. Very probably the army would cease to exist.[192] It seemed that after the disarray of the night the two Czechs still had some hope that the Berlin convention was aiming only at the liquidation of the Czech army. Chvalkovský even hoped that Bohemia would maintain diplomatic representation abroad.[193]

The return to Prague was depressing. The Czech officials assembled at the railroad station had to wait in icy weather for almost two hours. The train did not arrive until 7:35 P.M. On the platform, instead of the company of honor of the Czechoslovak army,[194] were 96 men of a German army unit which greeted the President with a strident Prussian military march. The small, stooping figure of Hácha at the side of the six feet of the representative of the German Protocol, Gustav Adolf von Halem, was a living symbol of the humiliation of the country. The ceremony was short at the station and the President left without delay for the castle where the cabinet had already assembled. The President reported his conversations with Hitler. Beran again offered the resignation of the cabinet. Hácha accepted and asked the ministers to take care of the current affairs.[195]

At that moment, however, Hácha was not the only master of the castle. He had been preceded by an unexpected guest: Chancellor Hitler himself. For Hitler had decided after the signature of the documents to inspect personally the army in the occupied territory and to spend the night at the ancient royal castle in Prague. Only some months earlier he derided foreign heads of state for residing in ancient castles and named the Prague *Hradčany* twice in this context. "I am not going to the castles" (*Ich gehe nicht in die Schlösser*) he boasted in August 1938.[196] However, in March 1939, in spite of the most inclement weather, he was hastening uninvited to the ancient seat of the kings of Bohemia and emperors of the Roman Empire of the German Nation. The Berliners passing Wilhelmstrasse in the early morning of March 15 could see before the old chancellery a truck loading Hitler's personal luggage. From Česká Lípa in the occupied Sudeten region he set out for the Czech frontier, which he crossed at 4:45 P.M. A long convoy of automobiles preceded by armored cars labored slowly through a snowstorm and reached Prague about 7:00 P.M., shortly before the return of Hácha.[197]

Nobody was waiting for the German visitors and they presented themselves to nobody. When the rumor spread that Hitler was in the Prague castle, minister Havelka from the President's chancellery was charged with checking it out. Chvalkovský met Ribbentrop in the corridor and, surprised, asked him for the reasons for such an unexpected visit. Ribbentrop replied briefly that Hitler would explain it to Hácha himself. For the moment he did not want to disturb him.[198]

The Germans installed themselves in the western wing of the castle, where they spent the night deliberating how to consolidate the gained positions.[199] They did not need worry about the reactions abroad. The speech Chamberlain had delivered in the House of Commons the preceding afternoon was faint; nor was the French attitude marked by any excess of firmness.[200] The conclusion which Hitler drew was based on the declaration signed by Hácha in Berlin, the text of which had been published in the morning. Hitler had brought to Prague several legal experts whom he now ordered to give legal form to his political projects. He declared that he wished to grant the Czechs "some form of autonomy" and added that he had decided to establish a protectorate over their land. Only a few hours were at their disposal. The draft was drawn up by Dr. Hans Lammers, the head of the Reich Chancellery, Dr. Wilhelm Stuckart, the State Secretary in the Ministry of the Interior, and Dr. Friedrich Gaus, the director of the Legal Department of the Foreign Ministry, and some other experts. Dr. Lammers was on several occasions obliged to request information from Hitler as to what the Chancellor's idea really was. Later Dr. Stuckart claimed the main authorship of the decree instituting the protectorate and even admitted that some of its vagueness had been caused by lack of time.[201]

On the following day, March 16, at 1:00 P.M., Ribbentrop read on the radio the decree establishing the protectorate. From the preamble on, the style disclosed the hand of Hitler and his predilection for arguments of historical character. "For a thousand years the lands of Bohemia and Moravia formed part of the living space of the German people. By force and folly they were arbitrarily torn from their ancient historic setting and, by their ultimate fusion into the artificial structure of Czechoslovakia, became a center of constant unrest." Therefore, "in keeping with the law of self-preservation," the German Reich resolved to intervene. Hitler then summed up his decisions in thirteen points, among them: Art. 1. The areas of the former Czechoslovak Republic occupied by the German troops in March 1939, form part of the Greater German Reich as the Protectorate of Bohemia and Moravia and come under the protection of Germany.[202] Art. 3. "The Protectorate will be autonomous and self-governing. Art. 4. The supreme head of the Protectorate (i.e. President Hácha) will enjoy the protection of the Reich and honorary rights of the head of state. He must have the confidence of the Führer. 5. The Führer will appoint a Reich Protector in Bohemia and Moravia as guardian of the interests of the Reich whose headquarters will be in Prague.[203] 6. The Reich will take over the foreign affairs of the Protectorate. The Protectorate will have a representative with the Reich government with the rank of minister.[204] 7. The Reich will afford military protection to the Protectorate and will maintain garrisons and military installations there. The Protectorate may set up its own formations for the maintenance of internal security and order.[205] According to Article 9 the Protectorate was to come within the customs area of the German Reich.[206]

The decree instituting the Protectorate was the second painful surprise for Hácha in two days. Having read the text on the radio, Ribbentrop visited Hácha and handed it over to him. Hácha at first did not want to read it, thinking that it was only the communiqué for the press about Hitler's visit to Prague.[207] At 2:00 P.M. Hácha was invited to Hitler. The conversation lasted thirty minutes and dealt with the establishment of the Protestorate. Hitler assured Hácha that his functions would not be changed.[208]

Without losing time, the Germans began to install themselves in the central administration. The office of Chvalkovský was occupied by Ambassador Ritter. The codes and archives of the ministry were seized and sealed.[209] At the same time the Ministry of National Defense was occupied and the military equipment seized. The Germans acquired 1,582 planes, 501 antiaircraft guns, 2,175 pieces of light and heavy artillery, 785 mine throwers, 469 armored cars, 43,876 machine guns, 114,000 pistols, 1,090,000 rifles, more than one billion rounds of ammunition, more than 3 million shells and gas shells.[210]

On the evening of March 16, Hácha made a speech on the defunct liberty. He recalled that as early as 1918 his joy over independence was not without shadows. Twenty years later, in 1939, his fears had been painfully confirmed. "The events have shown that what we were taking for a solution for centuries was but a short episode of our national history," he declared.[211]

He was, however, not yet at the end of his disappointments. In his speech he expressed the hope that the Czech nation in its new legal status would find "a calm and prosperous life." Subsequently he had to witness a gradual deterioration of the situation and later in a private conversation he declared about the Berlin agreement: "Hitler has fooled me."[212] During the war he wrote to one of his friends: "The mischievous fate has burdened me with this task. My sacrifice has been more painful than I originally realized. I am exhausted by life and feel my forces escaping."[213]

CHAPTER V
VAIN PROTESTS

The two western signatories of the Munich Agreement witnessed passively the upheaval in Central Europe. At the moment when Slovakia seceded from Prague, the plans of Berlin still seemed obscure. Diplomatic circles in the German capital thought that Hitler would demand a reduction of the Czechoslovak army and might proceed to a token occupation of Bohemia and Moravia.[1] There were rumors that Prague could be occupied as a measure of protection for the German population of Jihlava.[2] However, the French ambassador Coulondre reported from Berlin that Hitler was inclined to extreme solutions and that the Reich would demand at least a complete disarmament of Bohemia.[3] Mastný, more and more isolated, had lost all contact with Weizsäcker.[4] On Monday, March 13, he met Henderson and Coulondre who advised him "to keep (if he can) in as close touch as possible with the German government and to endeavor to reassure the latter as to influence in Prague of adherents of late President Beneš."[5]

Neither Great Britain nor France was thinking of a demarche in Berlin. On the 13th Lord Halifax made in Sunderland a speech in every way conciliatory. Permanent Under-Secretary of the Foreign Office, Sir Alexander Cadogan, acknowledged that the British-German declaration of September 30 provided for a mutual consultation on questions concerning the two countries, but he was afraid that if Britain attempted to invoke the agreement Germany would retort that Britain had no interest whatever in Czechoslovakia. As to the guarantee promised by Britain in October, Cadogan, though admitting some moral obligation, declared that it could equally be maintained that Britain had been released from her promise by the fact that the negotiations had failed.[6] In the House of Commons, Chamberlain adopted the same passive attitude when the leader of the opposition, Attlee, asked him about the guarantee. He reminded him that the proposed guarantee was against unprovoked aggression on Czechoslovakia. "No such aggression has yet taken place," declared Chamberlain at the very moment when the presidential train was under steam to leave Prague for Berlin.[7]

In the morning of March 14, Henderson saw State Secretary Weizsäcker and according to his memoirs "adjured him to see that nothing was done to violate the Munich Agreement or to upset the Stanley-Hudson visit."[8] Weizsäcker was noncomittal and only assured the British ambassador that whatever was done would be done in a "decent manner." In his memoirs Henderson stated that after seeing Weizsäcker he left the Wilhelmstrasse "filled with the gloomiest forebodings."[9] However, in the report he sent on the same day to Halifax,[10] he hid his worries and only repeated Weizsäcker's words that Germany wished to arrange matters "in a decent way." As his general impression he added that no definite line of action had yet been decided upon, but that the use of force was certainly not excluded if Prague proved recalcitrant. He had tried to impress upon Weizsäcker "the extreme importance of the form in which Germany handled the situation."[11]

London was nevertheless uneasy. It was agreed not to make any empty threats, since Britain was "not going to fight for Czechoslovakia" and should not regard herself "as in any way guaranteeing Czechoslovakia."[12] In the evening of the 14th Halifax instructed Henderson to declare to the German government at his earliest opportunity that the British government would deplore any action in Central Europe which would cause a setback to a relaxation of tension. The wording of the message was, however, very mild. In its first sentence the British government almost excused itself for this demarche stating that it had "no desire to interfere unnecessarily in matters in which other governments may be more directly concerned" than Britain.[13]

The French government at the beginning was attempting to keep the same reserve as Great Britain. When Bonnet, the chairman of the Senate Foreign Relations Committee, Henri Bérenger, and General Maurice Gamelin were invited to a dinner at the British embassy on March 13, they did not seem "unduly perturbed" about the Slovak crisis. Both Bonnet and Bérenger felt that the less Britain interfered in this crisis the better. According to ambassador Phipps, they remarked that the renewed rift between the Czechs and Slovaks only proved that Britain and France nearly went to war last autumn to boost up a state that was not "viable."[14]

On the 14th, however, Bonnet was forced to warn Berlin. Probably under the impression of the false rumor that Germany sent an ultimatum to Prague, he asked the German ambassador Welczek to caution his government that the entry of German forces into Czechoslovakia would be a violation of the Munich Agreement and would ruin the peace efforts. Welczek replied that Hitler would never commit the error of annexing the Czechs and Slovaks.[15] At the same time Bonnet instructed

Coulondre to ask Ribbentrop urgently what the meaning of the German activity in Slovakia was. As in the case of the British demarche, it was only a purely informative sounding made on the basis of the French-German declaration of December 6 calling for mutual consultation.[16]

On the following day when the two ambassadors had to effectuate their modest demarches the situation was, however, entirely different. In the morning the big headlines of the German press announced the events of the night while the Wehrmacht was invading Bohemia and Moravia. Henderson carried out his demarche by simply sending a written communication to Ribbentrop.[17] A little later, on instruction from London, he informed the Wilhelmstrasse that his government felt that in view of the situation the visit of the two British ministers would be inopportune and was being postponed.[18] Henderson himself was upset and indignant. He realized that the situation was much more serious than indicated by Weizsäcker the preceding day. He felt that the State Secretary had deceived him when he said that everything would be arranged in a decent way. In the morning of the 15th he let Weizsäcker know through Coulondre that if this was his conception of "decency", it was not his, Henderson's.[19] To Halifax he wrote a letter complaining bitterly of the German behavior. The following day he wired to his chief: "The utter cynicism and immorality of the whole performance defies description."[20]

On March 15 Halifax and Chamberlain made a declaration in Parliament. Even this was only a mild protest against the German methods. "These events cannot fail to be a cause of disturbance of the international situation. They are bound to administer a shock of confidence, all the more regrettable since confidence was beginning to revive..." stated their identical declaration.[21] Later the same day Halifax received German ambassador Dirksen, and spoke to him in a more energetic and open way than to his own compatriots in the Parliament. He reproached him for the naked application of force which was in flat contradiction with the spirit of the Munich Agreement. Nobody felt the German promises to be worth very much. "I could well understand," Halifax continued, "Herr Hitler's taste for bloodless victories, but one of these days he would find himself up against something that would not be bloodless." Dirksen had no illusion about the consequences of Hitler's action and in his report to Berlin he described the general mood in Britain as "a feeling of suppressed fury."[22]

Coulondre saw Weizsäcker the same day (15th). His modest mission had been overtaken by events. Weizsäcker pointed out to him the declaration of the Slovak independence and stated that the agreement between Hitler and Hácha was a final settlement of the Czech problem. Coulondre, going beyond his instructions, expressed his indignation about this violation of the Munich Agreement and declared that the pressure made on Czechoslovakia was throwing a peculiar light on the conditions under which the agreement was concluded.[23] Weizsäcker's reply was sharp. Above all, he protested against the reference to Munich. In his opinion the Munich Agreement contained two elements, namely the maintenance of peace and the French désintéressement in the eastern European questions. France should turn her eyes to the west, to her empire and not to interfere where, as experience had shown, her participation had not served the cause of the peace. Weizsäcker did not recognize any demarche other than a purely informatory one. Toward the end, smoothing down his speech, he adopted "a more confidential tone." He expressed the hope that Coulondre would find fresh instructions when he returned to his embassy and that they would set his mind at rest. "In this question it is not worthwhile to exaggerate," he said, and pointed out the "common duty to see that Franco-German relations remained unaffected by it as far as possible."[24]

In Paris the German ambassador presented to the Foreign Ministry the text of the Berlin declaration. Like Dirksen in London, Welczek manifested "an uneasiness and embarrassment," an understandable uneasiness, for the document the two German diplomats had in their hands contradicted their affirmations of the preceding day. The conversation of the German ambassador with Bonnet was brief. "I protest," declared the latter, "in the name of the French government against this coup de force. We refuse to recognize it." The French minister stated that the German action in Bohemia was the heaviest blow yet struck against the friends of peace in Europe. The peace and the appeasement policy of the "men of Munich" had suffered a lamentable disaster.[25]

Which line of conduct was to be adopted after such a flagrant violation of the Munich Agreement? It seems that the initiative came from the French. In the evening of March 15, the French ambassador asked in London on his own authority whether the British government did not intend to make another official demarche in Berlin. The answer was negative. According to Halifax, the best action was the postponement of the planned visit of the two British ministers to Germany.[26] On the following day Bonnet invited London to a joint demarche in Berlin, for it was impossible "to assist today in silence the dismemberment of the Czech people and the annexation of their territory." Great Britain and France owed it to international opinion as well as to themselves to protest formally against the German use of force.[27]

Chamberlain was rather evasive on the 16th in the Chamber of Commons. However, in the evening of the 17th he made a speech in Birmingham which showed not only a radical change of his attitude, but a complete reversal of the British policy. The moderated tone of the preceding days changed into a new language, a bitter criticism, an eloquent protestation, a will to resist. "Is this the last attack upon a small State, or is it to be followed by others? Is this, in fact, a step in the direction of an attempt to dominate the world by force?" asked the Prime Minister.[28]

This change of attitude put London in line with the demarche proposed by Paris. The demarche took place on March 18. The ambassadors of the two great powers were received separately by Weizsäcker. Coulondre came in the morning to protest against "a fragrant violation of the letter and the spirit" of the Munich Agreement and to announce that France could not recognize the legitimacy of the new situation. Weizsäcker rejected the protest. His contracted face when he saw the document which Coulondre was handing to him showed that he guessed the aim of the demarche and had received instructions to make the ambassador take back his note. When Coulondre explained its contents, Weizsäcker refused to accept the note referring to the talks that Bonnet had with Ribbentrop in December.[29] Finally he accepted the note as if it had been delivered to him by mail, declaring, however, that he feared that the French government would regret its demarche.[30]

Henderson handed over his note to Weizsäcker in the afternoon. London protested against the changes in Czechoslovakia by German military action which in the British view were devoid of any legality. This time, too, Weizsäcker refused to accept the note. Probably he was afraid of the reaction of Hitler and later asked Henderson by telephone to reconsider the note. Henderson refused.[31]

The two ambassadors then left their posts: Henderson on the 18th, Coulondre on the 19th. They returned to Berlin only toward the end of April (Henderson the 24th, Coulondre the 26th) at a moment when the Polish crisis was beginning to loom on the horizon.

Moscow protested on March 18. Contesting the legality of the agreement with Hácha, it refused to recognize the incorporation of Bohemia and Moravia into the Reich and pointed out that the German methods were aggravating the dangers menacing the peace of the world.[32]

From the United States, where he lived since February as a professor at the University of Chicago, Beneš expressed his protests. In the morning of March 16 he sent to President Roosevelt, Prime Ministers Chamberlain and Daladier, to Maxim Litvinov, and the General Secretary of the League of Nations, Joseph Avenol, a telegraphic protest which he signed as "the former President of the Republic." Referring to article 10 of the Covenant of the League (about sanctions) he expressed the hope that no member of the League of Nations would recognize "this crime" and that all would in due time fulfill the obligations arising out of the Covenant.[33]

The United States protested on March 20. At his press conference, the Acting Secretary of State, Sumner Welles, condemned in the name of his government the acts which had resulted in the temporary extinguishment of the liberties of Czechoslovakia.[34] And on March 20, in the reply to the German note of March 17 announcing the assumption of a protectorate over Bohemia and Moravia, the American government declared that it did not recognize "any legal basis" for such status.[35]

Quite peculiar in these days of March was the German attitude toward Italy. Hitler left his ally without news and announced his decision to him—as in the case of the Anschluss a year ago—only at the moment when his plan was almost implemented. In Berlin, Attolico was as much in the dark as his British and French colleagues.[36] On the 10th, the Day of the Heroes (*Heldengedenktag*), he guessed by the tired face of Hitler that the Führer was on the eve of an action. He telephoned immediately to Cassel, to the residence of the Prince of Hesse, husband of the daughter of the King of Italy, Princess Mafalda of Savoy, whom Hitler used as messenger to communicate with Mussolini. He learned that the Prince had been urgently called to Berlin which confirmed Attolico's fears.[37] On March 11 he asked Walter Hewel, Ribbentrop's representative with the Führer, for information. The reply was evasive: The situation was obscure. However Berlin hoped—according to Hewel—that people like Chvalkovský could restore order.[38] The same evasiveness was manifested by Weizsäcker on the 12th, and by Ribbentrop in the evening of the 13th.[39]

Only in the evening of the 14th, while Hácha was on his way to Berlin was Ribbentrop more communicative. He received Attolico at about 6:00 P.M. to announce that the future of Bohemia and Moravia would be discussed with Hácha: "The Führer intends to lance the abscess. The liquidation of this problem is of interest not only to Germany, but also to the Axis."[40]

On the 15th, Attolico got from Weizsäcker some information by telephone[41] and the same day, at 3:00 P.M., the Prince of Hesse brought to Mussolini in the presence of Ciano the oral message from Hitler about the intervention in Prague. The Führer had acted because the Czechs did not want to demobilize, had continued their contacts with Russia and had mistreated the Germans. According to the telegram of the German ambassador, Mussolini received the message with thanks. However, the banality of the explanation was far from satisfying the two Italians: "Such pretexts may be good for Goebbels's propaganda, but they should not use them when talking with us," wrote Ciano. Mussolini was dissatisfied. He did not even want to transmit to the press the information that the Prince of Hesse had made him a visit and declared: "The Italians would laugh at me; every time Hitler occupies a country he sends me a message."[42] The news from Berlin depressed him. On the 16th, the secretary of the fascist party, Ettore Muti, found him tired and aged by several years.[43] On the 17th, Ciano stated: "The Duce was anxious and gloomy. It was the first time I had seen him thus. Even at the time of the Anschluss he had shown greater indifference."[44]

Relations between Italy and Germany were entering upon a critical stage. "What importance can one give in the future to other declarations and promises which concern us closer?" asked Ciano in his diary on March 15, and he stated: "It is useless to conceal that all this worries and humiliates the Italian people." The occupation of Prague was however not to be the last surprise for Italian politicians in the course of the year.

CONCLUSION

The Munich Agreement was a solution of short duration, a temporary settlement between Germany and Czechoslovakia as well as an interlude on the international scene. In Munich, France and Great Britain were not aware of the import of the concessions they were forcing on Czechoslovakia and they realized only later to what extent they had increased the stature of Germany.

For Hitler the Munich solution of the Sudeten problem was merely one step in his plan for the total annihilation of Czechoslovakia. The rigor with which he enforced the territorial clauses of the Agreement was a bad augury for the future. While the French and British members of the International Commission in Berlin were more or less merely passive onlookers he was gradually increasing his demands and inflicting new and painful territorial losses on Prague. The German minority which remained in Czechoslovakia, far from being appeased, again became a vanguard of a bellicose pangermanism.

The two other neighbors of Czechoslovakia, Hungary and Poland, used the favorable conjuction to assert their own territorial demands. Hungary saw here an opportunity to break the narrow frame into which she had been forced by the Treaty of Trianon. In her fear of a resuscitated German influence in the Danubian basin she preferred to rely mainly on Italy, for years a supporter of Hungarian revisionism. The oscillation between the two Axis powers explains the tortuous policy pursued by Budapest in September 1938, a policy which had so angered Hitler, himself anti-Magyar since his youth. While timid towards Berlin, Budapest assumed a forcible attitude toward Czechoslovakia and attempted to enforce even its maximum demands including the whole eastern part of the state, Slovakia and Subcarpathian Ruthenia. Though these hopes could not materialize, Hungary was able, with the help of Italy, to secure by the Vienna Award a large tract of fertile land on the southern border of eastern Czechoslovakia. Her aspirations in Subcarpathian Ruthenia (Carpatho-Ukraine) met later with stern rebuke from Berlin, which was averse to losing its grip on an area of potential importance for its plans in the East.

Whereas Budapest, aware of its military weakness, proceeded in a rather hesitant way, Poland was more resolute. Full of animosity toward Czechoslovakia and fascinated by the apple of discord between the two countries, the land of Těšín, Colonel Beck pushed his demands quite ruthlessly. Shortly after Munich Poland occupied the contested territory including the important railroad junction of Bohumín: a problematic victory, for a fortnight later Ribbentrop unfolded the German designs on Danzig and the Polish corridor before the surprised Polish ambassador.

The new Czechoslovakia struggled in the meantime with serious political and economic difficulties stemming from the new situation. The trunkated state, devoid of its strategic frontiers and its fortifications, was helplessly open to any German move. North of Prague, the German border was only about 25 miles away. The German legation was an invisible power behind the scenes. The German chargé d'affaires Hencke spoke confidently of a "vassal-relationship" and boasted that members of the Prague cabinet who were not approved by Germany could simply be forced to resign.[1] Similarly, his colleague, the press attaché Gregory watched over the Czech press.

Prague had to grant autonomy to Slovakia and Ruthenia where the new local governments nimbly introduced the totalitarian regime then current in Central Europe. Bohemia and Moravia, "the historic lands," were attempting to save some democratic façade, though it was only a very pale reflexion of the recent political past. Under the impact of the changed political situation in central Europe even here reactionary elements were gaining strength, foreshadowing in some respects the oppressive atmosphere which would pervade the Vichy France two years later.

The feeble government of post-Munich Czechoslovakia was composed mainly of experts without greater experience of active political life. The only real political minds were the head of the cabinet, Beran, and foreign minister Chvalkovský. Beran's background was, however, limited to domestic politics and his knowledge of the external world was insufficient. His attempts to approach leading German circles were not without a certain naive simplicity. In the sphere of foreign policy he had to rely above all on Chvalkovský, a man of the world, well-travelled, with practical knowledge of diplomacy. The threats he heard from Hitler in Munich in October were hanging like a dark cloud over Chvalkovský's head and influenced his total posture during this period. Though often unnecessarily pliant and almost subservient to Germany, he was nevertheless systematically endeavoring to reach the only goal of Czechoslovakia's post-Munich foreign policy, the guarantees promised in Munich.

In September 1938 Czechoslovakia agreed to capitulate and yield to the German demands only on the condition that the previous system of her alliances would be replaced by efficient guarantees of her new borders. The guarantees were, however, long in coming even when Prague had met all the required conditions. Great Britain and France evinced only mild interest in guaranteeing a state drawn more and more into the orbit of Greater Germany. The latter, expecting to occupy the country in the not too distant future, categorically refused any guarantees.

On the broader scene of European politics none of the hopes and promises which appeared in Munich were fulfilled. Relations between Germany and Great Britain as well as between France and Italy were deteriorating. The French-German Declaration signed in Paris two months after Munich proved still-born. Though conjectures abounded in diplomatic circles and foreign press it was not easy in the winter of 1938–39 to predict the future and to prognosticate about the plans of the German policy makers.

Hitler, disappointed that the Munich Agreement had prevented him from crushing Czechoslovakia once and for all, was in the seclusion of Berchtesgaden vaguely ruminating upon his future moves. The fall and the early winter of 1938–39 were for him a period of groping for new ideas. For the time being he issued to his military two directives concerning action against Czechoslovakia, but on the whole this former adversary was at the time relatively in the background.

In the forefront of Hitler's thoughts at that moment were his future moves in the East, Danzig and the Polish corridor. Only when Poland manifested a resistance to his overtures did he turn his attention again to Czechoslovakia. Thus the opening of the new year saw a revival of German initiatives. When the talks with Poland came to a temporary standstill, Hitler decided to deal Czechoslovakia the final blow and thus to facilitate his future actions.

Exploiting the separatist aspirations of the radical fringe of the Slovak Populist party he encouraged the proclamation of an independent Slovak state. Slovak Prime Minister Tiso, after some initial vacillation, gradually moved into the openly separatist camp. In the end it was his steps which led to the declaration of independence and contributed to the disintegration of Czechoslovakia. Having reached this stage Hitler imposed his conditions on Prague. He was helped in this to a certain degree by the maladresse of the Czechoslovak government. At the moment when Berlin was veiling itself in silence and was leaving the Czech queries without answer Prague wished to learn more about the German attitude. However, to send to Berlin for this end even the head of state was a misplaced gesture which Hitler was quick to turn to his advantage.

The sudden journey of President Hácha and Chvalkovský to Berlin forced Hitler to change his original plans and to withhold the ultimatum which he originally had intended to send to Prague. The presence of the two Czechs offered him the opportunity to attain his goal in an easier way and to lend a semblance of legitimacy to his brutal moves.

His position was made easier by another error made by Prague. Chvalkovský, and with him Prime Minister Beran, systematically underestimated the reports of German military preparations carried out in the last few days before their journey to Berlin. Even the news of German occupation of Moravská Ostrava in the evening of March 14 received only their cursory attention when the Czechs arrived in Berlin. Consequently Hácha was entirely out of touch with the situation when he attempted to enlighten Hitler on the juridical background of the Czech actions in Slovakia. Only when Hitler cut him short and when he was faced with Hitler's unexpected threats did he gather his strength and tried to resist. All was in vain and he was forced to put his name to two documents, one concerning the military capitulation and the second one pretending that the Czech president trusted the righteousness of the Führer's decisions. Even before Hácha returned home, Hitler preceded him impatiently to his own house and overwhelmed him on the following day with another surprise: the proclamation of the Protectorate Bohemia-Moravia, hastily drawn up the preceding night. During the discussions in Berlin, the term "protectorate" was not once used and in the night of March 15–16, the Czechs did not have the slightest idea what the Germans were hatching in the Prague castle.

Before Munich, Hitler declared that he did not want any Czechs within the Reich. Now he annexed their whole country and violated the letter and spirit of the Munich Agreement. The frail peace achieved at Munich was shaken. The policy of appeasement came to an end. "Thereafter, Hitler's word could never more be trusted," wrote one of the foremost protagonists of appeasement, the British ambassador in Berlin, Sir Nevile Henderson.[2] The initiator of the appeasement policy, British Prime Minister Neville Chamberlain, after some hesitation vigorously condemned these actions of Hitler and from that moment on set out to actively resist German policies. Not discouraged, Hitler pursued his projects unyieldingly. On his chessboard it was the Poland's turn. After some dismal negotiations German troops crossed the Polish border in the morning of September 1. The first anniversary of Munich saw a prostrate Poland and Europe in arms. The Second World War had begun.

APPENDIX I

Agreement Signed at Munich Between Germany, the United Kingdom, France, and Italy,[1] September 29, 1938

Germany, the United Kingdom, France, and Italy, taking into consideration the agreement, which has been already reached in principle for the cession to Germany of the Sudeten German territory, have agreed on the following terms and conditions governing the said cession and the measures consequent thereon, and by this agreement they each hold themselves responsible for the steps necessary to secure its fulfillment.

1) The evacuation will begin on October 1st.

2) The United Kingdom, France, and Italy agree that the evacuation of the territory shall be completed by October 10th, without any existing installations having been destroyed, and that the Czechoslovak Government will be held responsible for carrying out the evacuation without damage to the said installations.

3) The conditions governing the evacuation will be laid down in detail by an international commission composed of representatives of Germany, the United Kingdom, France, Italy, and Czechoslovakia.

4) The occupation by stages of the predominantly German territory by German troops will begin on October 1st. The four territories marked on the attached map will be occupied by German troops in the following order: the territory marked number I on the 1st and 2d of October, the territory marked number II on the 2d and 3d of October, the territory marked number III on the 3d, 4th, and 5th of October, the territory marked number IV on the 6th and 7th of October. The remaining territory of preponderantly German character will be ascertained by the aforesaid international commission forwith and be occupied by German troops by the 10th of October.

5) The international commission referred to in paragraph 3) will determine the territories in which a plebiscite is to be held. These territories will be occupied by international bodies until the plebiscite has been completed. The same commission will fix the conditions in which the plebiscite is to be held, taking as a basis the conditions of the Saar plebiscite. The commission will also fix a date, not later than the end of November, on which the plebiscite will be held.

6) The final determination of the frontier will be carried out by the international commission. This commission will also be entitled to recommend to the

four Powers, Germany, the United Kingdom, France, and Italy, in certain exceptional cases, minor modifications in the strictly ethnographical determination of the zones which are to be transferred without plebiscite.

7) There will be a right of option into and out of the transferred territories, the option to be exercised within 6 months from the date of this agreement. A German-Czechoslovak commission shall determine the details of the option, consider ways of facilitating the transfer of population and settle questions of principle arising out of the said transfer.

8) The Czechoslovak Government will, within a period of 4 weeks from the date of this agreement, release from their military and police forces any Sudeten Germans who may wish to be released, and the Czechoslovak Government will within the same period release Sudeten German prisoners who are serving terms of imprisonment for political offenses.

Adolf Hitler
Ed. Daladier
Mussolini
Neville Chamberlain

Munich, September 29, 1938.

Annex to the Agreement

His Majesty's Government in the United Kingdom and the French Government have entered into the above agreement on the basis that they stand by the offer, contained in paragraph 6 of the Anglo-French proposals of September 19th, relating to an international guarantee of the new boundaries of the Czechoslovak State against unprovoked aggression.

When the question of the Polish and Hungarian minorities in Czechoslovakia has been settled, Germany and Italy for their part will give a guarantee to Czechoslovakia.

Adolf Hitler
Neville Chamberlain
Mussolini
Ed. Daladier

Munich, September 29, 1938.

The four Heads of Government here present agree that the international commission, provided for in the agreement signed by them today, shall consist of the State Secretary in the German Foreign Office, the British, French, and Italian Ambassadors, accredited in Berlin, and a representative to be nominated by the

Government of Czechoslovakia.

Adolf Hitler
Neville Chamberlain
Mussolini
Ed. Daladier

Munich, September 29, 1938.

Supplementary Declaration

All questions which may arise out of the transfer of the territory shall be considered as coming within the terms of reference to the international commission.

Adolf Hitler
Neville Chamberlain
Mussolini
Ed. Daladier

Munich, September 29, 1938.

1. *DGFP, II,* no. 675.

APPENDIX II

Declaration by the German and Czechoslovak Governments, Berlin, March 15, 1939[2]

At their request the Führer today received the Czechoslovak President, Dr. Hácha, and the Czechoslovak Foreign Minister, Dr. Chvalkovsky, in Berlin in the presence of Foreign Minister von Ribbentrop. At the meeting the serious situation created by the events of recent weeks in the present Czechoslovak territory was examined with complete frankness. The conviction was unanimously expressed on both sides that the aim of all efforts must be the safeguarding of calm, order, and peace in this part of central Europe. The Czechoslovak president declared that, in order to serve this object and to achieve ultimate pacification, he confidently placed the fate of the Czech people in the hands of the Führer of the German Reich. The Führer accepted this declaration and expressed his intention of taking the Czech people under the protection of the German Reich and of guaranteeing them an autonomous development of their ethnic life as suited to their character.

In witness whereof this document has been signed in duplicate.

Adolf Hitler	Dr. E. Hácha
Ribbentrop	F. Chvalkovský

2. *DGFP*, IV, no. 22g.

APPENDIX III

Comparative Tables of Place - Names

Central Europe belongs to the areas where the same geographical place-names occur in two and even more different languages. In the present volume Czech names are used for places located in Czechoslovakia. In the diplomatic documents and literature these names are, however, often mentioned in their German, Hungarian (Magyar), or Polish form. To facilitate the orientation of the reader comparative tables are added here. Table A contains the Czech and Slovak names first, followed by their equivalent in the other languages, while table B reverses the listings and equivalents for easy cross-reference.

Table A

Aš - Asch
Berehovo - Beregszás
Bohumín - Bogumin. Oderberg
Bratislava - Pressburg, Pozsony
Břeclav - Lundenburg
Brno - Brünn
Bruntál - Freudenthal
Český Dub - Böhmisch Aicha
Český Krumlov - Böhmisch Krumau
Cheb - Eger
Čop - Csap
Devín - Theben
Domažlice - Taus
Dvůr Králové - Königinhof
Frývaldov - Freiwaldau
Jasina - Körösmözö
Jihlava - Iglau
Jindřichův Hradec - Neuhaus
Karlovy Vary - Karlsbad
Komárno - Komárom, Komorn
Konice - Konitz
Košice - Kassa, Kaschau
Krnov - Jägerndorf

Liberec - Reichenberg
Litice - Lititz
Lučenec - Losoncz
Moravská Ostrava - Mährisch Ostrau
Moravský Krumlov - Mährisch Kromau
Mukačevo - Munkács
Nitra - Nyitra, Neutra
Nové Mesto pod Šatorom - Sátoraljaújhely
Nový Jičín - Neutitschein
Olomouc - Olmütz
Opava - Troppau
Petržalka - Engerau, Pozsonyligetfalu
Plzeň - Pilsen
Rimavská Sobota - Rimaszombat
Rožňava - Rozsnyó, Rosenau
Šahy - Ipolyság
Stará Paka - Altpaka
Šumava - Böhmerwald, Bohemian Forest
Svitavy - Zwittau
Těšín - Teschen, Ciezsyn
Vel'ký Žitný ostrov - Csálloköz, Grossschütt
Verecky - Vereczke

Table B

Altpaka - Stará Paka
Asch - Aš
Beregszás - Berehovo
Bogumin - Bohumín, Oderberg
Böhmerwald - Šumava, Bohemian Forest
Böhmisch Aicha - Český Dub
Böhmisch Krumau - Český Krumlov
Ciezsyn - Těšín, Teschen
Csálloköz - Vel'ký Žitný ostrov, Grossschütt
Eger - Cheb
Engerau - Petržalka, Pozsonyligetfalu
Freiwaldau - Frývaldov
Grossschütt - Vel'ký Žitný ostrov, Csálloköz
Iglau - Jihlava
Ipolyság - Šahy
Jägerndorf - Krnov
Karlsbad - Karlovy Vary
Kaschau, Kassa - Košice
Komárom, Komorn - Komárno
Königinhof - Dvůr Králové

Konitz - Konice
Körösmözö - Jasina
Lundenburg - Břeclav
Mährisch Kromau - Moravský Krumlov
Mährisch Ostrau - Moravská Ostrava
Munkács - Mukačevo
Neuhaus - Jindřichův Hradec
Neutitschein - Nový Jičín
Neutra - Nitra, Nyitra
Oderberg - Bohumín, Bogumin
Olmütz - Olomouc
Pilsen - Plzeň
Pozsonyligetfalu - Petržalka, Engerau
Pressburg - Bratislava, Pozsony
Reichenberg - Liberec
Rimaszombat - Rimavská Sobota
Rosenau, Rozsnyó - Rožňava
Sátoraljaújhely - Nové Mesto pod Šatorom
Taus - Domažlice
Teschen - Těšín, Ciezsyn
Theben - Devín
Troppau - Opava
Ungvár - Užhorod
Vereczke - Verecky
Zwittau - Svitavy

BIBLIOGRAPHY

I. Documents

Beran Rudolf. "Bývalý předseda vlády Rudolf Beran před Národním soudem. Jeho obhajovací řeč pronesená 28. a 29.III. 1947" [Former Prime Minister Rudolf Beran before the National Tribunal. His Plea Delivered on March 28 and 29, 1947]. Mimeographed. Prague, 1947 (?).

Biddle, A.J. Drexel, Jr. *Poland and the Coming of the Second World War. The Diplomatic Papers of A.J. Drexel Biddle, Jr., United States Ambassador to Poland, 1937–1939.* Edited by Philip V. Cannistraro, Edward D. Wybot, and Theodore P. Kovaleff. Columbus, 1976.

Bubeníčková R., and Helešicová V. "Deset říjnových dnů roku 1938" [Ten October Days of 1938] *Odboj a revoluce,* vol. 6, no. 4 (1968), pp. 111–88.

Bubeníčková R., Helešicová V., and Machotková R. "Tiskové pokyny pomnichovské republiky" [Press Directives of the post-Munich Republic] ibid, vol. 7, no. 1 (1969), pp. 126–98.

Ciano, Galeazzo. *L'Europa verso le catastrofe.* Milan, 1948. Czechoslovak Ministry of Information. *Český národ soudí K.H. Franka* [K.H. Frank on Trial before the Czech People]. Prague, 1946.

______, *Zpověď K.H. Franka. Podle vlastních výpovědí v době vazby u krajského soudu trestního na Pankráci* [Confession of K. H. Frank. According to His Own Depositions at the Regional Criminal Court at Pankrác]. Prague, 1946.

DeWitt C. Poole Mission. National Archives, Washington, D.C. M. 679, rolls 1–3.

Diplomáciai iratok Magyárország külpolitikájához 1936–1945 [Diplomatic Documents on Hungarian Foreign Policy, 1936–1945]

II. *A müncheni egyezmény létrejötte és Magyárország külpolitikája 1936–1938* [The Coming of the Munich Agreement and Hungarian Foreign Policy 1936–1938]. Budapest, 1965.

III. *Magyárország külpolitikája 1938–1939* [Hungarian Foreign Policy 1938–1939]. Budapest, 1970. Both volumes edited by Magda Ádám.

Documents diplomatiques français 1932–1939. 2e série (1936–1939), vols. XI, XII. Paris, 1977, 1978.

Documents on British Foreign Policy 1919–1939, Third Series, vol. III, 1938–9. London, 1950. Vol. IV, 1939. London, 1951. Both volumes edited by E.L. Woodward, and Rohan Butler.

Documents on International Affairs 1938. Vol. II. Edited by Monica Curtis. London, 1943.

Documents on Interantional Affairs 1939–1946. Vol. I, *March–September 1939.* Selected and edited under the direction of Arnold J. Toynbee. London, 1951

Dokumente der deutschen Politik. Edited by Paul Meier-Benneckenstein. VI. *Grossdeutschland 1938.* Berlin, 1939. VII. *Das Werden des Reiches 1939.* Berlin, 1940.

Europäische Politik 1933–1938 im Spiegel der Prager Akten. Edited by Friedrich Joseph Berber, 2nd ed., Essen, 1942.

Les événements survenus en France de 1933 à 1945. Témoignages et documents recueillis par la Commission d'enquête parlementaire. 11 vols. Paris, 1949–51.

German Army High Command. *Records of the Headquarters of the German Army High Command.* National Archives, Washington, D.C. Microcopy T-78

German Foreign Ministry. *Records of the German Foreign Ministry Archives.* National Archives, Washington, D.C. Microcopy T-120.

———, COLLECTION ENTITLED: *Tschecho-Slowakische Dokumente.* National Archives, Washington, D.C., Microcopy T-120, Serial 1809H, rolls 1039–1041. (Documents of the Czechoslovak Foreign Ministry, seized by the Germans in March 1939 and translated into German).

Germany and Czechoslovakia 1918–1945. Documents on German Policies. Edited by Koloman Gajan and Robert Kvaček. Prague, 1969.

Helešicová V., and Machotková R. "Mnichovská krise v jednáních ministerské rady [The Munich Crisis in the Proceedings of the Council of Ministers]. *Odboj a revoluce,* vol. 7, no. 5 (1969), pp. 138–230.

Hitler Adolf. "Hitler's Private Testament of May, 1938." Edited by G. L. Weinberg. *Journal of Modern History* 27 (1955), pp. 415–19.

——— "Rede Hitlers vor der deutschen Presse (10. November 1938)," Edited by Wilhelm Treue. *Vierteljahrshefte für Zeitgeschichte,* 6 (1958), pp. 181–91.

———, *Le Testament politique de Hitler.* Notes recueillies par Martin Bormann. Paris, 1959.

International Military Tribunal. *Trial of the Major War Criminals before the International Military Tribunal. Nuremberg. 14 November 1945* – 1 October 1946. 42 vols. Nuremberg, 1947–49.

———, *Trials of War Criminals before the Nuremberg Military Tribunal.* Vol. XII, XIII. Case 11. *US v. von Weizsäcker.* Washington, vol. XII, n.d.; XIII, 1952.

Jacobsen, Hans-Adolf. *1939–1945. Der zweite Weltkrieg in Chronik und Dokumenten.* 5th ed., Darmstadt, 1961.

Kerekes, Lájos, ed. *Allianz Hitler-Horthy-Mussolini. Dokumente zur ungarischen Aussenpolitik (1933–1944).* Budapest, 1966.

Král, Václav, ed. *Das Abkommen von München 1938.* Prague, 1968.

———, *Die Deutschen in der Tschechoslowakei 1933–1947. Prague, 1964.*

———, "Nové dokumenty k historii 15. března 1939" [New Documents to the History of March 15, 1939]. *Mezinárodní Politika,* vol. 3 (1939), pp. 176–78, 181.

———, *Politické strany a Mnichov* [Political Parties and Munich]. Prague, 1961.

Lipski, Józef. *Diplomat in Berlin, 1933–1939; papers and memoirs of Józef Lipski,*

Ambassador of Poland. Edited by Waclaw Jędrzejewicz. New York, 1968.
Ministère des affaires étrangères (France). *Le Livre Jaune Français. Documents diplomatiques 1938–1939.* Paris, 1939.
Ministry for Foreign Affairs of the Czechoslovak Republic–Ministry for Foreign Affairs of the U.S.S.R. *New Documents on the History of Munich.* Edited by. V. F. Klochko et al. Prague, 1958.
Ministry for Foreign Affairs of the Union of Soviet Socialist Republics. *Documents and Materials Relating to the Eve of the Second World War.* Vol. I November 1937–1938. New York, 1948.
Mnichov v dokumentech [Munich in Documents]. 2 vols. Prague, 1958.
Sbírka zákonů a nařízení Československého státu [The Collection of Laws and Regulations of the Czechoslovak State]. Prague, 1938–39.
Schwarz, Karl, ed. *Chronik des Krieges. Dokumente und Berichte.* Berlin, 1940.
Der Sekretär des Führers. Führers Tagebuch 1934–1943. Hitler's Daily Activities from January 30, 1934 to June 30, 1943. German Material. Rehse Collection, Hitler Material, Appendix 5, 472E, Ac. 9705. Library of Congress, Washington, D.C.
Slovak Autonomous Government. *Pred súdom národa; proces s Dr. J. Tisom, Dr. F. Ďurčanským a A. Machom v Bratislave v dňoch 2. dec. 1946–15. apr. 1947* [Facing the Trial by the People: The Trial of Dr. J. Tiso, Dr. F. Ďurčanský, and A. Mach in Bratislava from December 2, 1946 to April 15, 1947]. 5 vols. Bratislava, 1947.
U.S. Department of State. Diplomatic correspondence 1938–39. National Archives, Washington, D.C.
______, *Foreign Relations of the United States. Diplomatic Papers, 1939.* Vol. I. Washington, 1956.
______, *Documents on German Foreign Policy 1918–1945.* Series D (1937–1945). II. *Germany and Czechoslovakia 1937–1938.* Washington, 1949. III. *The Aftermath of Munich. October 1938–March 1939.*, Wash., 1951. V. *Poland; The Balkans; Latin America; The Smaller Powers, June 1937–March 1939.* Wash., 1955.
"Wegry i Polska w okresie kryzysu czechoslowackiego 1938r." [Hungary and Poland in the Course of the Czechoslovak Crisis]. *Sprawy Międzynarodowe,* 11, no. 7/8 (1950), pp. 69–73.
Zápisy o schůzích poslanecké sněmovny Národního shromáždění republiky Československé. Schůze 1–159 (od 18. června 1935 do 16. prosince 1938) [Records of the Sessions of the Chamber of Deputies of the National Assembly of the Czechoslovak Republic, Session 1–159, from June 18, 1935 to December 16, 1938]. Prague, 1939.

II. Books

Abel, Karl-Dietrich. *Presselenkung im NS-Staat.* Berlin, 1968.
Anderle, Josef. "The Slovak Question in the Munich Crisis of 1938." Ph.D. dissertation, University of Chicago, 1961.
Andreas-Friedrich, Ruth. *Schauplatz Berlin.* Munich, 1962.
Avon, Earl of (Anthony Eden). *Facing the Dictators.* Cambridge, Mass., 1962.

Batowski, Henryk. *Krysys dyplomatyczny w Europie: Jesień 1936–Wiosna 1939* [The Diplomatic Crisis in Europe: Autumn 1938–Spring 1939]. Warsaw, 1962.
Beck, Joseph. *Dernier Rapport. Politique polonaise 1926–1939.* Neuchâtel-Paris, 1951.
Beneš, Edvard. *Paměti* [Memoirs]. Prague, 1947. (English translation: *Memoirs of Dr. Eduard Beneš.* London, 1954).
______, *Mnichovské dny. Paměti* [Days of Munich. Memoirs]. Prague, 1968.
______, *Où vont les Slaves?* Paris, 1948.
Berndt, Alfred-Ingemar. *Der Marsch ins Grossdeutsche Reich.* Munich, 1940.
Bewley, Charles. *Hermann Göring and the Third Reich.* New York, 1962.
Bonnet, Georges. *De Munich à la guerre. Défense de la paix.* Paris, 1967.
______, *Dans la tourmente 1938–1948.* Paris, 1971.
______, *Fin d'une Europe. De Munich à la guerre.* Geneva, 1948.
______, *Le Quai d'Orsay sous trois républiques, 1870–1961.* Paris, 1961.
Bosl, Karl, ed. *Handbuch der Geschichte der böhmischen Länder.* Vol. IV *Der Tschechoslowakische Staat im Zeitalter der modernen Massendemokratie und Diktatur.* Stuttgart, 1970.
Bramsted, Ernst K. *Goebbels and National Socialist Propaganda 1925–1945.* East Lansing, Mich., 1965.
Brügel, Johann Wolfgang. *Czechoslovakia before Munich; the German minority problem and British appeasement policy.* Cambridge (Eng.), 1973.
______, *Tschechen und Deutsche 1919–1938.* Munich, 1967.
Bullock, Alan. *Hitler. A Study in Tyranny.* New York, 1952.
Cadogan, Sir Alexander, *The Diaries of Sir Alexander Cadogan, O.M., 1938–1945.* Edited by David Dilks. New York, 1972.
Čelovský, Boris. *Das Münchener Abkommen.* Stuttgart, 1958
Černý, Bohumil *Most k novému životu. Německá emigrace v ČSR v letech 1933–1939* [The Bridge to a New Life. The German Emigration in the Czechoslovak Republic in the Years 1933–1939] Prague, 1967.
Češi a Poláci v minulosti [The Czechs and the Poles in the Past]. Edited by Václav Žáček, Vol, Prague, 1967.
Československo v mapách [Czechoslovakia in Maps]. Prague, 1954.
Chmela, Leopold. *The Economic Aspect of the German Occupation of Czechoslovakia.* Prague, 1948.
Ciano, Galeazzo. *The Ciano Diaries 1939–1943.* New York, 1946.
______, *Ciano's Hidden Diary 1937–1938.* New York, 1953.
Comnène-Petresco, Nicolai. *Preludi del grande dramma.* Rome, 1947
Coulondre, Robert. *De Staline à Hitler. Souvenirs de deux ambassades 1936–1939* Princeton, 1953.
Craig, Gordon A., and Gilbert, Felix, eds. *The Diplomats 1919–1939.* Princeton, 1953.
Crane, Katherine. *Mr. Carr of State.* New York, 1960.
Čulen, Konstantín. *Po Svätoplukovi druhá naša hlava. (Život Dr. Jozefa Tisu)* [After Svätopluk Our Second Head of State. The Life of Dr. Jozef Tiso]. Cleveland, 1947.
Danáš, Josef. *Luďácký separatizmus a hitlerovské Nemecko* [The Separatism of

the People's Party and Hitler's Germany]. Bratislava, 1963
Davignon, Jacques. *Berlin 1936–1940.* Paris, 1951.
Delfiner, Henry. *Vienna Broadcasts to Slovakia 1938–1939. A Case Study in Subversion.* New York–London, 1974.
Dérer, Ivan. *Slovenský vývoj a l'uďácká zrada* [The Slovak Development and the People's Party Betrayal]. Prague, 1946.
Dirksen, Herbert von. *Moscow, Tokyo, London. Twenty Years of German Foreign Policy.* Norman, Okla., 1952.
Donosti, Mario. *Mussolini e l'Europa. La politica estera fascista.* Rome, 1945.
Dreisziger, Nandor A.F. *Hungary's Way to World War II.* Astor Park, Fla., 1968.
Ďurčanský, Ferdinand. *Právo Slovákov na samostatnosť vo svetle dokumentov* [The Slovaks' Right to Independence in the Light of Documents]. Buenos Aires, 1954.
Ďurica, Milan Stanislas. *La Slovacchia e le sue relazioni politiche con la Germania 1938–1945.* Vol. I. *Dagli accordi di Monacho all'inizio della secunda guerra mondiale.* Padua, 1964.
______, *Die slowakische Politik 1938/39 im Lichte der Staatslehre Tisos.* Bonn, 1967.
Duroselle, Jean-Baptiste. *La décadence 1932–1939.* Paris, 1979.
______, *Les frontières européennes de l'U.R.S.S. 1917–1941.* Paris, 1957.
El Mallakh, Dorothea H. *The Slovak Autonomy Movement, 1935–1939: A Study in Unrelenting Nationalism.* Boulder–New York, 1979.
Feierabend, Ivo K. "The Pattern of a Satellite State: Czechoslovakia 1938–1939." Ph.D. dissertation, Yale University, 1960.
Feierabend, Ladislav, K. *Ve vládách Druhé republiky* [In the Governments of the Second Republic]. New York, 1961.
______, *Ve vládě Protektorátu* [In the Government of the Protectorate]. New York, 1962.
Feiling, Keith. *The Life of Neville Chamberlain.* London, 1946.
Fiala, Václav. *La Pologne d'aujourd'hui.* Paris, 1936.
Fierlinger, Zdeněk. *Ve službách ČSR* [In the Service of the Czechoslovak Republic]. 2 vols. Prague, 1947–1948.
François-Poncet, André. *Au Palais Farnèse. Souvenirs d'une ambassade à Rome 1938–1940.* Paris, 1961.
______, *Souvenirs d'une ambassade à Berlin. Septembre 1937–Octobre 1938.* Paris, 1946.
Frank, Ernst. *Karl Hermann Frank. Staatsminister im Protektorat.* Heusenstamm b. Offenbach/M., 1976.
Görlitz, Walter. *Generalfeldmarschall Keitel. Verbrecher oder Offizier? Göttingen, 1961.*
Graca, Bohuslav. 14. marec 1939 [March 14, 1939]. Bratislava, 1959.
Gromada, Thaddeus. "The Slovak Question in Polish Foreign Policy." Ph.D. dissertation, Fordham University, 1966.
Grosscurth, Helmuth. *Tagebücher eines Abwehroffiziers 1938–1940.* Stuttgart, 1970.
Guderian, Heinz. *Erinnerungen eines Soldaten.* Heidelberg, 1951.

Hagemann, Walter *Publizistik im Dritten Reich*. Hamburg, 1948.
Hagen, Walter (Wilhelm Hoettl). *Die geheime Front*. Stuttgart, 1952. (The English translation: *The Secret Front. The Story of Nazi Political Espionage*. London, 1955).
Hájek, Miloš. *Od Mnichova k 15. březnu* [From Munich to March 15]. Prague, 1959.
Hale, Oron James. *The Captive Press in the Third Reich*. Princeton, 1964.
Halifax, Earl of. *Fulness of Days*. London, 1957.
Harvey, Oliver. *The Diplomatic Diaries of Oliver Harvey 1937–1940*. Edited by John Harvey. London, 1970.
Hassell, Ulrich von. *Vom andern Deutschland. Aus den nachgelassenen Tagebüchern 1938–1944 von Ulrich von Hassell*. 2nd ed., Zurich, 1946. (The English translation: *The Von Hassell Diaries*. New York, 1947).
Henderson, Sir Nevile. *Failure of a Mission. Berlin 1937–1939*. New York, 1940.
Hildebrand, Klaus. *The Foreign Policy of the Third Reich*. Berkeley, and Los Angeles, 1973.
Hillgruber, Andreas. *Staatsmänner und Diplomaten bei Hitler*. Frankfurt, 1967.
Hitler, Adolf. *Mein Kampf*. 370th–371st ed., Munich, 1938.
Hitler's Secret Conversations 1941–1944. New York, 1953.
Hitlers zweites Buch. Ein Dokument aus dem Jahre 1928. Edited by G. L. Weinberg. Stuttgart, 1961.
Hore-Belisha, Leslie. *The Private Papers of Hore-Belisha*. Ed. by R. J. Minney. New York, 1961.
Horthy, Nikolaus von. *Ein Leben für Ungarn*. Bonn, 1953.
Jacobsen, Hans-Adolf. *Nationalsozialistische Aussenpolitik, 1933–1938*. Frankfurt, 1968.
Janeček, Oldřich. *Odboj a revoluce 1938–1945. Nástin dějin československého odboje* [Resistance and Revolution 1938–1945. An Outline of the History of the Czechoslovak Resistance]. Vol. I. Prague, 1965.
______ , *et al.*, *Z počátků odboje 1938–1941* [The Beginnings of the Resistance 1938–1941]. Prague, 1969.
Jelinek, Yeshayahu. *The Parish Republic: Hlinka's Slovak People's Party, 1939–1945*. Boulder, Colo., New York, 1976.
Káňa, Otakar, and Pavelka, Ryszard. *Těšínsko v polsko-československých vztazích 1918–1939* [The Těšín Region in the Polish-Czechoslovak Relations, 1918–1939]. Ostrava, 1970.
Kerner, Robert J. *Czechoslovakia: Twenty Years of Independence*. Berkeley, 1940.
Kirkpatrick, Sir Ivone. *The Inner Circle*. London, 1959.
Kirschbaum, Joseph M. *Slovakia: Nation at the Crossroads of Central Europe*. New York, 1960.
Kordt, Erich. *Nicht aus den Akten*. Stuttgart, 1950.
______ , *Wahn und Wirklichkeit*. Stuttgart, 1947.
Kozeński, Jerzy. *Czechoslowacja w polskiej polityce zagranicznej w latach 1932–1938* [Czechoslovakia in the Polish Foreign Policy 1932–1938]. Poznań, 1964.

Král, Václav. *Dny, které otřásly Československem* [The Days Which Shook Czechoslovakia]. Prague, 1975.

______, *Otázky hospodářského a sociálního vývoje v českých zemích v letech 1938–1945* [Questions of Economic and Social Development in the Czech Lands in 1938–1945]. 3 vols. Prague, 1957–59.

______, *Pravda o okupaci* [The Truth about the Occupation]. Prague, 1962.

Kramer, Juraj. *Slovenské autonomistické hnutie v rokoch 1918–1929* [The Slovak Autonomist Movement in 1918–1929]. Bratislava, 1962.

Křen, Jan. *Do emigrace. Buržoasní zahraniční odboj 1938–1939* [Into the Exile. The Bourgeois Resistance Abroad 1938–1939]. Prague, 1963.

Kuhn, Axel. *Hitlers aussenpolitisches Programm. Entstehung und Entwicklung 1919–1939.* Stuttgart, 1970.

Laffan, Robert G. D. and others. *Survey of International Affairs 1938.* Vol. III, ed. by Veronica M. Toynbee. London, 1953.

Lettrich, Jozef. *History of Modern Slovakia.* New York, 1955

Lukeš, František. *Podivný mír* [A Strange Peace]. Prague, 1968.

Luža, Radomír. *The Transfer of the Sudeten Germans.* New York, 1964.

Macartney, Carlile A. *October Fifteenth; a History of Modern Hungary 1929–1945.* 2 vols. Edinburgh. 1956–57.

______, *Independent Eastern Europe.* London, 1961.

Magistrati, Massimo. *L'Italia a Berlino 1937–1939.* Milan, 1956.

Magocsi, Paul R. *An Historiographical Guide to Subcarpathian Rus.* Harvard Ukrainian Research Institute, Offprint Series No. 1. Cambridge, Massachusets. (Offprint from *Austrian History Yearbook,* Vol. IX–X, 1973–74).

Mamatey, Victor S., and Luža, Radomír, eds. *A History of the Czechoslovak Republic 1918–1948.* Princeton, 1973.

Mastný, Vojtěch. *The Czechs under Nazi Rule. The Failure of National Resistance 1939–1942.* New York, 1971.

Meissner, Otto. *Staatssekretär unter Ebert-Hindenburg-Hitler.* 3rd ed., Hamburg, 1950.

Middlemass, Keith. *Diplomacy of Illusion. The British Government and Germany, 1937–39.* London, 1972.

Mikuš, Joseph A. *Slovakia. A Political History: 1918–1950.* Milwaukee, 1963.

Moravec, František. *Master of Spies. The Memoirs of General František Moravec.* London, Toronto, 1975.

Mueller-Hillebrand, Burkhart. *Das Heer 1933–45; Entwicklung des organisatorischen Aufbaues.* 3 vols. Vol. I. *Das Heer bis zum Kriegsbeginn.* Darmstadt, 1954.

Murgaš, Karol. *Národ medzi Dunajom a Karpatmi* [The Nation between the Danube and the Carpathians]. Bratislava, 1940.

Namier, Lewis B. *Diplomatic Prelude, 1938–1939.* London, 1948.

______, *Europe in Decay. A Study in Disintegration, 1936–1940.* London, 1950.

______, *In the Nazi Era.* London, 1952.

Newman, Simon. *March 1939: The British Guarantee to Poland. A Study in the Continuity of British Foreign Policy.* Oxford, 1976.

Noël, Léon. *L'agression allemande contre la Pologne*. Paris, 1946.

Odložilík, Otakar. *Odvěký úděl. Úvaha z žíjna 1938* [A Perennial Lot. A reflection from October 1938]. Prague, 1938.

Olšovský, Rudolf, *et al. Přehled hospodářského vývoje Československa v létech 1918–1945* [A Survey of the Economic Development of Czechoslovakia, 1918–1945]. Prague, 1961.

Paučo, Jozef, ed. *Dr. J. Tiso o sebe* [Dr. J. Tiso about himself]. Passaic, N.J., 1952.

Perman, Dagmar. *The Shaping of the Czechoslovak State: Diplomatic History of the Boundaries of Czechoslovakia, 1914–1920*. Leiden, 1962.

Petreas, Johann Oskar. *Die Slowakei im Umbruch*. Turč. Sv. Martin, 1941.

Picker, Henry. *Hitlers Tischgespräche im Führerhauptquartier 1941–42*. Edited by Percy Ernst Schramm. Stuttgart, 1963.

Piwarski, Kazimierz. *Polityka europejska w okresie pomonachijskim* [European Politics in the post-Munich Era]. Warsaw, 1960.

Procházka, Théodore. "La Tchécoslovaquie de Munich à Mars 1939." Unpublished doctoral dissertation, University of Paris, 1954.

Raubal Stanislas. *Formation de la frontière entre la Pologne et la Tchécoslovaquie*. Paris, 1928.

Rauschning, Hermann. *The Voice of Destruction*. New York, 1940.

Les relations franco-allemandes 1933–1939. Colloques internationaux du Centre National de la Recherche Scientifique. Paris, 1976.

Les relations franco-britanniques de 1935 à 1939. (CNRS), Paris, 1975.

Renouvin, Pierre. *Histoire des relations internationales*. Vol. 8, *Les Crises du XXe siècle*.II. *De 1939 à 1945*. Paris, 1958.

Reynaud, Paul. *Au coeur de la mêlée 1930–1945*. Paris, 1951.

Ribbentrop, Joachim von. *Zwischen London und Moskau*. Leoni am Starnberger See, 1953.

Rich, Norman. *Hitler's War Aims. Ideology, the Nazi State, and the Course of Expansion*. New York, 1973.

Ripka, Hubert. *Munich. Before and After*. London, 1939.

Robertson, E.M. *Hitler's Pre-War Policy and Military Plans*. London, 1963.

Rönnefahrt, Helmuth K. *Die Sudetenkrise in der internationalen Politik*. 2 vols. Wiesbaden, 1961.

Roos, Hans. *A History of Modern Poland from the Foundation of the State in the First World War to the Present Day*. London, 1966.

Rothermere, Viscount H.S.S. *My Campaign for Hungary*. London, 1939.

Sänger, Fritz. *Politik der Täuschungen. Missbrauch der Presse im Dritten Reich. Vienna, 1975.*

Schellenber, Walter. The Schellenberg Memoirs Edited and translated by Louis Hagen. London, 1956.

Schmidt, Paul. *Statist auf diplomatischer Bühne 1923–45*. Bonn, 1951. (The English translation of the second half of the German original: *Hitler's Interpreter*. Ed. by R. H. C. Steed, New York, 1951).

Seton-Watson, Hugh. *Eastern Europe between the Wars, 1918–1941*. Cambridge, 1946.

Sidor, Karol. *Moje poznámky k historickým dňom* [My Notes on the Historic Days] Edited by František Vnuk. Middleton, Pa., 1971.
______, *Slovenská politika na pôde pražského snemu, 1918–1938* [Slovak Politics in the Prague Parliament]. 2 vols. Bratislava, 1943.
Singbartl, Hartmut. *Die Durchführung der deutsch-tschechoslowakischen Grenzregelung von 1938 in völkerrechtlicher und staatsrechtlicher Sicht.* Munich, 1971.
Slávik, Juraj. *Moja pamät—živá kniha* [My Memory—a Living Book]. Memoirs published in the journal "Slovenský Denník", New York, 1956–60.
Soják, Vladimír, ed. *O československé zahraniční politice v letech 1918–1939* [The Czechoslovak Foreign Policy in the Years 1918–1939]. Prague, 1956.
Şpeer, Albert. *Erinnerungen.* Frankfurt-Berlin, 1969.
Šprinc, Mikuláš, ed. *Slovenská Republika, 1939–1949* [The Slovak Republic, 1939–1949]. Scranton, 1949.
Stanislawska, Stefania. *Polska a Monachium* [Poland and Munich]. Warsaw, 1967.
Stehlin, Paul. *Témoignage pour l'histoire.* Paris, 1964.
Strang, Lord. *Home and Abroad.* London, 1956.
Strauch, Rudi. *Sir Nevile Henderson, Britischer Botschafter in Berlin von 1937 bis 1939.* Bonn, 1959.
Sündermann, Helmut. *Die Grenzen fallen von der Ostmark zum Sudetenland.* Munich, 1939.
Szembek, Jean. *Journal 1933–1939.* Paris, 1952.
______, *Diariusz i teki Jana Szembeka (1935–1945)* [Diary and Notes of Jan Szembek, 1935–1945]. Vol. IV. *Diariusz i dokumentacja za rok 1938, 1939* [Diary and Documentation for 1938, 1939]. Edited by Józef Zarański. London, 1972.
Száthmaryová-Vlčková, V. *Putování za svobodou 1938–1945* [In Search of Liberty 1938–1945]. Prague 1946.
Táborský, Eduard. *Pravda zvítězila* [The Truth Has Prevailed]. Prague, 1947.
Tapié, Victor-L. *Le Pays de Teschen et les rapports entre la Pologne et la Tchécoslovaquie.* Paris, 1936.
Taylor, Telford. *Munich: the Price of Peace.* Garden City, N.Y., 1979.
Thomson, Harrison S. *Czechoslovakia in European History.* Princeton, N.J., 1944; rev. ed. 1953.
Tilkovszky, Loránt. *Južné Slovensko v rokoch 1938–1945* [Southern Slovakia in 1938–1945]. Bratislava, 1972.
Trapl, Miloš. *Politika českého katolicismu na Moravě 1918–1938* [The Policy of Czech Catholicism in Moravia 1918–1938]. Prague, 1968.
Turlejska, Maria. *Rok przed klęską* [The Year before the Defeat]. Warsaw, 1960.
Uhlíř, František. *Těšínské Slezsko* [The Těšín Silesia]. Moravská Ostrava-Prague, 1946.
Vallette, Geneviève, and Bouillon, Jacques. *Munich, 1938.* Paris, 1964.
Vávra, Ferdinand, and Eibel, Ján. *Viedeňská arbitráž—dôsledok Mníchova* [The Vienna Arbitration—a Consequence of Munich]. Bratislava, 1963.
Vietor, Martin. *Dejiny okupácie južného Slovenska 1938–1945* [History of the

Occupation of Southern Slovakia, 1938–1945]. Bratislava, 1968.
Vnuk, František. *Slovakia's Six Eventful Months (October 1938–March 1939).* Offprint from the "Slovak Studies", Cleveland-Rome, 1964.
Vondráček John F. *The Foreign Policy of Czechoslovakia 1918–1935.* New York, 1937.
Wagner, Eduard. *Der Generalquartiermeister. Briefe und Tagebuchaufzeichnungen des Generalquartiermeisters des Heeres, General der Artillerie Eduard Wagner.* Edited by Elisabeth Wagner. Munich-Vienna, 1963.
Wandycz, Piotr S. *France and Her Eastern Allies 1919–1925.* Minneapolis, 1962.
Warlimont, Walter. *Im Hauptquartier der deutschen Wehrmacht, 1939–1945; Grundlagen, Formen, Gestalten.* Frankfurt, 1962. (Engl. transl.: *Inside Hitler's Headquarters 1939–1945.* New York, 1964).
Weinberg, Gerhard L. *The Foreign Policy of Hitler's Germany. Diplomatic Revolution in Europe, 1933–1936.* Chicago, 1970.
Weizsäcker, Ernst von. *Erinnerungen.* Munich, Leipzig, Freiburg, 1950.
______, *Die Weizsäcker Papiere 1933–1950.* Edited by Leonidas E. Hill. Berlin, 1974.
Wheeler-Bennett, John W. *Munich, Prologue to a Tragedy.* London, New York, 1948.
Winch, Michael. *Republic for a Day* London, 1939.
Wiskemann, Elizabeth. *Czechs and Germans.* London, 1938.
Záděra, Vladimír. *Deset let parlamentní retrospektivy 1935–1945* [Ten Years of the Parliament Retrospective 1935–1945]. Prague, 1948.

III. Articles

Anderle, Josef. "The Establishment of Slovak Autonomy in 1938," *Czechoslovakia Past and Present,* M. Rechcigl, Jr. ed. The Hague, 1969, pp. 85–97.
Bareš Arnošt, and Pasák, Tomáš. "Odbojová organizace Zdeňka Schmoranz v roce 1939"[The Resistance Organization of Zdeněk Schmoranz in 1939] *Historie a vojenství,* 1968, nos. 6–7, pp. 1003–33.
Batowski, Henryk. "Le voyage de Joseph Beck en Roumanie en octobre 1938," *Annuaire polonais des affaires internationales 1950–1960,* pp. 137–60.
Bodensieck, Heinrich. "Das Dritte Reich und die Lage der Juden in der Tschecho-Slowakei nach München," *Vierteljahrshefte für Zeitgeschichte,*[11] (1961), pp. 249–62.
______, "Der Plan eines 'Freundschaftsvertrages' zwischen dem Reich und der Tschecho-Slowakei im Jahre 1938," *Zeitschrift für Ostforschung,* 10 (1961), pp. 462–76.
______. "Die Politik der Zweiten Tschechoslowakischen Republik," ibid., 6 (1957), pp. 54–71.
______, "Volksgruppenrecht und national—sozialistische Aussenpolitik nach dem Münchener Abkommen 1938," ibid., 7 (1958), pp. 502–18.
______, "Zur Vorgeschichte des 'Protektorats Böhmen und Mähren.' Der Einfluss volksdeutscher Nationalsozialisten und reichsdeutscher Berufsdiplomaten auf Hitlers Entscheidung," *Geschichte in Wissenschaft und Unterricht,* 19 (1968), pp. 713–32.

Bohmann, Alfred. "Die tschechoslowakischen Gebietsabtretungen an Polen und Ungarn 1938/39," *Zeitschrift für Ostforschung*, 20 (1971), pp. 465–96.

Böss, Otto. "Die zweite Tschecho-Slowakische Republik im Spiegel zeitgenossischer tschechischer Pressestimmen (Oktober 1938–März 1939)," *Bohemia. Jahrbuch des Collegium Carolinum*, 3 (1962), pp. 402–25.

Bouček, Jaroslav Alex. "Post Munich Czechoslovakia: A Few Historical Notes," *Canadian Slavonic Papers*, 17 (1975), pp. 45–64.

Břachová, Věra. "Francouzská vojenská misse v Československu" [The French Military Mission in Czechoslovakia] *Historie a vojenství*, (1967), pp. 883–910.

Budurowycz, Bohdan B. "The Ukrainian Problem in International Politics, October 1938 to March 1939," *Canadian Slavonic Papers*, 3 (1958), pp. 59–75.

Čarnogurský, Pal'o. "Deklaracia o únii Slovenska s Polskom z 28. septembra 1938"[Declaration about the Union of Slovakia with Poland from September 28, 1938] *Historický časopis*, 16 (1968), pp. 407–23.

———, "Z memoirových statí Pal's Černogurského"[From Pal'o Černogurský's Memoirs], *Slovanský Přehled*, 54 (1968), pp. 500–511.

César, Jaroslav, and Černý, Bohumil. "Die deutsche antifaschistische Emigration in der Tschechoslowakei (1933–1934)." *Historica*, 12 (1966), pp. 147–84.

Chudek, Józef, "Sprawa Bogumina v dokumentach polskich" [The Bogumin Question in the Polish Documents], *Sprawy miedzynarodowe*, XI, no. 9, Warsaw, 1958, pp. 108–114.

Cienciala, Anna M. "Poland and the Munich Crisis 1938.—A Reappraisal," *East European Quarterly*, 3 (1969), pp. 201–219.

Coulson, R. G. "Czechoslovakian Adventure," *The Quarterly Review*, no. 539, London, January 1939, pp.

Crkovský, František. "Ostravsko a 15. březen 1939" [The Ostrava Region and March 15, 1939] *Slezský sborník*, 59 (1961), pp. 475–490.

Danáš, Jozef. "O vzťahoch HSL'S s hitlerovským Nemeckom v predvečer vzniku t.zv. slovenského štátu" [The Relations of Hlinka's Populist Party with Hitler's Germany on the Eve of the Creation of the so-called Slovak State] *Historický časopis*, 7 (1959), pp. 53–73.

Dictionnaire Diplomatique, ed. by M.A.-F. Frangulis. S.v. "Hongrie", Paris, n.d., pp. 589–91.

Ďurčanský, Ferdinand. "Mit Tiso bei Hitler," *Politische Studien*, 7 (1956), pp. 1–10.

Faltys, Antonín. "Postavení českého pohraničí v rámci Velkoněmecké říše v letech 1938–1945" [The Situation of the Czech Border Region in the Framework of the Greater German Reich in 1938–1945] *Historie a vojenství*, no. 3 (1968), pp. 386–420.

Feierabend, Ivo K. "The Second Czechoslovak Republic, September 1938–March 1939: A Study in Political Change." Paper prepared for the Second Congress of the Czechoslovak Society of Arts and Sciences in America, New York, September 11–13, 1964.

Gromada, Thaddeus V. "The Slovaks and the Failure of Beck's 'Third Europe' Scheme," *The Polish Review*, 14 (1969), pp. 1–10.

Harna, Josef. "Českoslovenští národní socialisté v mnichovské krizi" [The Czechoslovak National Socialists in the Munich Crisis] *Československý časopis historický*, 22 (1974), pp. 57–79.

Heidrich, Arnošt. "International Political Causes of the Czechoslovak Tragedies of 1938 and 1948," Part I. Paper delivered before the Czechoslovak Society of Arts and Sciences in America, Washington, 1962.

Hoensch, Jörg Konrad. "Revision und Expansion. Überlegungen zur Zielsetzung, Methode und Planung der Tschechoslowakei-Politik Hitlers," *Bohemia*, 9 (1968), pp. 208–228.

______, "Účast Telekiho vlády na rozbití Československa (březen 1939)" [Teleki Government's Share in the Break-up of Czechoslovakia (March 1939)] *Československý časopis historický*, 17 (1969), pp. 351–74.

Holub, Ota. "Boje československé armády a jednotek Stráže obrany státu na Podparpatské Rusi (Karpatské Ukrajině) v březnu 1939" [The Engagements of the Czechoslovak Army and the Units of the Guard for the Defense of the State in Subcarpathian Russia (Carpathian Ukraine) in March 1959] *Odboj a revoluce*, 7 (1969), no. 9, pp. 5–74.

Hyndrák, Václav. "K otázce vojenské připravenosti v Československu v roce 1938" [Problem of Military Preparedness in Czechoslovakia in 1938] *Severní Čechy a Mnichov* [Northern Bohemia and Munich], edited by Jiří Procházka, Liberec, 1969, pp. 140–75.

______, "Polsko a československá krise na podzim 1938" [Poland and the Czechoslovak Crisis in the Fall of 1938] *Historie a* vojenství (1968), no. 1, pp. 84–98.

Jelinek, Yeshayahu. "Storm-troopers in Slovakia: the Rodobrana and the Hlinka Guard," *Journal of Contemporary History*, 6 (1971), no. 3, pp. 97–119.

Joza, Jaroslav. "Česká menšina v severních Čechách v letech 1938–1941 ve světle nacistických pramenů," [The Czech Minority in Northern Bohemia in 1938–1941 in the Light of the German Sources]" *Severní Čechy a Mnichov*, Liberec, 1969, pp. 176–213.

Kamenec, Ivan. "Snem Slovenskej republiky a jeho postoj k problému židovského obyvatelstva na Slovensku v rokoch 1939–1945" [The Diet of the Slovak Republic and its Attitude to the Problem of the Jewish Population in Slovakia in 1939–1945] *Historický časopis*, 17 (1969), pp. 329–362.

Kapras, Jan. "Jazykové a národnostní dějiny v české koruně" [History of Language and Nationality in the Lands of the Crown of Bohemia] in *Československá vlastivěda* [A Survey of Czechoslovakia], vol. V, Prague, 1931, pp. 173–92.

Kirschbaum, Jozef M. "Facts and Events behind the Scenes of Slovakia's Declaration of Independence," *Slovakia*, 9 (1959), pp. 1–7.

______, Medzinárodná situácia a vznik SR [The International Situation and the Origins of the Slovak Republic] *Slovenská republika 1939–1949* [The Slovak Republic 1939–1949] edited by Nicholas Sprinc, Scranton, Pa., 1949, pp. 61–72.

Krejčí, Ludvík. "Obranyschopnost ČSR 1938" [The Defense Capability of Czechoslovakia in 1938] *Odboj a revoluce*, 6 (1968), no. 2, pp. 14–41.

Kuklík, Jan. "Petiční výbor Věrni zůstaneme v období Mnichova a az druhé republiky [The Petition Committee 'We shall Remain Faithful' in the Era of

Munich and the Second Republic] *Československý časopis historický*, 17 (1969), pp. 681–711.

Künzl-Jizerský, Rudolf. "Jak vznikl tak zvaný protektorát,"[The Origins of the So-Called Protectorate] *Svobodné Noviny*, September 10, 1945.

Lipták, L'ubomír. "Autonómia slovenskej krajiny. Od Mnichova k 14. marcu 1939" [The Autonomy of the Slovak Land. From Munich to March 14, 1939] *Odboj a revoluce*, 4 (1966), no. 5, pp. 17–65.

Lukasiewicz, Juliusz. "Sprawa czechoslowacka w r. 1938 na tle stosunków polsko-francuskich" [The Czechoslovak Question in 1938 against the Background of Polish-French Relations] *Sprawy Międzynarodowe*, (London, 1948), no. 2–3, 6–7.

Lukeš, František. "Dvě tajné cesty Vladimíra Krychtálka do Německa" [Vladimír Krychtálek's Two Secret Trips to Germany] *Dějiny a současnost*, 1962, no. 2, pp. 28–29.

______, "K diplomatickému pozadí vídeňské arbitráže" [About the Diplomatic Background of the Vienna Award] *Historický časopis*, 10 (1962), pp. 51–67.

______, "Příspěvek k objasnění politiky české a německé buržoasie v předvečer 15. března [The Policy of the Czech and German Bourgeoisie on the Eve of March 15] *Časopis Národního Musea*, Social Science Series, 130 (1961), pp. 65–68.

______, "K volbě Emila Háchy presidentem tzv. Druhé republiky" [The Election of Emil Hácha as President of the So-Called Second Republic] ibid., 131 (1962), pp. 114–20.

Magocsi, Paul M. "The Nationality Problem in Subcarpathian Ruthenia 1938–1939. A Reapprisal." Paper prepared for the Seventh Congress of the Czechoslovak Society of Arts and Sciences in America, New York, November 17, 1974!

Mainuš, František. "České školství v pohraničí za nacistické okupace se zvláštním zřetelem k severní Moravě a Slezsku" [Czech Schools in the Border-Areas during the Nazi Occupation with Special Reference to Northern Moravia and Silesia] *Slezský sborník*, 37 (1959), no. 3, pp. 277–312.

Mares, Antoine. "La faillite des relations franco-tchécolslovaques. La mission militaire française à Prague (1926–1938), *Revue d'histoire de la deuxième guerre mondiale*, 28, no. 111 (July 1978), pp. 44–71.

Markus, Vasyl. "Carpatho-Ukraine under Hungarian Occupation (1939–1944)" *Ukrainian Quarterly*, 10 (1954), no. 3, pp. 252–56.

Mastny, Vojtech. "Design or Improvisation? The Origins of the Protectorate of Bohemia and Moravia 1939," *Columbia Essays in International Affairs*, New York, 1966, pp. 127–53.

Medlicott, W. N. "De Munich à Prague," *Revue d'histoire de la deuxième guerre mondiale*, 4 (1954), no. 13, pp. 3–16.

Megerle, Karl. "Deutschland und das Ende der Tschecho-Slowakei," *Monatshefte für Auswärtige Politik*, 6 (1939), no. 6, pp. 763–76.

Myška, Milan. "Ostravsko mezi Mnichovem a 15. březnem 1939"[The Ostrava Region between Munich and March 15, 1939] *Slezský sborník*, 61 (1963), no. 3, pp. 257–76.

Nesvadba, František. "Vládní vojsko a jeho odsun do Italie" [The Government Troops and Their Transfer to Italy] *Historie a vojenství,* 1968, nos. 6–7, pp. 924–961.

Pasák, Tomáš. "Vstup německých vojsk na české území v roce 1939" [The Entry of German Troops into Czech Territory in 1939] *Československý časopis historický,* 17 (1969), pp. 161–83.

______, "Vývoj Vlajky v období okupace" [The Evolution of the 'Vlajka' during the Occupation] *Historie a vojenství,* 1966, no. 5, pp. 846–95.

Pradelle, A. de La. "La Tchécoslovaquie de Munich à Prague," *Revue de droit international,* 22 (1938), pp. 353–740, 23 (1939), pp. 74–100.

Procházka, Theodore. "The Delimitation of Czechoslovak-German Frontiers after Munich," *Journal of Central European Affairs,* 21 (1961), no. 2, pp. 200–218.

______, "The Second Republic, 1938–1939" in *A History of the Czechoslovak Republic 1918–1948,* edited by Victor S. Mamatey and Radomír Luža, Princeton, 1973, pp. 255–270.

______, "Some Aspects of Carpatho-Ukrainian History in Post-Munich Czechoslovakia," in *Czechoslovakia Past and Present,* ed. by Miloslav Rechcigl, Jr., vol. I, The Hague, 1968, pp. 104–114.

Revay, Julian. "The March to Liberation of Carpatho-Ukraine," *The Ukrainian Quarterly,* 10 (1954), no. 3, pp. 227–34.

Sakmyster, Thomas L. "Hungary and the Munich Crisis. The Revisionist Dilemma," *Slavic Review,* 32 (1973), pp. 725–40.

Schiefer, Hans. "Deutschland und die Tschechoslowakei von September 1938 bis März 1939," *Zeitschrift für Ostforschung,* 4 (1955), pp. 48–66.

Schubert, Miroslav. "Konec Druhé republiky [The End of the Second Republic] *Naše Hlasy,* Toronto, March 14, 1964.

Shandor, Vincent. "Carpatho-Ukraine in the International Bargaining of 1918–1939," *The Ukrainian Quarterly,* 10 (1954), no. 3, pp. 235–46.

Sidor, Karol. "Ako došlo k vyhlaseniu SR" [How the Slovak Republic Was Proclaimed] *Slovenská republika 1939–1949* [The Slovak Republic 1939–1949], edited by Nicholas Sprinc, Scranton, Pa., 1949, pp. 42–58.

Stenzel, David B. "Second Thoughts on Prague, 1939." Paper presented to the 74th annual convention of the American Historical Association, Chicago, December 30, 1959.

Strankmüller, Emil. "Československé ofensívní zpravodajství v letech 1937 do 15. března 1939 [The Czechoslovak Intelligence Service from 1937 to March 15, 1939] *Odboj a revoluce,* 6 (1968), no. 2, pp 42–73.

Suško, Ladislav. "German Policy towards Slovakia and Carpatho-Ukraine in the Period from the September Crisis in 1938 up to the Splitting of Czechoslovakia in March 1939," *Studia Historica Slovaca,* 8 (1975), pp. 111–55.

Szinai, Miklós, and Szücs, László. "Prispevok k dejinám nemeckých a maďarských agresívnych plánov proti Československu v rokoch 1920–1939" [A Contribution to the History of German and Hungarian Aggressive Plans against Czechoslovakia in 1920–1939] *Historický časopis,* 14 (1968), no. 4, pp. 595–607.

"La Tchécoslovaquie pendant la guerre," *Revue d'histoire de la deuxième guerre mondiale*, 13 (1963), no. 52.

Trevor-Roper, Hugh R. "Hitlers Kriegsziele," *Vierteljahrshefte für Zeitgeschichte, 8 (1960), pp. 121–33.*

Valenta, Jaroslav. "Cesta k Mnichovu a válce (1938–1939)" [The Road to Munich and the War (1938–1939] in *Češi a Poláci v minulosti* [The Czechs and the Poles in the Past], vol. 2, edited by Václav Žáček, Prague, 1967, pp. 581–619.

Vnuk, František. "The German Zone of Protection," *Slovakia*, 9 (1959), no. 29, pp. 7–23.

Vrbata, Jaroslav. "Přehled vývoje veřejné správy v odtržených českých oblastech v letech 1938–1945" [A Survey of the Evolution of Public Administration in Severed Czech Regions in 1938–1945] *Sborník archivních prací*, 12 (1962), no. 2, pp. 45–67.

Wagner, Eduard. "Die Besetzung der Tschechoslowakei," *Politische Studien*, 14 (1963), no. 151, pp. 578–84.

Weinberg, Gerhard L. "Czechoslovakia and Germany, 1933–1945." *Czechoslovakia Past and Present*. Vol. I. ed. by Miloslav Rechcigl, Jr. The Hague-Paris, 1968, pp. 760–69.

Wierzbiański, Kazimierz. "Czechy a Polska" [Bohemia and Poland] *Niepodległość*, 4, London, 1952, pp. 93–106.

Winchester, Betty Jo. "Hungary and the 'Third Europe' in 1938," *Slavic Review*, 32 (1973), pp. 741–56.

Winters, Stanley B. "The Health of Edvard Beneš: An Unpublished Letter from 1948," *East Central Europe*, 4, no. 1 (1977), pp. 60–66.

Woytak, Richard A. "Polish Military Intervention into Czechoslovakian Teschen and Western Slovakia in September–November 1938," *East European Quarterly*, 6 (1972), no. 3, pp. 376–87.

Wucher, Albert. "Hitlers letzte Phrasen," *Politische Studien*, 11 (1960), pp. 798–805.

Young, Robert J. "The Aftermath of Munich: The Course of French Diplomacy, October 1938 to March 1939," *French Historical Studies*, 8 (1973), no. 2, pp. 305–22.

Zorach, Jonathan. "Czechoslovakia's Fortifications. Their Development and Role in the 1938 Munich Crisis," *Militärgeschichtliche Mitteilungen*, 2 (1976), pp. 81–91.

IV. Newspapers and Periodicals

Newspapers

A-Zet, Prague.

České Slovo, Prague.

The Chicago Tribune.

Czas, Warsaw.

Frankfurter Zeitung, Frankfurt am Main.

Lidové Noviny, Prague, Brno.
Národní Osvobození, Prague.
The New York Times.
Pester Lloyd, Budapest
Prager Presse, Prague.
Rudé Právo, Prague.
Svobodné Noviny, Prague.
Svobodné Slovo, Prague.
Le Temps, Paris.
The Times, London.
Völkischer Beobachter, Berlin-Munich.
Bulletin périodique de la presse tchécoslovaque, Paris, 1938–39.
Přehled denního tisku pražského [Survey of the Prague Daily Press]. Published by the Press Division [Tiskový odbor] of the Presidium of the Council of Ministers in Prague. Quotations from this source are followed in the text by the abbreviation T.O.
Tschechische Presseauszüge, Berlin-Dahlem. (Quotations in the text followed by the abbreviation T.P.).

Periodicals

The Central European Observer.
Československý časopis historický.
Dějiny a současnost.
L'Europe Centrale.
L'Europe nouvelle.
L'Esprit international.
Historický časopis.
Historie a vojenství.
The Journal of Central European Affairs.
Odboj a revoluce.
Osteuropa.
Přítomnost.
Revue d'histoire de la deuxième guerre mondiale.
Sprawy międzynarodowe.
Vierteljahrshefte für Zeitgeschichte.
Zahraniční politika.
Zeitschrift für Ostforschung.

NOTES

Notes to Introduction

1. Josef Vítězslav Šimák, *Středověká kolonisace v zemích českých* [Mediaeval Colonization in the Czech Lands] in *České dějiny*, [History of Bohemia] ed. by Kamil Krofta, vol. I, part. 5 (Prague, 1938), pp. 510–15; Jan Kapras, "Jazykové a národnostní dějiny v české koruně" [History of Language and Nationality in the Lands of the Crown of Bohemia] in *Československá vlastivěda* [A Survey of Czechoslovakia], vol. V (Prague, 1931), pp. 173–91.

2. V. S. Mamatey, "The Development of Czechoslovak Democracy, 1920–1938," in *A History of Czechoslovak Republic 1918–1948*, edited by Victor S. Mamatey and Radomír Luža (Princeton, 1973), p. 154; Johann Wolfgang Brügel, *Tschechen und Deutsche*, 1918-1938 (Munich, 1967), pp. 232, 263, 266.

3. Hermann Rauschning, *The Voice of Destruction* (New York, 1940), pp. 37–38. The same contemptuous tone may be found in his talks during the Second World War (as contained in Henry Picker, *Hitlers Tischgespräche* (Stuttgart, 1963, especially pp. 161–62, 333).

4. Alfred Rosenberg, edit. *Das Parteiprogramm. Wesen, Grundsätze und Ziele der NSDAP* (Munich, 1941), p. 15.

5. *Documents on German Foreign Policy 1918–1945*, Series D (1937–1945), vol. I (Washington, 1949), no. 19. (This collection will be hereafter quoted as *DGFP*, followed by Roman numeral indicating the respective volume).

6. For the history of the Munich crisis see: Keith Eubank, *Munich* (Norman, 1963); Boris Čelovský, *Das Münchener Abkommen von 1938* (Stuttgart, 1958); John Wheeler-Bennett, *Munich: Prologue to Tragedy* (New York, 1948); Helmut K. Rönnefahrt, *Die Sudetenkrise in der internationalen Politik. Entstehung—Verlauf—Auswirkung* (Wiesbaden, 1961); Telford Taylor, *Munich: The Price of Peace* (Garden City, N.Y., 1979).

7. In 1930 there were 719,569 Magyars in Czechoslovakia. For Hungarian policy see Jörg K. Hoensch, *Der ungarische Revisionismus und die Zerstörung der Tschechoslowakei* (Tübingen, 1967).

8. Carlile A. Macartney, *October Fifteenth: A History of Modern Hungary 1929–1945* (2 vols., Edinburgh, 1956), vol. I, p. 285; Galeazzo Ciano, *L'Europa verso la catastrofe* (Milan, 1948), January 1, 1939.

9. Nandor A. F. Dreisziger, *Hungary's Way to World War II* (Astor Park, Fla., 1968), pp. 79–80.

10. *DGFP*, II, no. 383.

11. Ibid.; *Diplomáciai iratok magyárország külpolitikájához 1936–1945* [Diplomatic Documents on Hungarian Foreign Policy 1936–1945], vol. II. *A müncheni egyezmén létrejötte és Magyarország külpolitikája 1936*–1938], ed. by Magda Ádám (Budapest, 1965), nos.292, 307. At the end of each volume of this Magyar-language series is a short summary of published documents in German; hereafter the collection will be quoted as *D. ir.*, followed by Roman numeral indicating the respective volume.

12. *DGFP,* II, No. 506; *D. ir.*, II, nos. 347, 361.

13. *D. ir.*, II, nos. 334, 351, 363, 367, 387.

14. Macartney, *October Fifteenth,* I, p. 265; Betty J. Winchester, "Hungary and the 'Third Europe' in 1938," *Slavic Review,* 32 (Dec. 1973), p. 750; *Records of Headquarters, German Armed Forces High Command* (National Archives, Washington, D.C.), T-77, Serial 269, Roll 301, frame 6252037; *Documents on British Foreign Policy 1919–1939,* ed. by E. L. Woodward and Rohan Bulter. Third Series, vol. III, 1938–9 (London, 1950), no. 16. This series will hereafter be quoted as *DBFP,* followed by Roman numeral indicating the respective volume. *D. ir.*, II, no. 358.

15. *DBFP,* III, no. 9.

16. *D. ir.*, II, nos. 327, 329, 422.

17. *DGFP,* II, no. 554.

18. *DBFP,* III, no. 29, annex p. 21.

19. *DGFP,* II, no. 630.

20. Ibid., no. 658; *DBFP,* III, no. 63.

21. *DGFP,* II, nos. 506, 586: IV, no. 29; *DBFP, III,* nos. 52, 64; *D. ir.*, II, nos. 380, 381, 424; Macartney, *October Fifteenth,* I, p. 264; Dreisziger, *Hungary's Way,* p. 75; Winchester, "Hungary and the 'Third Europe'", p. 749; Josef Anderle, "The Slovak Question in the Munich Crisis of 1938" (Ph. D. diss., University of Chicago, 1961), p. 242.

22. *D. ir.*, II, nos. 317, 319, 320, 343, 364, 372, 377; Jean Szembek, *Journal 1933–1939* (Paris, 1952), September 8, 1938; Anna M. Cienciala, *Poland and the Western Powers 1938–1939* (London, Toronto, 1968), p. 110, n. 11.

23. *D. ir.*, II, nos. 337, 354, 357, 369.

24. For the Polish-Czechoslovak relations see also Piotr S. Wandycz, "The Foreign Policy of Edvard Beneš, 1918–1938," in *A History of the Czechoslovak Republic, 1918–1948,* pp. 216–38. Beck's memoirs contain numerous remarks highly critical of Czechoslovakia (*Dernier Rapport: Politique polonaise 1926–1939* (Neuchâtel, 1951), pp. 9–10, 34, 41, 51–54, 108–109, for the period preceding Munich. For the contemporary Czechoslovak view see Václav Fiala, *La Pologne d'aujourd'hui* (Paris, 1936). Cf. also Čelovský, *Das Münchener Abkommen,* pp. 230–38.

25. Georges Bonnet, *Défense de la paix. De Washington au Quai d'Orsay* (Geneva, 1946), p. 132.

26. *DGFP,* II, no. 500.

27. *DBFP,* III, nos. 4, 5; Bonnet, *De Washington,* pp. 256, 362.

28. *DBFP,* III, nos. 11, 28.

29. On September 30. *Documents and Materials Relating to the Eve of the Sec-*

ond World War, vol. I (Moscow, 1948), no. 23 (hereafter cited as *Documents and Materials*).

30. *DGFP*, II, no. 553, subenclosure 2; Lewis B. Namier, *Europe in Decay* (London, 1950), pp. 285–86.

31. Richard A. Woytak, "Polish Military Intervention into Czechoslovakian Teschen and Western Slovakia in September–November 1938," *East European Quarterly*, VI (1972), p. 379.

32. Text in Namier, *Europe in Decay*, p. 288.

33. Beck, *Dernier Rapport*, p. 342.

34. Ibid., p. 343.

35. *DBFP*, III, no. 71, n. 2, according to a Czechoslovak aide-mémoire submitted in London by Jan Masaryk on September 29.

36. Namier, *Europe in Decay*, pp. 296–97.

37. See the text to the Munich Agreement, p. 159.

38. *DGFP*, IV, no. 1; *Documents and Materials*, no. 38.

39. *Documents and Materials*, no. 37.

40. *Documents diplomatiques français 1932–1939, 2ê série (1936–1939)*, vol. XI (Paris, 1977), no. 480. Hereafter cited as *DDF*.

41. *DBFP*, II, no. 1225.

42. I am following the description given by Hubert Ripka in his book written shortly after the events, *Munich, Before and After* (London, 1939), p. 230. See also *Lidové Noviny*, the evening edition, October 1, 1938. The official minutes of the meeting in *Mnichov v dokumentech* [Munich in Documents] vol. II (Prague, 1958), no. 170.

43. *Mnichov. Vzpomínková kronika* [Munich. A Chronicle of Reminiscences] ed. by Věra Holá and Míla Lvová (Prague, 1969), p. 343.

44. V. Helešicová and R. Machotková, "Mnichovská krise v jednáních ministerské rady" [The Munich Crisis in the Deliberations of the Cabinet Council] *Odboj a revoluce*, 7, no. 5 (1969), no. 11. About the Soviet assistance he declared: "If Russia alone gave us help a war of all against Russia would ensue, and England would be against us." He repeated the same argument to the delegation of several politicians, both leftist and righ-wing, who attempted to dissuade him from any concessions. He received them in the early afternon and replied to their remonstrances: "We are alone and encircled on all sides. To wage an isolated war would mean to massacre the whole nation." (Václav Král, *Politické strany a Mnichov* [Political Parties and Munich] Prague, 1961, no. 88).

45. The official communiqué, *Lidové Noviny*, October 1, 1938.

46. *Documents and Materials*, no. 38.

47. *Documents diplomatiques français*, vol. XI, no. 482; *DGFP*, IV, no. 3.

48. *Lidové Noviny*, October 1, 1938.

49. G. E. R. Gedye in *The New York Times*, October 1, 1938.

50. About this abortive attempt on October 2 and 3 see František Lukeš, *Podivný mír* [A Strange Peace] (Prague, 1969), p. 46; Ludvík Krejčí, "Obranyschopnost ČSR 1938" [Defense Capability of Czechoslovakia in 1938] *Odboj a revoluce*, 6, no. 2 (1968), pp. 30–33.

51. *Memoirs of Dr. Eduard Beneš* (London, 1954), p. 50.

52. Communicated by Arnošt Heidrich to the author.

53. Lukeš, *Podivný mír,* p. 59; Míla Lvová, *Mnichov a Edvard Beneš* [Munich and Edvard Beneš] (Prague, 1968), pp. 176–77; Král, *Politické strany a Mnichov,* no. 88; Vlastimil Klíma in *Mnichov, Kronika,* p. 356.

54. Born in 1885, at first attorney in Prague, Cracow and Bolzano. After the First World War minister in Tokyo, Washington, Berlin, and from 1932 in Rome.

55. *Memoirs of Dr. Eduard Beneš,* p. 293.

56. Ibid., p. 51; Adolf Maixner, "Mnichov na pražském hradě" [Munich at the Castle of Prague] in *Svobodné Noviny,* September 30, 1945; Stanley B. Winters, "The Health of Edvard Beneš: An Unpublished Letter from 1948," *East Central Europe,* 4, no. 1 (1977), pp. 60–66.

57. Later he was invited to the United States by Brown and Harvard Universities. Other organizations, like the Council of Foreign Relations in New York, invited him to a series of lectures if he came to America. On October 8, the minister of the United States, Wilbur J. Carr, handed over to him a cable from the University of Chicago inviting him for a one-year stay. On October 15, Carr reported from Prague that Beneš was accepting the proposal of the President of the University, Robert M. Hutchins (U.S. Department of State, Diplomatic Correspondence, National Archives, Washington, D.C., 860F.001/95-100, 760F.62/1883. Hereafter cited as *Dept. St.*). See also Katherine Crane, *Mr. Carr of State* (New York, 1960), p. 350. Beneš's close collaborator, the newspaperman Hubert Ripka, left for France on October 10, 1938 (Miloš Hájek, *Od Mnichova k 15. březnu* From Munich to March 15 Prague, 1959, p. 52).

Notes to Chapter I

Notes to Negotiations with Germany

1. Sir Nevile Henderson, André François-Poncet, Bernard Attolico.

2. Heidrich was summoned to go to Berlin directly from Geneva, where he had been attending the meeting of the Assembly of the League of Nations (Communicated by Heidrich to the author).

3. *Records of the German Foreign Ministry Archives,* National Archives, Washington, D.C. Collection entitled *Tschechoslowakische Dokumente.* Microcopy T-120, Serial 1809H, Roll 1040, frames 412729–30. (Documents of the Czechoslovak foreign ministry, seized by the Germans in March 1939 and translated into German. Hereafter quoted as *Czechosl. Doc.*).

4. According to *DGFP,* iv, no. 2; at 5:00 P.M. according to *DBFP,* III, nos. 79, 165.

5. *DGFP* IV, no. 2.

6. Territory no. I in south-western Bohemia to be occupied on the 1st and 2nd of October; no. II, two salients in northern Bohemia (Oct. 2 and 3); no. III, western Bohemia (Oct. 3, 4, and 5) and no. IV, northern Moravia-Silesia (Oct. 6 and 7).

7. Colonel F. N. Mason-MacFarlane in his report to the British ambassador Henderson, *DBFP,* III, no. 191, enclosure, p. 164.

8. *DGFP*, IV, no. 2.

9. The geographical names are given in their Czech form. When they are mentioned for the first time their German equivalent is added.

10. *DBFP*, III, no. 191, p. 164.

11. Ibid., p. 163.

12. Ibid., no. 191, enclosure, p. 165. So the town of Český Krumlov (Böhmisch Krumau) in southern Bohemia was terrorized by members of the Sudeten German party during the night of September 20–October 1. Shooting was spread throughout the Vltava valley during the same night. "It was significant," a British observer reported, "that two Czech police were killed and ten wounded but that no Sudeten party casualty was reported" (*DBFP*, III, no. 104; cf. no. 118). From northern Bohemia came reports that the armed Sudeten German *Ordners* attacked post offices on the Czech side of the demarcation line and forced the officials to evacuate the buildings (R. Bubeníčková—V. Helešicová, "Deset říjnových dnů roku 1938" [Ten October Days of 1938] in *Odboj a revoluce*, VI, 1968, no. 4, doc. no. 11).

13. *DBFP*, III, Enclosure to no. 191, p. 165.

14. R. G. Coulson, "Czechoslovak Adventure," *The Quarterly Review*, London, no. 539, January 1939, p. 138.

15. On October 23 and November 3 (Microfilmed German documents in the National Archives, Washington, D.C., T-120, Serial 4824H, Roll 2443, frames E240024-34, 240168-72. - Hereafter cited as *G. Doc.*). The German High Command tried to explain this by the fact that there was a slight difference between the Czech and German maps because in the printing process of the German maps the line was by a technical error shifted by a few millimeters (ibid., fr. E240085).

16. Coulson, loc. cit.

17. *DGFP*, IV, no. 10.

18. Ibid., no. 12.

19. Communicated by A. Heidrich to the author.

20. The report of Mastný quoted by Edward Táborský, *Pravda zvítězila* [The Truth Prevailed], (Prague, 1947), p. 12.

21. *DBFP*, III, no. 165, pp. 131–32.

22. Ibid.

23. Ibid., no. 150, p. 117.

24. *British White Paper*, Cmd. 5847, no. 2.

25. To increase the influence of the German population in Austria's western part, the "Cisleithania," the Habsburg monarchy had based its census on the principle of the *Umgangssprache*, i.e. the language used in daily life. Thus the Czechs in the mixed regions who spoke German in their contacts with the Austrian authorities or their German employers were registered as Germans.

26. Václav Král, ed., *Das Abkommen von München 1938. Tschechoslowakische diplomatische Dokumente, 1937–1939* (Prague, 1968), no. 276, p. 309. Probably it was on this occasion that François-Poncet, frustrated by a protracted and fruitless discussion and by the unyielding posture of the Czechs nervously rebuked Heidrich: "Eh bien, mon ami, voulez-vous que l'on vous dicte de nouveau le tracé de la frontière?" According to Heidrich, the French am-

bassador was at this moment clearly afraid of possible complications (communicated by Heidrich to the author).

27. *DGFP*, IV, no. 25.

28. Ibid.

29. André François-Poncet, *Souvenirs d'une ambassade à Berlin. Septembre 1931–Octobre 1938* (Paris, 1946), p. 335. *DDF*, XII, no. 25.

30. *DBFP*, III, nos. 125, 135.

31. Ibid., no. 165, par. 24.

32. Ibid., no. 125.

33. Ibid., no. 127, n. 2.

34. Král, *Das Abkommen von München*, no. 276, p. 310.

35. *DBFP*, III, no. 128. See also Sir Nevile Henderson, *Failure of a Mission* (New York, 1940), p. 175.

36. *DGFP*, IV, no. 32.

37. Helešicová-Machotková, "Mnichovská krise," doc. no. 16, p. 226.

38. *DGFP*, IV, no. 36.

39. In Prague the Czechoslovak Prime Minister Syrový announced at 6:00 P.M. the resignation of President Beneš and at 7:00 P.M. Dr. Beneš delivered his farewell address over the radio.

40. Král, *Das Abkommen von München*, no. 276, p. 310. *DDF*, XII, no. 27, François-Poncet's report of 8:35 P.M. This time the French ambassador said that he had yielded to the necessities of the situation with *la mort dans l'âme*. Cf. his summary, ibid., no. 52.

41. *DGFP*, IV, no. 31.

42. Cf. p. 20.

43. *DGFP*, IV, no. 33.

44. Helešicová-Machotková, "Mnichovská krise," no. 17.

45. *DGFP*, IV, no. 41. For the "fifth zone" see the sketch map published in *DBFP*, III. Cf. *Prager Presse*, October 7, 1938.

46. *Lidové Noviny*, October 12, 1938.

47. Germany thus occupied the first line of Czechoslovak fortifications. According to General Heinz Guderian "it was not so strong as we had thought, but it was good that Germany did not have to conquer it in a bloody fight" (*Erinnerungen eines Soldaten*, Heidelberg, 1951, p. 51). Keitel reported that experimental bombardment of the fortifications which were modeled on the Maginot Line, proved that even break-through of the French line was "perfectly possible" (*DGFP*, IV, no. 411, p. 531). Albert Speer on the contrary states that "the Czech border fortifications caused general astonishment." The most massive fortifications extended from Moravská Ostrava to Trutnov. Hitler himself went to the former frontier to inspect them and according to Speer returned impressed. To the surprise of experts a test bombardment showed that the German weapons would not have prevailed against them. "Given a resolute defense, taking them would have been very difficult and would have cost us a great many lives," declared Hitler (Albert Speer, *Inside the Third Reich*, New York, 1970, p. 111). However, talking to Chvalkovský in October 1938 Hitler declared contemptuously: "How amateurish" (*Wie dilettantisch.*—Communicated by Chvalkov-

ský to the author). After the German occupation of Bohemia the armored turrets of the fortifications were dismantled and transferred to the Western Wall. See Wenzel Mattausch, "Tschechische Panzerkuppeln für den Westwall", in *Der Sudetendeutsche*, Hamburg, nos. 10, 11, 14–16, 20 in 1954. Cf. Jonathan Zorach, "Czechoslovakia's Fortifications. Their Development and Role in the 1938 Munich Crisis, " in *Militärgeschichtliche Mitteilungen*, 2 (1976), pp. 81–91.

48. See p. 17.

49. *DBFP*, III, nos. 177, 179.

50. *DGFP*, IV, no. 52.

51. Ibid., no. 53.

52. Ibid., no. 56.

53. Ibid., no. 101. Many of these claims were submitted by Sudeten Germans whose representative in Berlin, Dr. Quido Klieber, supported by K. H. Frank, was especially active. Emotional dispatches and entirely false reports about alleged Czech excesses in Brno, Jihlava, Olomouc and Moravská Ostrava were sent to Berlin and incidents were planned. A Dr. Hugo Preibsch of Brno suggested: "The best would be to transport—as a prove of Czech terrorism—a dead or a wounded man across the frontier. Only in this way could one move Berlin to intervention" (*G. Doc.*, T–120, S. 4824H, R. 2443, fr. E239910–11).

54. *DGFP*, IV, no. 108.

55. Ibid., no. 102.

56. Concerning the *Autobahn* see *DGFP*, IV, nos. 53, 55, 103, 108, 116, and 117.

57. Ibid., no. 108.

58. Král, *Abkommen von München*, no. 276, p. 320.

59. *DGFP*, IV, no. 100. See also *G. Doc.*, T–120, S. 2064H, R. 1098, fr. 448758–62.

60. The Czechoslovak documents (*Mnichov v dokumentech*, no. 231) sum up the desiderata of the delimitation commission of the Czechoslovak General Staff. According to a memorandum of November 10, 1938, the surrender of the Jihlava region with its 16,490 Germans could not be compensated for by the German occupation of the purely Czech compact areas of Opava, Bílovec, Zábřeh, Šumperk, Šternberg, Lanškroun and Moravský Krumlov, with 11,465 Czechs. The commission suggested the demand for the return of all these purely Czech areas as well as of the areas which had importance for the national economic life, especially in the region of Plzeň, Jindřichův Hradec, Dvůr Králové and the coal basin of Most-Duchcov. This proposal, drawn up probably in the first days of November, is dated November 10, i.e. the day when the new radical demands of Germany became known in Prague. See also *DGFP*, IV, no. 102.

61. Weizsäcker showed the map to Mastný on October 31 (Král, *Abkommen von München*, no. 280, p. 321). A few days later Mastný reported that the Prague government had forbidden it (*G. Doc.*, T–120, S. 140, R. 154, fr. 76123. - Altenburg's note). Similarly Germany protested in Prague when the State Statistical Office published a list of localities and districts attached to Germany, Hungary and Poland with a table indicating their ethnic composition. The German legation in Prague was immediately ordered to warn the Czechoslovak authorities that cir-

culation of such "propagandistic figures" would raise a strong displeasure (*starkes Befremden*) in Berlin (Václav Král, ed., *Die Deutschen in der Tschechoslowakei, 1933–1947*. Prague, 1964, no. 269).

63. *DGFP*, IV, no. 110; Král, *Abkommen von München*, no. 280, p. 321. On this occasion Richthofen too pointed out that this reversal to the worse had been caused by the propaganda map which Weizsäcker had already shown to Mastný. He told the same to Count Hanuš Kolovrat on November 11 (ibid., p. 323).

64. *DGFP*, IV, no. 113.

65. Ibid., no. 115.

66. Mastný's text speaks about *territorial* demands. *DGFP*, IV, no. 114 omits the word "territorial" which in this connection makes a great difference.

67. Ibid. See also Heidrich's letter in Ladislav Feierabend, *Ve vládách Druhé republiky* [In the Governments of the Second Republic] (New York, 1961), pp. 176–77.

68. Probably from Munich. Cf. *DGFP*, IV, no. 116, note 2.

69. Ibid., no. 114.

70. Ibid., no. 116. The *Autobahn* treaty was signed on November 19.

71. Ibid., no. 125.

72. Král, *Abkommen v. München*, no. 280, p. 327.

73. To be exact, there were two maps. One on the scale 1:300,000, and another, more detailed, on the scale 1:75,000. A map based on the first of these was published in the *British White Paper*, Cmd. 5908 of 1938. It is reprinted in *DBFP*, III.

74. *DBFP*, III, no. 264.

75. Ibid., no. 266.

76. Ibid., no. 265.

77. Ibid., no. 261.

78. *DGFP*, IV, no. 135, enclosure.

79. Král, *Abkommen v. München*, no. 280, p. 328.

80. Antonín Boháč, "Páté a šesté pásmo" [The Fifth and the Sixth Zone] *Přítomnost*, 16, no. 9, March 1, 1939, p. 143.

81. *DGFP*, IV, no. 121.

82. See p. 25.

83. *Mnichov v dokumentech*, II, no. 226; *G. Doc.*, T-120, S. 2367, R. 1307, fr. 489588–89.

84. *Lidové Noviny*, November 25, 1938.

85. *DGFP*, IV, no. 46.

86. *G. Doc.* T-120, S. 379, R. 281, fr. 209869-70.

87. *DGFP*, IV, no. 112.

88. Ibid., no. 119.

89. *Lidové Noviny*, December 11 and 17, 1938.

90. *Statistisches Jahrbuch für das Protektorat Böhmen und Mähren* (Prague, 1941), p. XXX. See also *DBFP*, III, no. 275; *DGFP*, IV, no. 121; *Prager Presse*, November 27, 1938; *Československo v mapách* [Czechoslovakia in Maps] (Prague, 1954), map no. 9. The population figures in these sources differ slightly.

Cf. Radomír Luža, *The Transfer of the Sudeten Germans* (New York, 1964), p. 158.

91. *DBFP*, III, no. 157.

92. Ibid., no. 180.

93. Ibid., no. 157.

94. Feierabend, *Ve vládách Druhé republiky*, p. 42. In a conversation with the Czech journalist Hubert Ripka the speaker of the French National Assembly, Edouard Herriot, was more outspoken. He declared that according to his information these men behaved "comme des cochons et des brutes" (quoted by Jan Křen, *Do emigrace* [Into Exile], Prague, 1963, p. 134, no. 98).

95. See p. 13.

96. *DBFP*, III, p. 649.

97. *DGFP*, IV, no. 111. "For example, we could not tolerate the following: A Czech State Secretary for the Czech minority, an extensive Czech educational system and Czech colleges, open activity by the pan-Slav-oriented *Sokol* with flags and uniforms, uncontrolled relations abroad for Czech national organizations, cultural autonomy, nationalistic organizations in Czech-language enclaves."

98. Text in *DBFP*, III, p. 653.

99. Communicated to the author by Mr. Miroslav Schubert. See *DBFP*, III, nos. 175, 176.

100. Ibid., p. 645.

101. *DGFP*, IV, no. 53.

102. Ibid., no. 55.

103. Ibid., no. 103.

104. Ibid., no. 116.

105. Ibid., nos. 117, 123, n. 2.

106. *G. doc.*, S. 2313, R. 1279, fr. 484803.

107. *DGFP*, IV, no. 124.

108. Jaroslav Vrbata, "Přehled vývoje veřejné správy v odtržených českých oblastech v letech 1938–1945" [A Survey of the Development of Public Administration in the Separated Czech Regions 1938–1945], *Sborník archivních prací* [Miscellany of Archival Writings], 12 (1962). pp. 47–51.

109. *G. Doc.*, T-120, S. 3011, R. 1450, fr. D588321–32, 38–41;588346–56, 72–87; 588396–403.

110. Antonín Faltys, "Postavení českého pohraničí v rámci Velkoněmecké říše v letech 1938–1945" [The Situation of the Czech Borderlands in the Framework of Greater Germany in the Years 1938–1945] *Historie a vojenství* (Prague, 1968), no. 3, pp. 386–420; Jaroslav Joza, "Česká menšina v severních Čechách" [The Czech Minority in Northern Bohemia] *Severní Čechy a Mnichov* [Northern Bohemia and Munich] (Liberec, 1969), pp. 176–213; František Mainuš, "České školství v pohraničí za nacistické okupace se zvláštním zřetelem k severní Moravě a Slezsku" [Czech Schools in the Borderland under the Nazi Occupation with Special Regard to Northern Moravia and Silesia] *Slezský sborník* [Silesian Miscellany] (Opava, 1959), vol. 57, no. 3, pp. 277–312.

Notes to Negotiations with Hungary

1. Lukeš, *Podivný mír*, p. 120.
2. *DBFP*, III, nos. 149, 160; *DGFP*, IV, no. 47.
3. *DGFP*, IV, no. 9; V, no. 229.
4. Ibid., V, no. 254; Nicolai Comnène-Petresco, *Preludi del grande dramma* (Rome, 1947), p. 223.
5. *DGFP*, IV, no. 9; *D. ir.*, II, no. 438.
6. *DGFP*, IV, nos. 26, 39. Cf. p. 100.
7. Ibid., no. 45.
8. Hungary considered Petržalka as an old part of the Burgenland, a Hungarian region parts of which were ceded to Austria after the plebiscite of 1922. Minister Sztójay accompanied his demarche of October 6 by a naive suggestion that Hitler, after taking possession of Petržalka, could make "a very happy gesture" and cede it to Hungary. He met with Weizsäcker's stern refusal (*DGFP*, IV, no. 42).
9. *Ciano's Hidden Diary, 1937–1938* (New York, 1953), October 3, 1938.
10. *DGFP*, IV, no. 26. "Italy did not wish to displease Yugoslavia in this matter," declared Weizsäcker.
11. *D. ir.*, II, no. 432; *DBFP*, III, nos. 108, 113.
12. *DGFP*, IV, no. 22; *D. ir.*, II, no. 449.
13. *D. ir.*, II, nos. 473, 476, 476a, 477.
14. Ferdinand Vávra and Ján Eibel, *Viedeňská arbitráž: dôsledok Mnichova* [The Vienna Arbitration: A Consequence of Munich] (Bratislava, 1965), p. 65; *D. ir.*, II, nos. 485, 491a; Feierabend, *Ve vládách*, p. 51.
15. *D. ir.*, II, 487.
16. According to General Viest it was not easy to parry the arguments of this well-informed Hungarian delegate (Communicated by Ladislav Feierabend to this author).
17. Macartney, *October Fifteenth*, I, p. 284, n.7. Kánya even insisted that the discussions be conducted in French, which few of the Slovak representatives knew and not in Magyar which would have been an acceptable alternative to some of them (Dreisziger, *Hungary's Way*, p. 212, n. 114). Eventually it was decided that the official language would be the French, but practically the talks would be conducted in Magyar or Slovak (*D. ir.*, II, no. 487b).
18. The Czechoslovak government had decided on October 7 to comply with this Hungarian demand (*DBFP*, III, no. 172; *D. ir.* II, no. 487, 487a; Vávra-Eibel, *Viedeňská arbitráž*, p. 65).
19. *DBFP*, III, no. 182. According to the Hungarian figures (*Le Temps*, October 24, 1938) the territory demanded by Hungary measured 14,153 sq. km. with 1,090,596 inhabitants of which 848,969 were Hungarians, i.e. 77% (census of 1910). The Slovak population according to these statistics was 13.5%. See also the report of the Czechoslovak delegation quoted by Vávra-Eibel, *Viedeňská arbitráž*, p. 67.
20. *D. ir.*, II, no. 487b. On October 13 the Czechoslovak authorities in Moravia intercepted a pro-Hungarian leaflet in Slovak promising the Slovaks

"wine, wheat and love" (Bubeníčková-Helešicová, "Deset říjnových dnů," no. 29).

21. *D. ir.*, nos. 488, 491b.

22. *DGFP*, IV, no. 68.

23. *D. ir.*, II, no. 491b.

24. Ibid., no. 491. The island, lying between Bratislava and Komárno, is known under several names: Csáloköz in Magyar, Grossschüttinsel in German, and Vel'ký Žitný ostrov in Slovak. The English translation would be the Great Rye Island.

25. *G. doc.*, T. 120, S. 379, R. 281, fr. 210154–55; see also the telephonic report from Komárno quoted by Vávra-Eibel, *Viedeňská arbitráž*, p. 71; *D. ir.*, II, no. 492.

26. *G. doc.*, T-120, S. 379, R. 281, fr. 210200, 210157; *D. ir.*, II, no. 493a.

27. Miklós Szinai and László Szücs, "Prispevok k dejinám nemeckých a maďarských agresívnych plánov proti Československu v rokoch 1920–1939," [A Contribution to the History of the German and Hungarian Aggressive Plans against Czechoslovakia in 1920–1939] *Historický časopis*, 14, no. 4 (1966), p. 605; *DGFP*, IV, no. 59; *G. doc.*, T-120, S. 140, R. 154, fr. 75828.

28. Macartney, *October Fifteenth*, I, pp. 30, 238; Thomas L. Sakmyster, "Hungary and the Munich Crisis. The Revisionist Dilemma," in *Slavic Review*, 32 (December 1973), p. 736.

29. *D. ir.*, II, p. 755, note 81.

30. *Allianz Hitler—Horthy—Mussolini. Dokumente zur ungarischen Aussenpolitik (1933–1944)*, edited by Magda Ádám, Gyula Juhász, and Lájos Kerekes (Budapest, 1966), p. 41.

31. *D. ir.*, II, no. 512; Macartney, *op. cit.*, p. 294, no. 5.

32. *The Times* (London), October 17, 1938; *České Slovo*, October 17, 1938.

33. On October 16, 25, and 31 (*D. ir.*, II, nos. 545, 581, 619).

34. Cf. similar Hungarian proposals concerning Petržalka (n. 8); *D. ir.*, II, no. 471; *Sprawy Międzynarodowe*, 12, nos. 7/8 (Warsaw, 1958), pp. 69–73; Beck, *Dernier rapport*, p. 169; Cienciala, *Poland*, p. 153; Thaddeus Gromada, "The Slovak Question in Polish Foreign Policy" (Ph.D. diss., Fordham University, 1966), pp. 203, n. 18, 204.

35. *D. ir.*, II, nos. 463, 518, 595.

36. *DGFP*, V, nos. 75, 80, 81; Józef Lipski, *Diplomat in Berlin, 1933–1939, papers and memoirs of Józef Lipski, Ambassador of Poland.* Edited by Waclaw Jędrzejewicz (New York, 1968), no. 124. *Les relations polono-allemandes et polono-soviétiques au cours de la période 1933–1939* (Paris, 1940), no. 44. Almost at the same time Foreign Minister Beck made an unsuccessful attempt to secure Rumania's support for the annexation of this province by Hungary. (For an account of his visit to Galati see his *Dernier Rapport*, pp. 172–73).

37. *DGFP*, IV, nos. 57, 59; *D. ir.*, II, nos. 522, 526.

38. *DGFP*, IV, no. 53, IX.

39. Ibid., no. 62. See also Hitler's statements to François-Poncet on October 17

(*Le Livre Jaune Français*, no. 18, p. 28).

40. *D. ir.*, II, nos. 529, 531, 533; *DGFP*, IV, no. 60; *Allianz Hitler—Horthy—Mussolini*, no. 41.

41. *Ciano's Hidden Diary*, October 14, 1938; *DGFP*, IV, nos. 60, 64.

42. Ciano, *loc. cit.*

43. *DGFP*, IV, no. 65; *D. ir.*, II, nos. 542, 549a.

44. *DGFP*, IV, nos. 66. 72.

45. Galeazzo Ciano, *L'Europa verso la catastrofe*, October 22, 1938.

46. Ibid., October 28, 1938; *DGFP*, IV, no. 400.

47. *Dictionnaire diplomatique*, IV (Paris, n.d.), s.v. "Hongrie", p. 591.

48. October 14 and 23, 1938.

49. *DGFP*, IV, no. 83; *G. doc.*, T-120, S. 379, R. 281, fr. 209975-78; *D. ir.*, II, no. 578.

50. *DGFP*, IV, no. 86; *D. ir.*, II, no. 580; *Le Temps*, October 26, 1938. About four or five days earlier, the Polish Foreign Minister Beck declared to the Italian ambassador in Warsaw that he would submit the Polish candidacy for the fifth place, were the four Munich powers to reconvene (*G. doc.*, T-120, S. 379, R. 281, fr. 210031, 210063). The possibility of the Polish participation, this time in the arbitration proceedings of the Axis powers only, was also mentioned by Kánya (*D. ir.*, II, no. 566). Rumania was moving in the same direction and intended to present her views to the four powers through an observer (*G. doc.*, S. 379, R. 281, fr. 210063; *DGFP*, V, no. 75, n. 2).

51. *DGFP*, IV, no. 92; *Mnichov v dokumentech*, no. 236; *D. ir.*, II, no. 585.

52. *DGFP*, IV, no. 98.

53. Ibid., nos. 93–96; *D. ir.*, II, nos. 602, 604, 606, 607.

54. *DGFP*, IV, no. 79.

55. *D. ir.*, II, nos. 575, 592.

56. *DBFP*, III, nos. 227, 229; *D. ir.*, II, nos. 589, 597, 603.

57. *Ciano's Hidden Diary*, November 2, 1938.

58. *DGFP*, IV, no. 99; "Węgry i Polska w okresie kryzysu czechoslowackiego 1938 r." [Hungary and Poland in the Time of the Czechoslovak Crisis in 1938], *Sprawy międzynarodowe*, II (no. 7/8, 1958), pp. 69–73; *Mnichov v dokumentech*, II, no. 237 (Chvalkovský's report).

59. November 3, 1938.

60. Ibid.

61. Text in *DGFP*, IV, no. 99/II–IV.

62. Vávra-Eibel, *Viedeňská arbitráž*, pp. 112–13. According to the Hungarian census 1,032,356 inhabitants were in the occupied territory on December 15, 1938 (*Lidové Noviny*, February 9, 1939). *Československo v mapách*, map no. 9, has somewhat different figures (1,052,930).

63. Martin Vietor, *Dejiny okupácie južného Slovenska, 1938–1945* [History of the Occupation of Southern Slovakia, 1938–1945] (Bratislava, 1968), p. 20; Dreisziger, *Hungary's Way*, p. 109.

64. *Lidové Noviny*, November 12, 1938.

65. *Pester Lloyd*, November 9, 1938.

66. Lord Rothermere, *My Campaign for Hungary* (London, 1939), p. 202; *G. Doc.*, T-120, S. 1962H, R. 1078, fr. 437618.

67. Vietor, *Dejiny okupácie*, p. 61; Loránt Tilkovsky, *Južné Slovensko v rokoch 1938–1945* [Southern Slovakia in the Years 1938–1945] (Bratislava, 1972), p. 144.

68. Vietor, *op. cit.*, pp. 62–63; Tilkovszky, *op. cit.*, p. 146.

69. *Allianz Hitler—Horthy—Mussolini*, p. 44.

70. *DGFP*, IV, no. 118.

71. Ibid., no. 127; *D. ir.*, III, no. 50.

72. *Ciano's Hidden Diary*, November 18, 1938; *DGFP*, IV, no. 128; *D. ir.*, III, nos. 51, 52.

73. Ciano, *op. cit.*, November 20, 1938. The exact date of the Szabo–Mussolini conversation is uncertain.

74. *DGFP*, IV, no. 130; Ciano, *op. cit.*, November 21, 1938.

75. *DGFP*, IV, no. 128.

76. Ibid., no. 129; Ciano, *op. cit.*, Nov. 20, 1938.

77. *DGFP*, IV, no. 131; *D. ir.*, III, no. 56.

78. *DGFP*, IV, no. 131, note 1.

79. *DGFP*, IV, nos. 132–33; *D. ir.*, III, nos. 58, 59.

80. *DGFP*, IV, no. 140.

Notes to Negotiations with Poland

1. Cienciala, *Poland and the Western Powers*, p. 139–41.

2. Beck, *Dernier rapport*, p. 167.

3. Szembek, *Journal*, September 30, 1938, p. 342. Several members of the government saw, however, the dangers of Polish participation in the dismemberment of Czechoslovakia, and thus, for instance, Vice-Premier Eugeniusz Kwiatkowski was against the ultimatum. While the ultimatum was under discussion a group of both leftist and rightist members of the opposition assembled in the palace of Prince Ździslaw Lubomirski intending to express their concern to President Mościcki. There was, however, not much time at their disposal and on October 1 it was already too late to take further steps (Hans Roos, *Polen und Europa*, Tübingen, 1957, p. 357).

4. Text in Namier, *Europe*, pp. 294–96.

5. Józef Chudek, "Dwie instrukcje Becka z wrzesnia 1938r." [Beck's Two Instructions from September 1938] *Sprawy międzynarodowe*, 2, 1958, pp. 112–16. See also Henryk Batowski, *Kryzys dyplomatyczny w Europie, jesień 1938 a wiosna 1939* [The Diplomatic Crisis in Europe, Autumn 1938 and Spring 1939] (Warsaw, 1962), pp. 62–63.

6. The text of the note published in Namier, *Europe*, pp. 297–300.

7. *DBFP*, III, no. 86.

8. Ibid., no. 136, par. 7.

9. *DGFP*, V, no. 54.

10. Ibid, no. 55. Lipski, *Diplomat in Berlin*, no. 115. At the same time Ribbentrop promised "a far more than friendly attitude" in case of a Polish–Soviet conflict.

11. Here he was immediately rebuked—probably by Ribbentrop or Hitler himself—for after his return to the embassy Lipski received a telephone call from Göring asking "somewhat embarrassedly" that the Polish ambassador not repeat his remarks about Moravská Ostrava to Warsaw (Lipski, *op. cit.*, no. 115, p. 438). A few days later, on October 4, Göring told Weizsäcker that the territory "south of the southwestern corner of Silesia" must "by all means" become German. Should a dispute develop about it with the Poles, a deal could be made over Danzig. "Otherwise it would be best to pass it to the Czechs" (*DGFP*, V, no. 58).

12. Lipski, *op. cit.*, p. 435; *DBFP*, III, no. 92.

13. Lipski, *op. cit.*, p. 436.

14. *Hidden Diary*, October 1, 1938.

15. *DBFP*, III, nos. 76, 86.

16. Bonnet, *De Washington*, p. 298.

17. Léon Noel, *L'agression allemande contre la Pologne* (Paris, 1946), p. 236.

18. *DBFP*, III, no. 93.

19. Helešicová-Machotková, "Mnichovská krise", nos. 13, 14.

20. Namier, *Europe*, p. 302. See also *Mnichov v dokumentech*, nos. 234, 235.

21. Beck, *Dernier rapport*, p. 167.

22. Namier, *Europe*, pp. 301–302.

23. *Le Temps*, October, 4, 1938.

24. Czechoslovak Press Agency (ČTK), October 2, 1938.

25. *Documents and Materials*, no. 23.

26. *DGFP*, IV, no. 17.

27. Ibid., V, no. 62. "He was not going to haggle with the Poles about every single city but would be generous toward those who were modest in their demands" (Memorandum by Hewel).

28. *The New York Times*, October 10, 1938; Szembek, *Journal*, Oct. 10, 1938; Woytak, "Polish Military Intervention", pp. 386–87; *DGFP*, V, no. 68.

29. Otakar Káňa and Ryszard Pavelka, *Těšínsko v polsko-československých vztazích 1919–1939* [The Land of Těšín in the Polish-Czechoslovak Relations 1918–1939] (Ostrava, 1970), P. 241; *Statistický lexikon obcí v republice Československé*, II, *Země moravskoslezská* [Statistical Lexicon of Communities in the Czechoslovak Republic, II, The Land of Moravia-Silesia] (Prague, 1935), pp. 29–31, 106–110. According to the Polish statistics there were about 110,000 Poles in the two districts (*Polonia*, October 6, 1938).

30. František Uhlíř, *Těšínské Slezsko* [The Těšín Silesia] (Ostrava-Prague, 1946), pp. 241–42.

31. Kána-Pavelka, *op. cit.*, p. 248.

32. Jaroslav Valenta, "Cesta k Mnichovu a válce (1938–1939)" [The Road to Munich and the War, 1938–1939] in *Češi a Poláci v minulosti* [The Czechs and the Poles in the Past], ed. by Václav Žáček (Prague, 1967), pp. 607, 610; Káňa and Pavelka, *Těšínsko*, p. 244; *G. Doc.*, T-120, S. 2388H, R. 1320, fr. 499846–51.

33. "I have the impression that our notes are of no avail here," reported Czechoslovak Minister Juraj Slávik to Prague (Slávik, "Moja pamät—živá kniha" [My Memory—a Living Book] in *Newyorský Denník*, no. 227, July 29, 1958;

ibid. no. 238, August 13, 1958). On December 15 Ribbentrop turned the attention of the Polish Ambassador Lipski to these conditions and pointed out that the Germans should not be treated in such a way that they would feel "as though they had fallen from the frying pan into the fire" (*DGFP*, V, nos. 112, 113; Lipski, *Diplomat in Berlin*, no. 131).

34. October 11. See Szembek, *Journal*, Oct. 11, pp. 351–52. In the Polish-Czechoslovak territorial disputes the Conference of the Ambassadors decided on July 28, 1920 generally in favor of Czechoslovakia and also the massif of Javorina in the Tatras was awarded to Czechoslovakia in March 1924. Cf. Stanislas Raubal, *Formation de la frontière entre la Pologne et la Tchécolslovaquie* (Paris, 1928), p. 76.

35. Hoensch, *Der ungarische Revisionismus*, pp. 198–211.

36. Szembek, *Journal*, October 11, 1938.

37. Lukeš, *Podivný mír*, p. 80; Ivan Dérer, *Slovenský vývoj a luďácká zrada* [Slovak Development and the People's Party Betrayal] (Prague, 1946), p. 306.

38. "Here Sidor assumed a very whimpering tone," remarks Szembek dryly (*Journal*, October 19, 1938).

39. *DGFP*, V, no. 83. Any hopes of obtaining the industrial towns of Moravská Ostrava and Vítkovice that Poland might have harbored were quashed by the decision of Hitler as communicated by Weizsäcker to Lipski on October 12 (*DGFP*, IV, no. 53; V, nos. 68, 69). Cf. Lipski, *Diplomat in Berlin*, no. 119.

40. Slávik, "Moja pamäť," *Newyorský Denník*, no. 227, July 29, 1958. France protested in Warsaw against these new demands on October 20 and Léon Noël declared to Szembek that Paris was concerned about the Polish-Czech talks regarding the frontier problems. According to the French ambassador the problems in question were above all the mines in the Slezská Ostrava area. "In case they should come to Poland as a result of partition it would be a severe blow to the Czechoslovak economy which would become still more dependent on the Reich," declared the French diplomat (Szembek, *Journal*, October 20, 1938), *DDF*, XII, no. 152.

41. *DGFP*, V, no. 83.

42. *G. Doc.*, *T*-120, S. 2376H, R. 1316, fr. D496887.

43. Ibid., S. 1340, R. 747, fr. 353469.

44. Years later Chvalkovský recalled with disgust the incessant visits of the Polish diplomat with continuously increasing demands (Communicated to the author by Chvalkovský).

45. Text in Namier, *Europe*, p. 304. The Czechoslovak answer ibid., p. 307.

46. Václav Hyndrák, "Polsko a československá krise na podzim 1938" [Poland and the Czechoslovak Crisis in the Fall of 1938] in *Historie a vojenství*, no. 1 (1968), p. 98. Woytak, "Polish military intervention," p. 387.

47. See also Szembek, *Journal*, November 22, 1938; Hoensch, *Der ungarische Revisionismus*, pp. 206–07; *Bulletin périodique de la presse tchécolslovaque*, no. 61, p. 12; Gromada, "The Slovak Question,", pp. 226–27; *G. Doc.*, T–120, S. 28, R. 12, fr. 18145; Beck, *Dernier rapport*, p. 168.

48. *DBFP*, III, no. 396.

49. After her victory, Germany, by the treaty of November 21, 1939, returned to Slovakia not only the territory lost in 1938, but even the regions ceded in 1920 and 1924 (Alfred Bohmann, "Die tschechoslowakischen Gebietsabtretungen an Polen und Ungarn 1938/39" *Zeitschrift für Ostforschung*, 20, no 3 (1971), pp. 476, 479–81). As for the Těšín region, the government of the Protectorate Bohemia-Moravia asked the Protector to exert his influence on Hitler and the German government to reunite the area with the Protectorate. However, the German foreign ministry and the *Volksdeutsche Mittelstelle* declared themselves against the return. On October 12, 1939, Woermann, director of the political department of the ministry, noted that Hitler's decision in this matter seemed to had already been made (*G. doc.*, S. 331, R. 257, fr. 195885, 195887; Bohmann, *op. cit.*, p. 476). The part acquired by Poland in 1938 was joined with the Prussian province of Upper-Silesia and the town of Těšín became a district capital. After the Second World War the pre-Munich line was restored.

Notes to Chapter II

1. The official Collection of the Laws and Regulations used the hyphen for the first time on November 26.
2. *Mnichov v dokumentech*, II, enclosure to no. 248. Each state immediately after Munich published statistics about its losses or acquisitions. Though these statistics were for the major part based on official sources they differed in some cases considerably. For instance, the Czechoslovak figures were based on the census of 1930, eight years anterior to Munich.
3. Rudolf Olšovský et al. *Přehled hospodářského vývoje Československa v letech 1919–1945* [A Survey of Economic Development of Czechoslovakia 1919–1945] (Prague, 1961), pp. 474–75.
4. *Statistický zpravodaj* [The Statistical Bulletin], 1939, nos. 1–2, quoted by Hájek, *Od Mnichova*, p. 112, no. 38.
5. Klumpar, *Memoirs*, pp. 45–47. After Hitler's seizure of power and occupation of Austria and Sudetenland the refugees from these areas increased the number of Jews in Prague to about 56,100 in March 1939 (35,463 in 1930). See *Encyclopaedia Judaica*, vol. 13, Jerusalem, 1971, s.v. "Prague," p. 974.
6. *L'Europe Centrale*, Prague, 1938, p. 621. *DBFP*, III, Appendix IV, (I), p. 629. *Czechosl. Doc.*, R. 1039, fr. 411980, 412031.
7. J.W. Wheeler—Bennett, *Munich. Prologue to Tragedy* (London, 1948), pp. 197–98; Feierabend, *Ve vládách druhé republiky*, p. 98.
8. *Dept. St.*, 860F. 48–41.
9. *DBFP*, III, Appendix IV, I, p. 629.
10. Ibid., Appendix IV (II–XV), pp. 630–35.
11. *Dept. St.*, 860F.51/695.
12. *Czechosl. Doc.*, S. 1809H, R. 1039, fr. 412209.
13. Ibid., fr. 412036.
14. *DBFP*, III, p. 636–XVI.
15. Ibid., p. 633–XII, Krno to Newton on January 2, 1939.

16. Ibid., p. 638.

17. *DBFP*, IV, no. 25.

18. Jaroslav Werstadt, "Hlas odporu z přítmí druhé republiky a z prvních měsíců nacistické okupace" [A Voice of Resistance from the Dusk of the Second Republic and the First Months of the Nazi Occupation] in *Historie a vojenství*, 1968, no. 3, p. 421. Otakar Odložilík, *Odvěký úděl* [The Immemorial Lot] (Prague, 1938).

19. *Mnichov. Vzpomínková kronika*, p. 441.

20. Carr's despatch of October 20, 1938 (*Dept. St.*, 760F.62-1873).

21. Chvalkovský, too, succumbed to this psychosis when he reproached the chief of the official press service Zdeněk Schmoranz for not allowing the publication of the translation of a sarcastic article on Beneš written by Mussolini (Communicated to the author by Z. Schmoranz). Cf. *DGFP*, IV, no. 159, n.198.

22. Subsequently Jan Masaryk's uninhibited ways of expression caused some trouble to the Prague government anxious not to provoke the ire of Berlin. On his arrival in New York on January 6, 1939, Masaryk made some scathing remarks about the Prague regime and the situation in Central Europe in general (*New York Times*, January 7, 1939). On January 25 Chvalkovský complained to American minister Carr about "unnecessary worries" to which he was subjected and showed the American diplomat a clipping from the New York paper with Masaryk's remarks (*Dept. St.*, 760 F.62/1930). After Chvalkovský's visit to Berlin in January, the Foreign Ministry "on the order of the minister" asked the legation in Washington for a detailed report on Masaryk's activities. (*Czechosl. Doc.*, S. 1809H, R. 1039, fr. 412269).

23. On the same day, the Council of Ministers decided to admit Hitler's *Mein Kampf* to Czechoslovakia where it had been banned until then (*G. Doc.*, T-120, S. 28, R. 12, fr. 18251.

24. Karel Čapek died on December 25, 1938.

25. *Bulletin périodique de la presse tchécoslovaque*, no. 61, p. 15.

26. The text of Matoušek's proposal in *G. Doc.*, T-120, S. 1916H, R. 1072, fr. 430845-49, enclosure to Hencke's letter of Nov. 11, 1938.

27. *Czechosl. Doc.*, S. 1809H, R. 1039, fr. 412098, 412103-04. Feierabend, *Ve vládách*, p. 66. *L'Europe Nouvelle*, December 3, 1938, p. 1320. *Le Temps*, November 19, 1938.

28. *G. Doc.*, T-120, S. 1613H, R. 916, fr. 387198-99.

29. The Czech text of the programmatic proclamation in *G. Doc*, S. 3109, R. 1501, fr. D629722-23. Letter to the German legation ibid., fr. D629738-42. Hencke's telegram to Berlin of Nov. 15, 1938, ibid., R. 1321, fr. 511142.

30. *Pražský List*, November 11, 1938; *Národní Politika*, Nov. 13, 1938; "Bývalý předseda vlády Rudolf Beran před Národním soudem. Jeho obhajovací řeč pronesená 28. a 29. III. 1947" [Former Prime Minister Rudolf Beran before the National Tribunal. His Plea Delivered on March 28 and 29, 1947]. Mimeographed (Prague, 1947?), pp. 37-38.

31. Bubeníčková R., Helešicová V., and Machotková R. "Tiskové pokyny pomnichovské republiky" [Press Directives of the post-Munich Republic] *Odboj*

a revoluce, vol. 7, no. 1 (1969), nos. 41, 45, 57; *G. Doc.*, T-120, S. 3109, R. 1501, fr. D629732-37.

32. *G. Doc.*, S. 1613H, R. 916, fr. 387131-32, 387153-54; S. 28, R. 12, fr. 18139-40; S. 2377, R. 1317, fr. 497904-918.

33. The penalties for disobeying were moderate: a fine of 10 to 5,000 crowns or jail from 12 hours to 14 days.

34. Josef Novotný, "KSČ v ilegalitě (1938-1939)" [The Czechoslovak Communist Party in Illegality] in *Z počátků odboje* [The Beginnings of the Resistance], ed. by Oldřich Janeček (Prague, 1969), p. 43.

35. Hájek, *Od Mnichova*, pp. 133-35.

36. Cis, "Konec sociální demokracie a vznik strany práce" [The End of the Social Democracy and the Origins of the Labor Party] *Přítomnost*, 15, no. 52. December 29, 1938, pp. 819-20; *Právo Lidu*, October 26 and 28, 1938 (T.O.).

37. Ferdinand Peroutka, "Tvrdá slova" [Harsh Words] *Přítomnost*, 15, no. 46, November 16, 1938, pp. 721-22.

38. Otto Böss. "Die zweite Tschecho-Slowakische Republik im Spiegel zeitgenossischer tschechischer Pressestimmen (Oktober 1930-März 1939)," *Bohemia*. Jahrbuch des Collegium Carolinum, Vol. 3 (Munich, 1962), pp. 402-425. Heinrich Bodensieck. "Zur 'Spiegelung' der nach-Münchener tschechoslowakischen Politik in der zeitgenossichen tschechischen Publizistik (Herbst 1938-Frühjahr 1939)," *Zeitschrift für Ostforschung*, 16, 1967, pp. 79-101. Cf. instructions of the Press Division of the Presidency of the Council, December 19, 1938, and January 12, 1939 (*Tiskové pokyny*, nos. 29, 35).

39. *Tiskové pokyny*, no. 24.

40. Václav Beneš, "Czechoslovak Democracy and its Problems," in *A History of the Czechoslovak Republic, 1918-1948*, ed. Radomír Luža and Victor S. Mamatey (Princeton, 1973), pp. 56-58, 73-86; Mamatey, "The Development of Czechoslovak Democracy; 1920-1938," ibid., pp. 114-26, 135-39, 148-52. Yeshayahu Jelinek, *The Parish Republic: Hlinka's Slovak People's Party 1939-1945* (New York and London, 1976). Josef Anderle, "The Slovak Question in the Munich Crisis of 1938" (Unpublished doctoral dissertation, U. of Chicago, 1961).

41. Josef Anderle, "The Establishment of Slovak Autonomy in 1938," in *Czechoslovakia Past and Present*, ed. by Miloslav Rechcigl Jr. (The Hague, 1969), p. 85.

42. Dérer, *Slovenský vývoj*, pp. 178-79.

43. For the text of the proposal see Edvard Beneš, *Où vont les Slaves*, (Paris, 1946), pp. 278-81.

44. Anderle, "The Slovak Question," p. 187.

45. Pal'o Čarnogurský, "Proklamácia unii Slovenska s Polskom z 28. septembra 1938" [The Declaration of the Union of Slovakia with Poland on September 28, 1938] *Historický časopis* 16 (1968), pp. 407-23. According to Čarnosgurský the declaration had an important reservation: It proposed the union "in the case when the territory of the Czechoslovak Republic was attacked by an enemy from the outside and a part of the Republic was permanently occupied so that Slovakia

would be forced to declare independence."

46. Anderle, "The Slovak Question," pp. 207–11. Lubomír Lipták, "Autonómia slovenskej krajiny. Od Mníchova k 14. marcu 1939" [The Autonomy of the Slovak Land. From Munich to March 14, 1939] *Odboj a revoluce*, 4 (1968), no. 5, p. 19.

47. Josef Lettrich, *History of Modern Slovakia* (New York, 1955), pp. 296–97.

48. Vladimír Záděra, *Deset let parlamentní retrospektivy* [Ten Years of the Parliament Retrospect] (Prague, 1948), p. 76. Lipták, "Autonómia slovenskej krajiny," p. 21.

49. Záděra, *Deset let*, p. 81. Lipták, *op. cit.*, pp. 31–39. *Nedělní List*, December 18, 1938 (T.O.).

50. *Lidové Noviny*, December 15, 1938. *Právo Lidu*, Dec. 23, 1938 (T.P.). Lipták, *op. cit.*, p. 44–45.

51. Lipták,*op. cit.*, pp. 51–52. Jozef Danáš, *L'uďácký separatizmus a hitlerovské Nemecko* [The People's Party Separatism and the Hitlerite Germany] (Bratislava, 1963), p. 55. Yeshayahu Jelinek, "Storm-troopers in Slovakia: the Rodobrana and the Hlinka Guard," *Journal of Contemporary History*, 6, no. 3 (1971), p. 103.

52. Georges Luciani, "La Tchécoslovaquie après Munich" *Le Temps*, March 2, 1939. This nationalism led to the removal of a bust of an old friend of the Slovak nation, the British historian, R. W. Seton-Watson, from the parish building at Ružomberok. Before the First World War, Seton-Watson defended the Slovaks against Hungarian oppression. In the critical period preceding Munich he warned them, however, against a radical autonomism. The bust was removed during a manifestation organized by the Hlinka Guard. (*Lidové Noviny*, November 2, 1938).

53. George F. Kennan, *From Prague After Munich* (New Jersey, 1968), p. 25.

54. *Bulletin périodique de la presse tchécoslovaque*, no. 61, p. 28.

55. Lipták, "Autonómia slovenskej krajiny," p. 44.

56. Feierabend, *Ve vládách*, pp. 83–84.

57. *Právo Lidu*, December 20, 1938 (Tschechische Presseauszüge, Berlin; hereafter quoted as T.P.).

58. *Národní Listy*, February 22, 1939 (T.O.).

59. *Lidové Noviny*, February 20, 1939 (T.O.).

60. According to the 1930 census there were 135,918 Jews in Slovakia. Only about 25,000 of them survived "the final solution." (*Encyclopaedia Judaica*, Jerusalem, 1971, V, s.v. "Czechoslovakia", p. 1195).

61. This term is used by the American historian of Ukrainian descent, Paul R. Magocsi ("The Nationality Problem in Subcarpathian Ruthenia, 1938–1939. A Reapprisal." Lecture delivered at the 4th meeting of the Czechoslovak Society of Arts and Sciences, New York, November 17, 1974).

62. Ladislav Suško, "German Policy towards Slovakia and Carpatho-Ukraine in the period from the September crisis in 1938 up to the splitting of Czechoslovakia in March 1939," in *Studia Historica Slovaca*, 16, Bratislava, 1975, pp. 112–17.

63. Ibid., p. 132.

64. Feierabend, *Ve vládách,* p. 94: The German legation was very quickly informed about the discussions in the Council of Ministers.

65. *G. Doc.*, S. 1647H, R. 1004, fr. 391085.

66. *D. ir.*, II, no. 469.

67. Lukeš, *Podivný mír,* p. 130.

68. *G. doc.*, T-120, S. 2036H, R. 1141, fr. 445671-3.

69. *D. ir.*, II, no. 474.

70. *Pester Lloyd,* October 28, 1938, March 7, 1939; Feierabend, *Ve vládách,* p. 50.

71. *Pester Lloyd,* November 18, 1938.

72. *Sbírka zákonů a nařízení Československého státu* [Collection of Laws and Regulations of the Czechoslovak State], no. 328, issue 109, December 16, 1938. The law used the term of *Podkarpatská Rus* (Subcarpathian Ruthenia), leaving the final decision about the name to the future autonomous diet. Similarly the decision about the official language was to be the task of the new diet.

73. Government regulation of November 19, 1938 (ibid., no. 99, issue 98, Nov. 22, 1938).

74. *Národní Politika,* December 23, 1938 (T.P.).

75. *Frankfurter Zeitung,* December 8, 1938.

76. *Lidové Listy,* January 3, 1939 (T.P.).

77. *A-Zet,* January 23, 1939.

78. *T.O.*, February 14, 1934.

79. *DGFP,* IV, no. 39.

80. Ibid., no. 45.

81. Ibid., no. 46.

82. Ibid., no.109.

83. Ibid., no. 140.

84. Ibid., no. 146.

85. See p.

86. *DGFP,* IV, no. 104.

87. Král, *Die Deutschen,* no. 261.

88. See below, p. 108.

89. *DGFP,* IV, no. 145.

90. Ibid., no. 155.

91. Ibid., nos. 147, 151.

92. Communicated by Chvalkovský to the author.

93. Feierabend, *Ve vládách,* p. 73; Lukeš, *Podivný mír,* p. 191.

94. *Zápisy o schůzích poslanecké sněmovny Národního shromáždění Republiky Československé* [Records of the Sessions of the Chamber of Deputies of the National Assembly of the Czechoslovak Republic] (Prague, 1939), session of November 30, 1939.

95. Communicated by Minister Vojtěch Mastný to the author. Cf. Hencke's assessment of Hácha in *DGFP,* IV, no. 143, p. 176. About the state of Hácha's health see Dr. Adolf Maixner, "Kdo tedy rozhodoval?" [Who actually made the

decisions?] *Svobodné Noviny*, October 14, 1945. Maixner was Hácha's personal physician, his description seems, however, too negative.

96. Born in Pracejovice near Strakonice in southern Bohemia in 1887. From 1918 Deputy of the Agrarian party, Prime Minister December 1938–April 1939. During the Second World War he was interned in German concentration camps, in 1947 sentenced by a Czechoslovak court to 20 years' imprisonment for his activities between 1938 and 1941. He died in prison in 1954. Cf. Luža-Mamatey, *A History of the Czechoslovak Republic*, pp. 139, 155.

97. December 29, 1938 (*Dept. St.*, 740.00/555).

98. *Le Petit Parisien*, December 5, 1938.

99. Law no. 330 (*Sbírka zákonů a nařízení*, issue 110, December 17, 1938).

100. Klumpar, *Memoirs*, p. 16.

101. *Memoirs of Dr. Beneš*, p. 293.

102. Wheeler-Bennett, *Munich*, p. 198, n. 2. In the same vein General Louis-Eugène Faucher, chief of the French military mission in Prague, in a letter to Daladier (*DDF*, XII, no. 49). Chvalkovský himself experienced this hatred. He went walking in Prague one evening with his wife. As usual they spoke French, since she was not a Czech. Suddenly a student came up and spat at them. (As told by Chvalkovský to ambassador von Hassell: *The Von Hassell Diaries*, Garden City, N.Y., 1947, p. 127).

103. *DGFP*, IV, no. 4.

104. Ibid., no. 36.

105. Edvard Táborský, *Pravda zvítězila* [The Truth Has Prevailed] (Prague, 1947), p. 14.

106. *DGFP*, IV, no. 37.

107. Ibid., no. 46.

108. Ibid., no. 49.

109. Ibid., no. 54.

110. Ibid., no. 55.

111. Ibid., no. 61; Král, *Das Abkommen von München*, nos. 266, 269; Feierabend, *Ve vládách*, p. 53; see also the despatch of minister Carr of October 21 (*Dept. St.*, 760F.62/1751).

112. Conversation of Göring with Mastný (*DGFP*, IV, no. 67).

113. *České Slovo*, December 14, 1938.

114. *Trials of War Criminals before the Nuremberg Military Tribunal* (Nuremberg, 1946–49), XII, p. 826. (Hereafter quoted as *Trials*).

115. Hájek, *Od Mnichova*, p. 46; František Lukeš, "Dvě tajné cesty Vladimíra Krychtálka do Německa" [Vladimír Krychtálek's Two Secret Trips to Germany] *Dějiny a současnost*, 1962, no. 2 pp. 28–29.

116. Feierabend, *Ve vládách*, pp. 57, 131; Klumpar, *Memoirs*, p. 7.

117. Feierabend, *op. cit.*, p. 78.

118. In Zohor on December 6, in Trnava on Dec. 8 (*Bulletin périodique*, no. 61, pp. 26–27); Klumpar, *Memoirs, p. 7.*

119. Klumpar, Memoirs, p.7.

120. *G. Doc.*, T–120, S. 397. R. 281, fr. 212721.

121. Slávik, "Moja pamäť," *Newyorský Deník*, no. 247, August 26, 1958.

122. *DGFP*, V, no. 111; *G. Doc.*, T-120, S. 140, R. 154, fr. 76230-31; Lukeš, *Podivný mír*, p. 147; Jan Křen, *Do emigrace*, pp. 144-45. Cf. Henryk Batowski, *Kryzys diplomatyczny*, p. 168.

123. *Cz. Doc.*, S. 1809H, R. 1039, fr. 412075.

124. *Le Temps*, November 13, December 17 and 19, 1938; Antoine Mares, "La faillite des relations franco-tchécoslovaques. La mission militaire française à Prague (1926–1938)" *Revue d'histoire de la deuxième guerre mondiale*, 28, no. 111 (July 1978), pp. 44–71.

125. *L'Europe Centrale*, November 12, 1938, p. 706.

126. *Cz. Doc.*, R. 1039, fr. 412080-83.

127. Václav Král, *Otázky hospodářského a sociálního vývoje v českých zemích v letech 1938–1945* [Problems of the Economic and Social Development in the Czech Lands in the Years 1938–1945], vol. II (Prague, 1958), pp. 74–75; Olšovský, *Přehled hospodářského vývoje*, p. 481.

128. See four documents from the archives of the Czechoslovak Foreign Ministry, published by the *Deutsches Nachrichtenbüro* on December 9, 1939, reprinted in *Chronik des Krieges. Dokumente und Berichte*, ed. by Karl Schwarz (Berlin, 1940), p. 194.

129. *DDF*, XI, no. 266; Szembek, *Journal*, p. 398.

130. *Cz. Doc.*, R. 1041, fr. 414186.

131. Ibid., S. 1809H, R. 1039, fr. 412424–27.

132. Ibid., fr. 412062–63.

133. Feierabend, *Ve vládách*, pp. 96–97. Testimony of General Heliodor Pika in Beran's trial in Prague (*Svobodné Noviny*, February 18, 1939).

134. See the text in Wheeler-Bennett, *Munich*, p. 456–57.

135. Ibid., pp. 449–55.

136. *House of Commons Debates*, October 3, 1938, col. 156.

137. Ibid., col. 303.

138. Hodža's statement of September 21, 1938 (*Mnichov v dokumentech*, no. 158). Cf. Beneš's statement on September 30: "Perhaps the guarantees will not be entirely worthless." (Lukeš, *Podivný mír*, p. 29).

139. Chvalkovský to Hencke, October 17, 1938 (*DGFP*, V, no. 74). Feierabend, *Ve vládách*, p. 86.

140. *DBFP*, III, no. 163.

141. *DGFP*, IV, no. 37.

142. Ibid., no. 61.

143. Ibid., no. 114.

144. Ibid., no. 116, 408. Cf. *G. Doc.*, S. 1647H, R. 1004, fr. 591105.

145. *Cz. Doc.*, R. 1039, fr. 412107–8; R. 1040, fr. 412969–70.

146. *DGFP*, IV, no. 136; *DDF*, XII, no. 352.

147. *DBFP*, III, no. 325, pp. 300–306.

148. *DGFP*, IV, no. 370. Coulondre, *De Staline*, p. 225. Georges Bonnet, *Fin d'une Europe*. (Geneva), 1948, pp. 35–42.

149. Communicated by Bonnet to Osuský. Osuský's dispatch, December 9,

1938, *Cz. Doc.*, R. 1039, fr. 412234–37.

150. *DGFP*, IV, no. 370; Král, *Das Abkommen von München*, no. 282.

151. *Le Livre Jaune*, no. 32. Coulondre, *De Staline*, p. 249.

152. On September 19, 1938 (*The Private Papers of Hore-Belisha*, (New York, 1961), p. 142.

153. *Le Livre Jaune*, no. 33.

154. *DBFP*, III, nos. 413, 414.

155. Ibid., no. 408.

156. Ibid., no. 423. *Documents and Mat.*, no. 43.

157. *DGFP*, IV, no. 373. *Le Livre Jaune*, no. 35. Coulondre, *De Staline*, p. 249.

158. *DGFP*, IV, no. 154.

159. *DBFP*, III, no. 496, enclosure.

160. Ibid., no. 500, pp. 527–28. Cf. *Ciano's Diplomatic Papers*, pp. 265–66.

161. *DBFP*, IV, nos. 446, 552.

162. *Le Livre Jaune*, no. 47. The atmosphere in the German capital was not particularly favorable. Two days earlier the French ambassador had had a talk with Ribbentrop. The German minister appeared to be "more violent than usual, wishing doubtless to express thus the stiffening of the German policy." Coulondre describes him in the following terms: "The head thrown back, his lips clipped, he declared once more that it was the lamb who had sullied the water of the river" (*De Staline*, p. 250).

163. *DBFP*, IV, no. 91. By a rather unfortunate coincidence at the very time the staunch opponent of the Munich Agreement, Sir Alfred Duff Cooper, made a speech highly skeptical about the possibility of a guarantee. On February 7 he declared in the House of Commons that no guarantee could be given by any sane government to the frontiers of Czechoslovakia "because the frontiers were where Germany cared to say." These words could be read in the report of *The Times* of London on February 8 on the very day of the French and British demarche.

164. Coulondre, loc. cit.

165. Bonnet, *De Washington*, p. 239.

166. *DBFP*, III, no. 164.

167. Laffan, *Survey of International Affairs 1938*, III, p. 207.

168. *DBFP*, III, no. 325, pp. 300–301.

169. Ibid., no. 408.

170. Fierlinger, *Ve službách ČSR*, I, p. 185; Král, *Das Abkommen v. München*, no. 264.

171. *DGFP*, IV, no. 54.

Notes to Chapter III

1. No monograph based on primary sources and devoted exclusively to this period so far exists. There is only an older study critical of Beck and the western democracies by the Polish historian Henryk Batowski, *Kryzys diplomatyczny w Europie: Jesién 1938–wiosna 1939* [The Diplomatic Crisis in Europe: Autumn 1938–Spring 1939] (Warsaw, 1962). There are several relevant contributions in

two publications of the "Centre National de la Recherche Scientifique": *Les relations franco-britanniques 1935–1939* (Paris, 1975), and *Les relations franco-allemandes 1933–1939* (Paris, 1976). See also Keith Middlemas, *Diplomacy of Illusion. The British Government and Germany 1937–39* (London, 1972), and R. G. D. Laffan, *Survey of International Affairs 1938*, vol. III (London, 1953).

2. At Chvalšiny (Kalsching) on October 20. See Helmuth Grosscurth, *Tagebücher eines Abwehroffiziers 1938–1940* (Stuttgart, 1970), pp. 151–52: *Frankfurter Zeitung*, October 22, 1938; General Walter Warlimont's deposition (DeWitt C. Poole, M–879, roll 3, fr. 0682–83). In his deposition, made after the war, on September 22, 1945, Warlimont mistakenly speaks of December instead of October. Cf. *Führers Tagebuch, 1934–1943*, Reese Collection in the Library of Congress, Washington, D.C., 472E, p. 31.

3. Weizsäcker, *Erinnerungen*, p. 212; *Die Weizsäcker Papiere* (Berlin, 1974), p. 173.

4. Hitler's speech to the press, November 10, 1938 ("Rede Hitlers vor der deutschen Presse," ed. by Wilhelm Treue, *Vierteljahrshefte für Zeitgeschichte*, 6, 1958, p. 185).

5. *DGFP*, II, no. 676.

6. *Le Livre Jaune*, no. 28.

7. Conversation with Oswald Pirow, South African Minister of Defense, Commerce and Industry, *DGFP*, IV, no. 271.

8. *Ciano's Hidden Diary*, November 30, 1938.

9. *Le Livre Jaune*, Annex II, pp. 423–25.

10. *DGFP*, IV, nos. 387, 389; *Le Livre Jaune*, nos. 38, 39; Coulondre, *De Staline*, p. 250; Léon Noël, *L'agression allemande contre la Pologne* (Paris, 1946), pp. 294–95.

11. Georges Bonnet, *Fin d'une Europe. De Munich à la guerre* (Geneva, 1948), p. 101.

12. Chamberlain's letter, December 11, 1938, quoted in Middlemas, *Diplomacy of Illusion*, p. 437.

13. Coulondre to Bonnet, December 15, 1938 (*Le Livre Jaune*, no. 33); DBFP, IV, nos. 5, 40, 77, 98.

14. *DBFP*, IV, no. 109.

15. Ibid., no. 118.

16. *The Times* (London), March 10, 1939.

17. Ibid., March 11, 1939.

18. *DBFP*, IV, no. 165.

19. Václav Král, *Die Deutschen in der Tschechoslowakei*, no. 148.

20. Ibid., no. 239. Cf. Woermann's memorandum of September 19, 1939 (ibid., no. 233).

21. *G. Doc.*, S. 1977H, R. 1081, fr. 439192–97.

22. Král, *Die Deutschen*, no. 261.

23. Ibid., no. 256. In 1940, at the height of the German military successes, the Sudeten-German politicians suggested still more radical measures: abolition of the unity of Bohemia and Moravia and an extreme germanization of the space and its inhabitants (ibid., nos. 313,315).

24. Hitler to Gauleiter Forster, *DBFP*, III, p. 659.

25. Albert Speer, *Erinnerungen* (Berlin, 1968), p. 117. Cf. commentary of François-Poncet in *Le Testament politique de Hitler* (Paris, 1959), p. 184.

26. *Trial of the Major War Criminals before the International Military Tribunal*, vol. XII. (Nuremberg, 1947), p. 531.

27. *Le Testament politique de Hitler*, pp. 118–19. See also Groscurth, *Tagebücher*, p. 133. Cf. Hitler's declaration to the supreme commanders on November 23, 1939 (*Trial of the Major War Criminals*, III, p. 172, XXVI, pp. 327–36).

28. See note 2.

29. André François-Poncet, *Au Palais Farnèse* (Paris, 1961), p. 8.

30. Hassell, *Diaries 1938–44*, p. 9.

31. Jacques Davignon, *Berlin 1936–1940* (Paris, 1951), p. 100.

32. Otto Meissner, *Staatssekretär unter Ebert-Hindenburg-Hitler* (Hamburg, 1950), p. 474.

33. *DGFP*, IV, no. 54.

34. Ibid., no. 55.

35. Ibid., no. 61.

36. Ibid., no. 81.

37. Ibid., no. 152.

38. Woermann's notes for a conference with Chvalkovský, November 25, 1938 (*Trials of War Criminals before the Nuremberg Military Tribunal*, vol. XII, p. 835–39). The text of the proposed treaty ibid., Doc. 116, Woermann defense exhibit 46, pp. 833–34; Weizsäcker, *Erinnerungen*, pp. 212–13; Hencke's deposition, DeWitt C. Poole Mission, M. 679, box 2, p. 11, fr. 0020.

39. *DGFP*, IV, no. 137. Final text of December 3, resp. 9, 1938 (*G. Doc.*, T–120, S. 401, R. 283, fr. 213658–61). In January Hitler saw in an English illustrated magazine a picture of a Czech heavy cannon supposedly produced by the Škoda Works. He immediately ordered Göring to protest in Prague that the Czechoslovak government had given Germany "incorrect information about the state of its armaments." It turned out, however, that the gun in question was but an old Austrian 38cm. cannon which had been under repair at Plzeň since the fall of 1938. The protest was then countermanded (*G. Doc.*, T–120, S. 367H, R. 1801, fr. E03520).

40. Ibid., S. 140, R. 154, fr. 75815–17; S. 401, R. 283, fr. 213665–76.

41. *DGFP*, IV, no. 151.

42. *Frankfurter Zeitung*, January 5, 1939.

43. Ibid., January 19.

44. Ibid., February 15; *Völkischer Beobachter*, February 19, 1939. Cf. *DBFP*, IV, no. 124.

45. *Bulletin périodique*, no. 62, pp. 17–18; *Národní Politika*, January 15 (T.O.); *Lidové Listy*, Jan. 18, 1939 (T.O.); Lukeš, *Podivný mír*, p. 286.

46. *DBFP*, IV, no. 124.

47. Quoted in Lukeš, *op. cit.*, p. 285.

48. *DGFP*, IV, no. 107.

49. Ibid., no. 156.

50. *G. Doc.*, T–120, S. 2313, R. 1279, fr. 484811.

51. *DGFP*, IV, no. 159 (conversation with Ribbentrop), no. 158 (audience with Hitler).

52. As early as December 2, the German chargé d'affaires Hencke reported, however, from Prague that the conduct of the Czech press was generally satisfactory with relatively few exceptions (*G. Doc.*, T–120, S. 1977H, R. 1081, fr. 439223–24).

53. See also *DGFP*, IV, no. 138. Czechoslovakia attempted to secure the revision of the new frontier in the Chod region as early as November 24. On that day Czechoslovak minister Mastný told the head of the division for Austria and Czechoslovakia, Günther Altenburg, what a serious loss the cession of the territory west of Domažlice (Taus) represented for the Czechs. He emphasized that the news of the surrender had a very unfavorable influence on the process of readjustment among the Czech people and that it was uncomprehensible that the Reich was now making demands on genuinly Czech territory, merely in order to simplify problems of traffic.

54. *Hoffen wir das beste* (communicated by Chvalkovský to the author).

55. *DBFP*, IV, no. 6.

56. *Le Livre Jaune*, nos. 45, 48; cf. *DBFP*, IV, no. 188; Lukeš, *Podivný* mír, pp. 230–31.

57. About Tuka see Dérer, *Slovenský vývoj*, pp. 19–88; Jelinek, *The Parish Republic*, pp. 7, 9, 10.

58. Feierabend, *Ve vládách*, pp. 54–55; *Ranní Noviny*, October 24, 1938 (T.O.).

59. *G. Doc.*, T–120, S. 2003H, R. 1141, fr. 442361.

60. When Mastný enquired about Tuka's stay in Germany, he was assured that Tuka had only economic talks with Keppler and that the German authorities did not attribute any particular importance to the visit. But he was not told that Tuka was received by Göring (Altenburg's memorandum, *G. Doc.*, T–120, S. 2002H, R. 1141, fr. 442226).

61. *T.O.*, December 7, 1938; *Lidové Noviny*, January 8, 1939 (T.O.).

62. Ďurčanský's conversation with Druffel on October 10, 1938 (*G. Doc.*, S. 140, R. 154, fr. 75744).

63. Král, *Die Deutschen*, nos. 255, 258, 266; Lukeš, *Podivný mír*, pp. 179–80.

64. *DGFP*, IV, no. 39.

65. Ibid., nos. 45, 46. See also *G. Doc.*, S. 2002H, R. 1141, fr. 442188.

66. *DGFP*, IV, no. 68. Ďurčanský, "Mit Tiso bei Hitler," p. 2.

67. *DGFP*, IV, no. 73.

68. Ibid., no. 112. However, Ďurčanský denied later visiting Göring on that day and affirmed that the German documents confused him with someone else ("Mit Tiso," p. 9). Ribbbentrop declared that he was at the disposition of the Slovak leaders if they needed to discuss their problems with him (dispatch of Woermann, October 21, 1938, *G. Doc.*, S. 2003H, R. 1141, fr. 442193).

69. *DGFP*, IV, no. 120. Nevertheless, Ribbentrop instructed Seyss-Inquart to keep in touch with Tuka without, however, taking up any position or "activating" Tuka (*G. Doc.*, T–120, S. 2003H, R. 1141, fr. 442362).

70. The principal source of information about Hácha's trip is the testimony of Ladislav Feierabend who accompanied the President (*Ve vládách*, pp. 110–19).

71. Záděra, *Deset let parlamentní retrospektivy*, p. 76,

72. Dérer, *Slovenský vývoj*, p. 314. *Slovók*, February 7, 1939.

73. Feierabend, *Ve vládách*, pp. 137–41; Lukeš, *Podivný mír*, pp. 254–55.

74. DeWitt C. Poole, Roll 2, p. 16 of the interrogation (no. of frame illegible).

75. See p. 89.

76. *DGFP*, V, no. 272.

77. Walter Schellenberg, *The Schellenberg Memoirs* (London, 1956), p. 56. Cf. Hencke's note about January 30 as the date of Hitler's decision to support the Slovaks (Hoensch, *Die Slowakei*, p. 131, n. 43).

78. Görlitz, *Generalfeldmarschall Keitel*, p. 199.

79. Lukeš, *op. cit.*, p. 250. *G. Doc.*, T–120, S. 140, R. 154, fr. 76265.

80. *DGFP*, IV, no. 168.

81. *Slovák*, February 22, 1939. Even Tuka found Tiso's declaration satisfactory. In a conversation with the German Consul Druffel he remarked that Tiso differed from the radicals only as far as the timing of the separation from Prague was concerned: whereas the radicals favored the spring 1939, Tiso would consider only the fall. (Druffel's report of February 23, 1939, *G. Doc.*, T–120, S. 2002H, R. 1141, fr. 442243–46.

82. Luciani, "La Tchécoslovaquie après Munich," *Le Temps*, March 2, 1939.

83. *G. Doc.*, T–120, S. 2003H, R. 1141, fr. 442380–84.

84. Druffel about his talk with Tuka on February 23 (see note 81).

85. DeWitt C. Poole, R. 3, p. 6, fr. 0636.

86. Josef M. Kirschbaum's "Doslov" [Postscript] in Karol Sidor, *Moje poznámky k historickým dňom* [My Notes to Historic Days] (Middletown, 1971), pp. 185–86.

87. *Večer*, January 9, 1939 (T.O.); *Naše Doba*, 46 (1939), p. 229.

88. *D. ir.*, III, no. 233; Kennan, *From Prague*, p. 65.

89. Czechoslovak note to Hungary, January 10, 1939 (*G. Doc.*, T–120, S. 28, R. 12. fr. 17730, 17741–44; *D. ir.*, III, nos. 209–209a.

90. *DGFP*, IV, nos. 272, 273.

91. *Ciano's Diary*, January 10, 1939; *D. ir.*, III, no. 201.

92. *G. Doc.*, T–120, S. 140, R. 154, fr.76232, 76243; *D. State*, 7600.62/418. Even the Ukrainian minority in Rumania began to stir. Though professing their loyalty to the Rumanian state, the cautious declarations of their leaders were betraying their admiration for Germany and Hitler and their hope that with the German help the dream of Greater Ukraine would materialize (*Cz. Doc.*, R. 1040, fr. 413007–10, Czechoslovak minister Veverka's report of January 20, 1939).

93. For instance, the Ukrainian demonstrators attacked the Polish consulate at Sevljuš on January 10, 1939, and Prague had to present its excuses to Poland (*A-Zet*, January 16, 1939; *G. Doc.*, T–120, S. 1340, R. 747, fr. 353513–14; *D. State*, 7600.62/434).

94. *České Slovo*, January 18, 1939; Suško, "German Policy towards Slovakia and Carpatho-Ukraine," pp. 147–48.

95. Kennan, *From Prague*, p. 67.

96. *Lidové Noviny*, February 17, 1939 (T.O.). *Dept. St.*, 860F00/597.
97. *České Slovo*, January 25, March 7, 1939.

Notes to Chapter IV

1. Hitler declared: "May Czechoslovakia, too succeed in establishing internal order in a manner which will exclude any possibility of a relapse into the tendencies of former President Dr. Beneš." (*DBFP*, IV, no. 161, editor's note).
2. *Venkov*, December 28, 1938 (T.O.).
3. According to official directives of October 13, 1938 "all news instigating to hatred, envy, vengeance or violence against Jews should be unconditionally suppressed." (Bubeníčková et al., "Tiskové pokyny," p. 130). Prime Minister Beran in his government declaration of December 13 stated that the attitude toward the Jews who had been settled for a long time in Czechoslovakia and who had a positive attitude to the necessities of the state "would not be hostile." (*České Slovo*, December 14, 1938). Streicher's anti-Semitic weekly *Der Stürmer* was banned in Czechoslovakia as late as February 1939 (*Našinec*, February 21, 1939).
4. *Sb. zákonů a nařízení, issue 11, no. 20*; Helešicová-Machotková, "Tiskové pokyny," nos. 46, 48.
5. *DGFP*, IV, no. 161.
6. Walter Hagemann, *Publizistik im Dritten Reich* (Hamburg, 1948), pp. 378–79.
7. The text of the undated proposal in Král, *Die Deutschen*, no. 272; Lukeš, *Podivný mír*, pp. 286–87; Havelka's letter to Mr. Schubert, February 25, 1939.
8. *G. Doc.*, T-120, S. 1957H, R. 1078, fr. 43127–41.
9. Lukeš, *op. cit.*, p. 287.
10. According to Mr. Schubert's information (his letter to Havelka, March 7, 1939).
11. For instance Vlastimil Kybal in Mexico (*G. Doc.*, T-120, S. 2370, R. 1307, fr. 495394–96).
12. *DGFP*, IV, no. 161; *G. Doc.*, T-120, S. 1977H, R. 1081, fr. 439200; S. 3109, R. 1501, fr. 629576–83; S. 28, R. 12, fr. 17703, 18089.
13. Georges Luciani, "La Tchécoslovaquie après Munich," *Le Temps*, February 26, 1939.
14. *Cz. Doc.*, R. 1040, fr. 412714–23.
15. *G. Doc.*, T-120, S. 1613H, R. 916, fr. 387271–75; *Mnichov v dokumentech*, no. 251; *DGFP*, IV, nos. 170, 201; Leopold Chmela, *The Economic Aspects of the German Occupation of Czechoslovakia* (Prague, 1948), pp. 56–57.
16. *DBFP*, IV, no. 63 with the text of the agreement.
17. *DGFP*, IV, nos. 172–73.
18. *DBFP*, IV, no. 188.
19. *Le Livre Jaune*, no. 65; *DBFP*, IV, no. 230, n. 4. Cf. similar information in the Hungarian documents (*D. ir.*, III, nos. 220, 301).
20. *Die Weizsäcker Papiere*, pp. 149–50.

21. Herbert von Dirksen, *Moskau, Tokio, London* (Stuttgart, 1949), p. 240.

22. Král, *Die Deutschen*, no. 246.

23. *Venkov*, January 27, 1939 (T.O.).

24. *Bulletin périodique*, 62, pp. 2–3.

25. Ripka's letters of February 10 and 19, 1939, quoted in Hájek, *Od Mnichova*, p. 111.

26. *Memoirs of Dr. Eduard Beneš*, pp. 54–57.

27. *DGFP*, IV, no. 169.

28. *DBFP*, IV, no. 126.

29. Ibid., nos. 134, 138; Král, *Das Abkommen von München*, no. 296.

30. *DGFP*, IV, no. 171.

31. Ibid., no. 176.

32. Ibid., no. 166.

33. Communicated to the author by Arnošt Heidrich.

34. Letters exchanged between Miroslav Schubert (Berlin, February 24, March 7, 1939) and Jiří Havelka (Prague, Feb. 25, 1939).

35. Schubert's letter quoted in Feierabend, *Ve vládách*, p. 181.

36. Henry Delfiner, *Vienna Broadcasts to Slovakia 1938–1939* (New York, London, 1974), p. 15.

37. In the evening Altenburg invited Masařík to dinner. The Czech then made a mistake. Forgetting that his former colleague from Sofia had transformed himself into a supporter of the official policy of the Third Reich, he told him some anecdotes about Hitler. Altenburg reported this to Weizsäcker (communicated to the author by Mr. Schubert. Cf. his letter of May 18, 1956, quoted in Feierabend, *Ve vládách*, pp. 181–87).

38. *DGFP*, IV, no. 177.

39. *G. Doc.*, T–120, S. 1647H, R. 1004, fr. 391289–93.

40. František Lukeš, "Dvě tajné cesty Vladimíra Krychtálka do Německa [Two Secret Journeys of Vladimír Krychtálek to Germany] *Dějiny a současnost*, 4 (1962), no. 2, p. 29; Lukeš, *Podivný mír*, p. 290. At the same time Beran tried to improve the relations with Berlin by establishing contacts with the German National Socialist Party to which he wanted to send a delegation consisting of the members of the National Unity Party, "entirely remote from the political line of the now completely overriden regime" (his letter of February 14, 1939, to the *NSDAP* in Berlin, *G. Doc.*, T–120, S. 3109, R. 1501, fr. D629701–03).

41. *DGFP*, IV, no. 177, n. 1.

42. Ibid., no. 175.

43. Ibid., no. 178. Mastný would have liked to present Masařík to Weizsäcker, as he was also in the building, but Weizsäcker refused with a remark that he could not receive a man who was circulating anecdotes about the Führer (communicated to the author by Mr. Schubert). It was Masařík who brought the news of the German answer to Franco-British demarche to Prague.

44. *DGFP*, IV, no. 185. See communication of Mr. Schubert, published in Feierabend, *Ve vládách*, pp. 188–96. As early as January 12, Chvalkovský drew the attention of the German chargé d'affaires to the fact that a whispering propaganda campaign, evidently emanating from the Sudeten German party, was

spreading the rumor that the incorporation of Czechoslovakia in the Reich was imminent (*DGFP*, IV, no. 155).

45. "Výstava dokumentů, která poučuje a varuje"[The Exhibition of Documents Which Enlightens and Warns] *Svobodné Slovo*, March 15, 1959. See also Paul Stehlin, *Témoignage pour l'histoire* (Paris, 1964), p. 136.

46. Schubert's letter in Feierabend, *Ve vládách*, p. 195.

47. L'ubomír Lipták, "Autonómia slovenskej krajiny," pp. 61–63; *Venkov*, February 7, 1939 (T.O.); *A-Zet*, Feb. 8, 1939 (T.O.); *Lidové Noviny*, March 1, 1939; *DGFP*, IV, no. 180.

48. Feierabend, *Ve vládách*, p. 144; Sidor, *Moje poznámky*, pp. 56–60.

49. The letter by which Pružinský announced the journey to Chvalkovský was dated February 24, but the minister received it only on March 1, when the Slovaks were already in Germany (*Karol Sidor o vzniku slovenského státu* [Karol Sidor on the Origins of the Slovak State], Bratislava, 1945, p. 9).

50. Ibid. Cf. Sidor, *Moje poznámky*, p. 67; Lukeš, *Podivný mír*, p. 258; Ďurčanský, "Mit Tiso bei Hitler," p. 5; Göring greeted the Slovaks with a heavy-handed geniality: "Now then, when are you going to be independent so that we don't have to give you to the Magyars?" (Testimony of Jozef Tiso before the National Tribunal in Bratislava, on December 4, 1946, quoted in Lettrich, *History of Modern Slovakia*, p. 105).

51. Dérer, *Slovenský vývoj*, p. 320.

52. Sidor, *Moje poznámky*, p. 67.

53. Ibid., p. 71. *České Slovo*, March 8, 1939.

54. Ripka, *Munich, p. 362.*

55. *Feierabend, Ve vládách*, p. 145.

56. *Venkov*, March 8, 1939.

57. Ripka, *op. cit.*, p. 363.

58. Ibid.

59. *G. Doc.*, *T*–120, S. 140, R. 154, fr. 76372.

60. "Z memoárových statí Pal'a Čarnogurského" [From Pal'o Čarnogurský's Memoirs], ed. by František Lukeš, *Slovanský Přehled*, 54 (1968), pp. 509–11; Lukeš, *Podivný mír*, pp. 252, 259–60, 266; Hoensch, *Die Slowakei*, pp. 244, 247–48; *DBFP*, IV, no. 186.

61. *DGFP*, V, no. 139; Lukeš, *op. cit.*, p. 266; Hoensch, *op. cit.*, p. 300, n. 103.

62. Sidor, *Moje poznámky*, pp. 73–75; Murgaš, *Národ medzi Dunajom*, p. 114. Seyss-Inquart's deposition (*Trial of the Major War Criminals*, vol. XV, p. 637) has no mention of a meeting at Bruck, nor is there any other document dealing with this alleged episode. During his trial after the war Tiso denied this allegation (Jozef Paučo, *Dr. Tiso o sobe* [Dr. J. Tiso about himself], Middletown, Pa., 1952, pp. 179–80). It is, however, hard not to give credence to the testimony of the two Slovaks, Sidor and Murgaš.

63. Feierabend, *Ve vládách*, pp. 145–49; Sidor, *Moje poznámky*, pp. 81–84.

64. *DGFP*, IV, no. 181.

65. Ibid., no. 184.

66. The official text of Hácha's decrees and broadcast declarations of March 10 in *České Slovo*, March 11, 1939; see also *DBFP*, IV, no. 198.

67. Feierabend, *Ve vládách*, p. 156; According to Ďurčanský's emissary V.

Kovár (as quoted in Lukeš, *Podivný mír*, p. 274) it was Ďurčanský who convinced Sivák to decline the offer.

68. *G. Doc.*, T-120, S. 2002H, R. 1141, fr. 442257.

69. Ibid., S. 28, R. 12, fr. 17637-38; S. 2002H, R. 1141, fr. 442254; *DGFP*, IV, no. 186.

70. *Frankfurter Zeitung*, March 11, 1939; *G. Doc.*, T-120, S. 1532H, R. 777, fr. 374320; S. 140, R. 154, fr. 76353, 76372.

71. Sidor, *Moje poznámky*, p. 110.

72. Ibid., pp. 103-104.

73. Ibid., pp. 113, 123; *Lidové Noviny*, March 12, 1939 (T.O.).

74. Graca, *14. marec*, p. 107, quotes the material of the Slovak General Ferdinand Čatloš. Cf. Sidor, *Moje poznámky*, pp. 114, 140.

75. Sidor, *op. cit.*, pp. 115-16.

76. *G. Doc.*, T-120, S. 140, R. 154, fr. 76391-93.

77. Sidor, *Moje poznámky*, pp. 126, 131, n. 67; *DGFP*, VI, p. 251. No such telegram from Ďurčanský to Hitler has been found (cf. *DGFP*, VI, no. 205, n. 4), but according to Göring (ibid., p. 251) it had been sent. The editor of Sidor's *Poznámky*, František Vnuk, discusses the history of the telegram on the basis of the unpublished notes of one of Ďurčanský's emissaries to Sidor, Vilo Kovár (*op. cit.*, p. 130, n. 67). See also Josef M. Kirschbaum, "Facts and Events behind the Scenes of Slovakia's Declaration of Independence," *Slovakia*, 9 (1959), p. 5.

78. Text in Sidor, *op. cit.*, pp. 123-25.

79. In the evening of March 11 (*G. Doc.*, T-120, S. 2383H, R. 1320, fr. D499697-98). See also Keppler's testimony in *Trials of War Criminals*, vol. XII, pp. 967-68.

80. Karol Murgaš, *Národ medzi Dunajom a Karpatmi* [The Nation between the Danube and the Carpathians] (Bratislava, 1940), p. 143; Sidor, *Moje poznámky*, p. 128.

81. *Völkischer Beobachter*, March 13, 1939; Sidor, *op. cit.*, p. 146, n. 75.

82. Keppler's testimony, *Trials of War Criminals*, vol. XII, pp. 969-70.

83. Ibid.; *DGFP*, IV, no. 193.

84. Before Dafčík's arrival Tiso got two invitations to Berlin communicated by Ďurčanský's emissaries. He accepted only the third one which had been brought by Dafčík and had the official confirmation by the German consulate (Sidor, *op. cit.*, pp. 148, 159, n. 78).

85. Ibid., pp. 148-49.

86. The details of this conversation with Ribbentrop are contained in Tiso's declaration in the Slovak Diet of March 14. The English translation in Josef M. Kirschbaum, *Slovakia, Nation at the Crossroads of Central Europe* (New York, 1960), pp. 258-59.

87. *DGFP*, IV, no. 202. For Tiso's version see Sidor, *op. cit.*, pp. 169-73. The English text in Kirschbaum, *op. cit.*, pp. 259-62. Sidor, "Ako došlo k vyhlaseniu S.R." [How the Slovak Republic Was Proclaimed], *Slovenská Republika 1939-1949* [The Slovak Republic 1939-1949] (Scranton, Pa., 1949), p. 55.

88. Sidor, *op. cit.*, pp. 157, 159.

89. Ďurčanský, "Mit Tiso bei Hitler," p. 8; *DGFP*, IV, no. 209; Fritz Sänger,

Politik der Täuschungen. Missbrauch der Presse im Dritten Reich. Weisungen, Information, Notizen 1933–1939 (Vienna, 1975), pp. 290, 292; Vnuk, *Slovakia's Six Eventful Months*, p. 118.

90. Sidor, *op. cit.*, pp. 164–68.

91. *Slovák*, March 15, 1939.

92. Lukeš, *Podivný mír*, p. 280.

93. Gromada, "The Slovak Question," p. 262.

94. *DGFP*, IV, no. 10.

95. *DGFP*, IV, no. 221; *Trials of War Criminals*, vol. 12, exhibit 3535, p. 866; *G. Doc.*, T–120, S. 401, R. 283, fr. 213383; *DBFP*, IV, no. 300. At the same time the Hungarian troops invaded eastern Slovakia and with German connivance attached to Ruthenia an area of 1,697 square kilometers with 69,639 inhabitants (26,981 Slovaks, 37,786 Ruthenes). See Vnuk, "Slovakia's Six Eventful Months," pp. 130–49.

96. *DGFP*, VI, no. 40. This delay may be explained by the German hope that an understanding with Poland was still possible in which case the Slovak problem could be raised as a part of a general settlement (*Les relations polono-allemandes*, no. 63). Cf. Vnuk, "Slovakia's Six Eventful Months," p. 127; Ďurčanský, *Právo Slovákov na samostatnosť*, pp. 195–200.

97. *DGFP*, no. 181; *G. Doc.*, T–120, S. 1969, R. 1081, fr. 437903–04; *D. ir.*, III, no. 390. After the formation of the Teleki government in February 1939 a new trait appeared in the Hungarian argumentation. Probably on the initiative of the new Prime Minister, a distinguished geographer, Hungary began to point out the alleged ruthless deforestation carried out by the new Carpatho-Ukrainian government which could have unfavorable effect on the water level of the rivers flowing from the Carpathians to the Hungarian plain. Though the Hungarian consul in Bratislava argued that the deforestation had not yet reached any larger proportions the argument was repeated everywhere to support the Hungarian claims and it was used by Vörnle in his talk with Chvalkovský (communicated to the author by Chvalkovský). Cf. *Allianz Hitler—Horthy—Mussolini*, no. 52; *D. ir.*, III, nos. 385, 386.

98. *G. Doc.*, T–120, S. 140, R. 154, fr. 76364–67.

99. Altenburg's note published by Milan S. Ďurica, *La Slovacchia e le sue relazioni con la Germania 1938–1945*, Padova, 1964, pp. 176–77; *D. ir.*, III, no. 413; Lukeš, *Podivný mír*, pp. 245–46; Hoensch, "Účast Telekiho vlády na rozbití Československa" [The Share of Teleki's Government in the Breaking-up of Czechoslovakia] *Československý časopis historický*, 17 (1969), p. 360.

100. *DGFP*, IV, no. 198.

101. Ibid., no. 199.

102. Ibid., no. 205.

103. Ibid., no. 214.

104. *The Ciano Diaries*, March 14, 1939.

105. *DBFP*, IV, nos. 243, 255; *DGFP*, IV, no. 217; *D. ir., III, nos. 423, 434.*

106. DGFP, IV, no. 210.

107. *G. Doc.*, T–120, S. 7587H, R. 3214, fr. 543255. Vološyn's further telegram asking for "the strong protection of the Reich" reached Berlin before midnight

(ibid., S. 140, R. 154, fr. 76480; cf. *DGFP*, IV, no. 210, n. 3). The third telegram sent by Vološyn to Ribbentrop was received in Berlin in the afternoon of March 15 (ibid., no. 236).

108. Záděra, *Deset let*, p. 90.

109. Vincent Shandor, "Carpatho-Ukraine in the International Bargaining of 1919–1939," *The Ukrainian Quarterly*, 10 (1954), p. 246.

110. *DGFP*, IV, no. 237.

111. Ibid., no. 243.

112. *D. ir.*, III, nos. 439, 445; *G. Doc.*, T–120, S. 401, R. 283, fr. 13404–05.

113. Ota Holub, "Boje československé armády a jednotek Stráže obrany státu na Podkarpatské Rusi (Karpatské Ukrajině) v březnu 1939" [The Engagements of the Czechoslovak Army and the Units of the Guard for the Defense of the State in Subcarpathian Ruthenia (Carpatho-Ukraine) in March 1939] *Odboj a revoluce*, 7 (1969), no. 5. pp. 65–71; *G. Doc.*, T–120, S. 1969H, R. 1081, fr. 437937; *Czas*, March 17, 1939.

114. Szembek, *Journal*, p. 425; *D. ir.*, III, nos. 450, 452, 453, 459. Cf. *DGFP*, IV, no. 240.

115. *DGFP*, IV, no. 243; *D. ir.*, III, nos. 471–72, 475, 477.

116. *DGFP*, IV, no. 294; *G. Doc.*, S. 2313, R. 1279, fr. 484483; *D. ir.*, III, nos. 482, 494.

117. Vasyl Markus, "Carpatho-Ukraine under Hungarian Occupation (1939–1944)," Carpatho-Ukrainian Quarterly, 10 (1954), no. 3, pp. 252–53.

118. *Trial of Major War Criminals*, IX, pp. 302–303. Göring omitted to indicate the date of Hitler's letter. He testified further that in his answer he tried to dissuade Hitler from such a radical step. For several days he heard nothing from Berlin, but then was recalled on a very short notice. According to newspaper reports he arrived in San Remo on March 5 (*The New York Times*, March 6, 1939) and left in the afternoon of March 13 (*Le Temps*, March 15, 1939). Cf. Paul Stehlin, *Témoignage pour l'histoire*, p. 136.

119. Král, *Das Abkommen von München*, no. 314. Chvalkovský, in his talks with this author, pointed out that according to his information the leading German circles themselves were surprised by the suddenness of Hitler's action. Even though Chvalkovský might have tried to shift from his shoulders the blame for the lack of perspicacity on the part of the Prague government, there is no doubt that there was a large amount of improvisation in Berlin.

120. *Records of Headquarters, German Army High Command*, T–78, S. 269, R.301, fr. 6252056–78.

121. See p. 90.

122. Burkhart Mueller-Hillebrand, *Das Heer 1933–1945; Entwicklung des organisatorischen Aufbaues*, vol. I, *Das Heer bis zum Kriegsbeginn* (Darmstadt, 1954), p. 64.

123. Keitel to the Foreign Ministry, March 11, 1939, *DGFP*, IV, no. 188.

124. *Records of Headquarters. German Armed Forces High Command*, T–77, R. 820, fr. 5555375–78.

125. The telegram was published by Král, *Die Deutschen*, no. 279, p. 380. It has no date. The editor places in on March 14. This author thinks the telegram

could have been drafted one or two days earlier.

126. *G. Doc.*, T–120, S. 1941H, R. 1077, fr. 435188–90. From the first days of March originate the undated studies worked out by the researchers of the Foreign Affairs Institute (*Deutsches Auslandswissenschaftliches Institut*, a part of the Berlin *Hochschule für Politik*) on the suggestion of Walter Hewel and P. O. Schmidt from the Foreign Ministry. The experts were ordered to present arguments for the institution of a protectorate over the Czech lands (Lukeš, *Podivný mír*, p. 304).

127. *Le Livre Jaune*, no. 55.

128. *DBFP*, IV, nos. 214, 236.

129. *Dept. St.*, 860F.00/612, 619, 818.

130. *Failure of a Mission* (New York, 1940), p. 214. Cf. *The Chicago Tribune*, March 14, 1939, announcing in a dispatch from Berlin that Czechoslovakia would be divided into three "independent" states.

131. *Le Livre Jaune*, no. 56.

132. *Master of Spies. The Memoirs of General Moravec* (London, 1975), pp. 151–54; Emil Strankmüller, "Československé ofensivní zpravodajství v letech 1937 do 15. března 1939" [The Czechoslovak Intelligence Service from 1937 until March 15, 1939] *Odboj a revoluce*, 6 (1968), no. 2, p. 65. There is a disagreement between Moravec's and Strankmüller's version as to the date of this information. According to Moravec, it reached Prague as early as March 3. Strankmüller speaks of March 11. General Moravec himself testified on February 18, 1947 (*Svobodné Noviny*, Feb. 19, 1947) that he received Thümmel's information "between March 10 and 12." Strankmüller's version seems to be the correct one.

133. Sänger, *Politik der Täuschungen*, pp. 290, 292.

134. Ernest K. Bramsted, *Goebbels and National Socialist Propaganda, 1925–1945* (East Lansing, Mich., 1965), p. 179. Cf. Hans Fritzsche's deposition in Nuremberg, *Trial of the Major War Criminals*, XXXII, pp. 319–20.

135. Král, *Die Deutschen*, no. 272a.

136. Hencke to the foreign ministry, March 13, 1939, *DGFP*, IV, no. 197. In Prague the German students attempted to stage anti-Czech demonstrations in the evening of March 12. The most serious skirmishes took place in the region of Jihlava and Brno (Hájek, *Od Mnichova*, p. 142; *Mnichov v dokumentech*, nos. 260–61). See also Luža, *The Transfer*, p. 175.

137. *G. Doc.*, T–120, S. 2370, R. 1307, fr. D495402; S. 28, R. 12, fr. 17609.

138. The Consul at Brno to the Foreign Ministry, *DGFP*, IV, no. 195.

139. Ibid., no. 208.

140. Ladislav Klumpar, *Memoirs* (manuscript), chapter II, p. 20; Klumpar, "Ukvapený úsudek" [A Hasty Conclusion] *Proměny*, 11, no. 4 (October 1974), p. 37; Lukeš, "Příspěvek k objasnění politiky české a německé buržoasie v předvečer 15. března" [A Contribution to the Explanation of the Policy of the Czech and German Bourgeoisie on the Eve of March 15]*Časopis Národního musea*, Social Sciences Series, 130 (1961), pp 65–66. Testimony of General Bohuslav Fiala in Beran's process, February 18, 1947 (*Svobodné Noviny*, Feb. 19, 1947). This is probably the basis of Chvalkovský's statement to the author that he originally intended to go to Berlin alone. About the genesis of Hácha's journey see Havelka's

testimony, February 5, 1947 (*Svobodné Noviny*, February 6, 1947). It was confirmed by Mr. Schubert, Havelka's brother-in-law (letter to this author, June 21, 1971). The same information was communicated to the author by Chvalkovský.

141. *Memoirs of Dr. Eduard Beneš*, pp. 96–97.

142. Deposition of minister Ludvík Krejčí, April 29, 1947; *Rudolf Beran před Národním soudem*, p. 15; Klumpar, "Ukvapený úsudek," p. 38.

143. Communicated to the author by Chvalkovský. Hencke's telephone conversations with Berlin were monitored by the Czechs. *G. Doc.*, T–120, S. 3100, R. 1502, fr. D630837.

144. Hencke to the Foreign Ministry, *DGFP*, IV, no. 204, n. 1, 206, 207. See also *G. Doc.*, T–120, S. 1613H, R. 916, fr. 387214.

145. *Trial of Major War Criminals*, X, p. 342.

146. Ribbentrop to the German legation in Prague, *DGFP*, IV, no. 204.

147. Hencke to the Foreign Ministry, ibid., no. 216.

148. At 12:25 A.M. Hencke to the Foreign Ministry, *G. Doc.*, T–120, S. 3110, R. 1502, fr. D630830; S. 28, R. 12, fr. 17598.

149. Cf. Walter Hagen, *Die geheime Front*, p. 177.

150. Memorandum, *G. Doc.*, T–120, S. 3110, R. 1502, fr. D630829.

151. Memorandum of Weizsäcker's secretariat, ibid., fr. D630831; DGFP, IV, no. 223.

152. *Le Livre Jaune*, Coulondre to Bonnet, nos. 56, 66. The American Embassy in Berlin reported the imminent invasion at 5:00 P.M. The dispatch stated that the German troops from Breslau, Dresden, and Leipzig areas would enter the Czech territory on Wednesday morning, at 8:00 (*Dept. St.* 860F.00/619).

153. Ludvík Jehl, "Pohřeb první třídy" [A Funeral of the First Class] *Svět práce*, March 17, 1969; Arnošt Bareš and Antonín Pasák, "Odbojová organizace Zdeňka Schmoranze v roce 1939" [The Resistance Organization of Zdeněk Schmoranz in 1939] *Historie a vojenství*, 1968, no. 6–7, p. 1007.

154. This information was telephoned from Berlin at 12:10 P.M. (*Cz. Doc.*, R. 1041, fr. 414192). Almost simultaneously Prague had a report from Chemnitz according to which German motorized army units were being transferred since Sunday to Dresden and farther east. The dispatch arrived in Prague at 1:30 P.M. on March 14, and was processed 15 minutes later (*Cz. Doc.*, T–120, S. 2376H, R. 1316, fr. D497045).

155. Havelka's testimony, February 5, 1947 (*Svobodné Noviny*, Feb. 6, 1947). Cf. Hájek, *Od Mnichova*, p. 186; Lukeš, *Podivný mír*, p. 306.

156. *Beran před Národním soudem*, p. 15; *Memoirs* of Dr. Ladislav Klumpar, manuscript, p. 21.

157. Feierabend, *Ve vládách*, p. 166.

158. Kennan, *From Prague After Munich*, p. 83.

159. *Mnichov v dokumentech*, no. 264; *G. Doc.*, T–120, S. 3110, R. 1502, fr. D630782–85.

160. *Memoirs of Dr. Eduard Beneš*, p. 58. See also fr. 630785 in *G. Doc.* quoted in note 159; ibid., S. 2050, R. 1094, fr. 447301.

161. *Records of Headquarters, German Army High Command*, T–78, S. 269, R. 301, fr. 6252074.

162. Beran's testimony, February 3, 1947 (*Svobodné Noviny*, Feb. 4, 1947); cf. note 168.

163. See Göring's remark to Henderson on May 27, 1939, that Germany wanted simply to forestall a Polish occupation of that area (*The British Blue Book*, no. 12). Cf. Keitel's testimony (*Trials of War Criminals*, XII, p. 877): "Hitler had told me that it was done in order to prevent the Poles from making a surprise attack from the north and thereby taking possession of the most modern rolling mill in the world."

164. Ribbentrop, *Zwischen London und Moskau*, p. 150.

165. Communicated by Chvalkovský to the author. According to Hitler's interpreter Paul Schmidt the reason why Hácha was kept waiting was that the German plans for occupation may have still been under consideration, or the agreement which Hácha was to sign may not have been completed (*DeWitt C. Poole Mission*, M 679, R. 3, 0223). Keitel explained this delay simply by Hitler's wish that the old man should repose himself after the journey (Görlitz, *Generalfeldmarschal Keitel*, p. 200). Mrs. Milada Rádlová, the daughter of the President, was after the arrival an object of rather painful attention. State Minister Meissner presented her with a box of candies and Hitler sent her a bouquet (Hácha's memorandum, *Mnichov v dokumentech*, no. 266).

166. Ribbentrop's version of the conversation in *Trial of the Major War Criminals*, X, p. 257.

167. Hewel's minutes in *DGFP*, IV, no. 228; Hácha's report, *Mnichov v dokumentech*, no. 266; Görlitz, *Generalfeldmarschal Keitel*, pp. 199–203; Schmidt, *Hitler's Interpreter*, pp. 122–26; Meissner, *Staatssekretär*, pp. 477–79; cf. Keppler's deposition, *DeWitt C. Poole*, R. 2, pp. 18–19.

168. Deposition of Mrs. Rádlová, *Trials of War Criminals*, XII, p. 905. When Mastný asked State Minister Meissner about this incident, the German official denied it. Weizsäcker was, however, not so positive. On Hácha's order, Mastný then reported to Prague that Germany was denying the news (Tomáš Pasák, "Vstup německých vojsk na české území v roce 1939" [Entry of German Troops into Czech Territory in 1939] *Československý časopis historický*, 17 (1969), p. 166.

169. Henry Picker, *Hitlers Tischgespräche in Führerhauptquartier 1941–1942*, p. 363.

170. Görlitz, *Generalfeldmarschal Keitel*, p. 200.

171. This insistence on the scope of the Czechoslovak army led Hácha and Chvalkovský to believe that the measure was taken under the pressure of the German military circles and that after their demilitarization the Czech lands would be able to lead a relatively independent life (communicated by Chvalkovský to the author).

172. Meissner, *Staatssekretär*, p. 477.

173. *DGFP*, IV, no. 229, enclosure 2.

174. Beran's testimony, February 3, 1947 (*Svobodné Noviny*, Feb. 4, 1947); Hájek, *Od Mnichova*, p. 151; Klumpar, *Memoirs*, p. 22; In Prague the Council of Ministers assembled shortly after 3:00 A.M. Although they had tendered demission before Hácha set out on his journey to Berlin, the ministers remained in of-

fice to take care of current affairs.

175. The German text in Hácha's report. Cf. Göring's declaration to ambassador Henderson on May 27, 1939 (*The British Blue Book,* no. 12). The threat—even in this form—would have been difficult to carry out, for there were severe snowstorms on March 15. It seems that Hitler would not have been averse to some air demonstration. In a rather inaccurate way—for him not unusual—he reminisced about it a few years later. Had the Czechs not accepted his proposals, German aircraft would have appeared over Prague. However, he had to concede: "I would have irremediably lost face if I had to put this threat into execution for at the hour mentioned fog was so thick over our airfields that none of our aircraft could have made its sortie." (*Hitler's Secret Conversations,* January 13, 1942, p. 168).

176. *DGFP,* IV, no. 229.

177. Communicated to the author by Mr. Miroslav Schubert. See also his article "Konec Druhé republiky" [The End of the Second Republic], *Naše Hlasy,* Toronto, March 14, 1964.

178. These details are for the major part contained in the testimonies of the accused and witnesses of the Beran trial: especially the testimony of Beran on February 3, 1947, of Syrový of February 4, of General Fiala of February 18, and Minister Krejčí of April 29, 1947.

In the German documents (*DGFP,* IV, no. 229), the declaration is followed by two enclosures. The second enclosure represets the ultimatum which Hitler submitted to the Czechs. In the first one, Hácha and Chvalkovský take congizance of the demands of the ultimatum (or memorandum as it was metaphorically named in the offical style). These two documents had probably been prepared in advance. It seems that they had been submitted to the Czech visitors first and only when Hácha and Chvalkovský had accepted them was the widely publicized declaration about placing the fate of the Czech people in Hitler's hands improvised. According to Mr. Schubert, the Germans united for formal, administrative reasons all three documents into a unit as it appears in the final edition of the Geman documents.

About Hácha's three telephone conversations with Prague see also Beran's written testimony of June 11, 1946 (*Národní Osvobození,* June 12, 1946). According to this version Hácha declared: "All my efforts have been in vain. I am sacrificing myself and if I cannot save the State, I will save at least the people." At one moment, when telephoning to Prague, Hácha did not feel well. Hitler's doctor was called and administered an injection of glucose (Communicated to the author by Chvalkovský).

179. Communicated to the author by Mr. Schubert.

180. *Le Livre Jaune,* no. 77.

181. Schubert, "Konec Druhé republiky", see note 177.

182. Görlitz, *Generalfeldmarschal Keitel,* p. 202. According to the Quartermaster-General of the German Army, General Eduard Wagner, the order was issued earlier, at 6:00 P.M. on March 14 (Wagner, "Die Besetzung der Tschechoslowakei," *Politische Studien,* 14, Sept.-Oct. 1963, p. 582).

183. Sänger, *Politik der Täuschungen,* p. 299; Jürgen Hagemann, *Die*

Presseleitung im Dritten Reich, p. 384.

184. *The Chicago Tribune*, March 15, 1939.

185. Beran had all the records of the cabinet proceedings transported to his native village of Pracejovice in southern Bohemia where they were buried in the barn of a farmer and only after the war were returned to the authorities (*Beran před Národním soudem*, p. 40).

186. "Praha, ráno 15. března 1939" [Prague on the Morning of March 15, 1939] *Přítomnost*, XVI, March 22, 1939, pp. 185–86.

187. *Records of Headquarters, German Army High Command*, T-77, S. 733, fr. 1959726–43; S. 734, R. 734, fr. 1961379–80. Erich Wagner, "Die Besetzung," p. 581.

188. *Národní Noviny*, March 16, 1939 (T.O.).

189. Moravec, *Master of Spies*, pp. 158–61; Strankmüller, "Ofensivní zpravodajství," pp. 69–73.

190. *German Army High Command*, T-77, S. 734, R. 734, fr. 1961368–70, 1961373–75

191. *České Slovo*, March 16, 1939.

192. Havelka's testimony, February 5, 1947 (*Svobodné Noviny*, Feb., 6, 1947).

193. Communicated by Chvalkovský to the author. Cf. also the statement of General Alois Eliáš, the Minister of the Railroads: "We believed that we would become a similar small state like Slovakia. It occurred to nobody that it could turn out like this" (Feierabend, *Ve vládě Protektorátu* [In the Government of the Protectorate] New York, 1962, p. 12). In the same vein *Beran před Národním soudem*, p. 41.

194. The Germans did not allow a Czech guard of honor (*G. Doc.*, T-120, S. 3110, R. 1502, fr. D630822).

195. Testimony of Beran, February 5, 1947 (Report of the Czechoslovak Press Agency).

196. Albert Speer, *Erinnerungen* (Berlin, 1970), p. 538. Cf. General Rudolf Schmundt's directive of March 15: "The Führer wishes to stay in the castle" (*Der Führer wünscht in der Burg zu wohnen*), *G. Doc.*, T-120, S. 3110, R. 1502, fr. 630802.

197. Ernst Frank, *Karl Hermann Frank, Staatsminister im Protektorat* (Heisenstamm b. Offenbach, 1976), pp. 75–76. *Přehled denního tisku pražského* [Survey of the Prague Daily Press] March 16, 1939.

198. Communicated to the author by Chvalkovský. The administrative office of the Prague castle, the President's residence, had been asked in the morning to place some rooms at the German disposal. At that time it seemed, however, that the bedrooms were to be used by a German commanding general (Klumpar, *Memoirs*, p. 24).

199. Even this visit to Prague was improvised. The visitors had brought no food, and hastily they ordered a cold dinner from a Prague delicatessen. Keitel (op. cit., p. 203) enumerates the courses: "cold Prague ham, rolls, butter, cheese, fruit and Pilsener beer." Hitler in his euphoria forgot his teetotalism and it was the only time Keitel saw him drink beer. The other members of the suite greatly enjoyed the famous beverage: "...uns schmeckte es ausgezeichnet, " says Keitel.

Amid the political projects connected with the occupation of Bohemia and Moravia Hitler was not forgetting his repressed artistic inclinations. Late in the evening, after his arrival, he made a tour of the old parts of the city which owing to the curfew was deserted. Prime Minister Beran, returning from the meeting with President Hácha, saw Hitler inspecting the neo-renaissance building of the Parliament (the former "Rudolfinum," the House of the Arts, with a concert hall and a picture gallery) (Beran's testimony, February 5, 1947, report of the Cz. Press Agency). When K.H. Frank called on Hitler next morning, on March 15, 1939, he found him standing by the window fascinated by the view of the city stretching below the castle of Hradčany. He immediately expounded to Frank his plans to build on the opposite hill of Petřín a colossal monument commemorating the incorporation of the Czech lands into the Reich (*Zpověď K.H. Franka*, p. 55; Ernst Frank, *Karl Hermann Frank*, p. 76).

200. See below, p. 147.

201. Deposition of Lammers, *Trials of War Criminals*, XII, pp. 986–87, 995; cf. Schubert, "Konec Druhé republiky."

202. *DGFP*, IV, no. 246. According to Lammers as told later to Chvalkovský, Hitler did not like this term because it was not a German word. But it expressed the notion of protection and Hitler eventually accepted the word though un-German (communicated by Chvalkovský to the author).

203. Ordinance concerning the authority of the Reich Protector, *Trials of War Criminals*, XII, p. 893. The first Protector was the former Minister of Foreign Affairs, Konstantin von Neurath. His deputy, with the title of State Secretary, was former deputy of the Sudeten German party, Karl Hermann Frank, an enemy of the Czech people (cf. Grosscurth, *Privattagebuch*, p. 171).

204. From May, 1939, this function was performed by Chvalkovský. He was from the first day of the occupation kept away from any contact with the diplomatic missions in Prague to make it clear that the Czechoslovak Foreign Ministry had ceased to exist (*G. Doc.*, T-120, S. 28, R. 12, fr. 17524). Chvalkovský was not a member of the diplomatic corps and was not accredited to the Reich Chancellor (ibid., S. 331, R. 257, fr. 195974–77). He was killed during an American air raid near the town of Belzig southwest of Berlin on February 25, 1945.

205. This "Army of the Protectorate," organized subsequently on the lines of the German constabulary (*Schutzpolizei*) had 7,000 men. It had only light military equipment. Toward the end of the war it was used to maintain order in northern Italy. Several of its soldiers joined the Italian resistance (František Nesvadba, "Vládní vojsko a jeho odsun do Italie" [The Government Troops and their Transfer to Italy] *Historie a vojenství*, 1968, no. 6–7, pp. 924–961).

206. The Protectorate was incorporated into the German customs zone only on October 1, 1940.

207. Communicated to the author by Chvalkovský. The Czech minister later compared these two moves by which Ribbentrop tried to circumvent Hácha—the declaration of Berlin and the decree instituting the Protectorate—to the maneuver Ribbentrop used on August 30, 1939, toward the British ambassador, Sir Nevile Henderson. To this British diplomat he read quickly the German proposals con-

cerning the settlement of the German-Polish dispute, but refused to hand them over to him.

208. Communiqué of the Czechoslovak Press Agency.

209. *G. Doc.*, T-120, S. 2050H, R. 1094, fr. 447284; S. 28, R. 12, fr. 17584.

210. Hitler's speech in the Reichstag on April 28, 1939. Hájek, *Od Mnichova*, p. 153, note 196, quotes slightly differing figures based on a summary of the Czechoslovak General Staff: 603,000 rifles, 14,000 heavy and 43,000 light machine guns, 1,966 anti-tank guns, 2,253 guns, 740 tanks, 70 light tanks, 1,231 planes; besides this in the factories material for the construction of 240 planes. The Czech tanks were used by Germany in Poland and France. Only in the Russian campaign had they to yield to heavier German models (Guderian, *Erinnerungen eines Soldaten*, p. 56). Hitler later stated that Czechoslovakia had "a clean and well balanced stock of arms, powder and munition" (*Tischgespräche*, p. 354, May 19, 1942).

211. *Přehled denního tisku*, March 17, 1939.

212. Testimony of Minister Krejčí, April 30, 1947.

213. *Národní Osvobození*, February 20, 1947. Hácha died in Prague on June 27, 1945, in the hospital of the Pankrác prison after a long period of total apathy and unconsciousness.

Notes to Chapter V

1. *DBFP*, IV, no. 246.
2. Ibid., no. 277.
3. *Le Livre Jaune*, no. 66.
4. *DBFP*, IV, no. 220.
5. Ibid.; Král, *Das Abkommen von Münechen*, no. 314.
6. Conversation with Corbin on March 14, *DBFP*, IV, no. 277.
7. *The Times* (London), March 15, 1939. On March 15, the very day of the German *Einmarsch* in Prague, the English satirical weekly, *The Punch*, comforted by the assurances of the British statesmen, even published a cartoon ridiculing the rumors of a crisis expected in the middle of March. In the cartoon John Bull was awaking from a bad dream, the fury of war scare was fleeing out of his bedroom window, and, relieved, he was saying to himself: "Thank goodness that's over!" (Reprinted in Wheeler-Bennett, *Munich*, p. 350).
8. *Failure of a Mission* (New York, 1940), pp. 211–12.
9. Ibid., p. 213.
10. *DBFP*, IV, no. 235.
11. Ibid., no. 248.
12. *The Diplomatic Diaries of Oliver Harvey*, p. 262.
13. *DBFP*, IV, no. 247.
14. Ibid., no. 234.
15. Bonnet, *Fin d'une Europe*, p. 150.
16. *Le Livre Jaune*, no. 64.
17. *DGFP*, IV, no. 234; *DBFP*, IV, no. 264.
18. *DGFP*, IV, no. 330; *DBFP*, IV, no. 266.

19. *DBFP,* IV, no. 265; Coulondre, *De Staline,* pp. 258–59.

20. *DBFP,* IV, no. 288.

21. *The Times* (London), March 16, 1939.

22. *DBFP,* IV, no. 279; *DGFP,* IV, no. 244.

23. *Le Livre Jaune,* no. 70. About Hácha's talks with Hitler Coulondre had a report from the secretary of the French embassy, Maurice Déjean, based on information from the secretary of the Czechoslovak legation, Ladislav Szathmáry (Coulondre, *De Staline,* p. 255, n. 1). This information, given under the direct impact of the events at the Reich Chancellery, was somewhat misleading which explains the dramatized tone of Coulondre's report to Paris (*Le Livre Jaune,* no. 77). For instance he described how the Germans were literally chasing Hácha and Chvalkovský around the table. Száthmáry did not assist the talks in the Chancellery and was not even in the Adlon Hotel. According to Chvalkovský (as communicated to the author) the description in the French Yellow Book was exaggerated. Even without this exaggeration the talks by themselves were dramatic enough. (In the same sense Mr. Schubert's communication to this author).

24. *Le Livre Jaune,* no. 70; *DBFP,* IV, nos. 270, 273; Coulondre, *De Staline,* p. 255; *DGFP,* IV, no. 233.

25. Bonnet, *Fin d'une Europe,* p. 151; *DGFP,* IV, no. 245.

26. *DBFP,* IV, no. 280.

27. *Le Livre Jaune,* no. 72; Bonnet, *op. cit.,* p. 151.

28. *The Times* (London), March 18, 1939.

29. See pp. 86–87.

30. *Le Livre Jaune,* no. 78; Coulondre, *De Staline,* p. 258.

31. *DGFP,* IV, nos. 308, 401. Cf. Coulondre, *op. cit.,* p. 258.

32. *Le Livre Jaune,* no. 82; *DBFP,* IV, no. 475, enclosure; *DGFP,* VI, no. 50. Cf. Beneš, *Memoirs,* pp. 296–97.

33. Beneš, *Memoirs,* p. 65.

34. *FRUS,* 1939, I, pp. 49–50.

35. Ibid., p. 56.

36. *DBFP,* IV, no. 220.

37. Mario Donosi, *Mussolini e l'Europa. La politica estera fascista* (Rome, 1945), p. 151.

38. *DGFP,* IV, no. 187.

39. Ibid., no. 205.

40. Ibid., no. 224.

41. Ibid., no. 232.

42. *Diary,* March 15, 1939. See also *DGFP,* IV, no. 463.

43. *Diary.,* March 16, 1939.

44. Ibid., March 17, 1939.

Notes to Conclusion

1. *DGFP,* IV, no. 150.

2. Henderson, *Failure of a Mission,* p. 218.

INDEX

EAST EUROPEAN MONOGRAPHS

The *East European Monographs* comprise scholarly books on the history and civilization of Eastern Europe. They are published by the *East European Quarterly* in the belief that these studies contribute substantially to the knowledge of the area and serve to stimulate scholarship and research.

Political Ideas and the Enlightenment in the Romanian Principalities, 1750-1831. By Vlad Georgescu. 1971.

America, Italy and the Birth of Yugoslavia, 1917-1919. By Dragan R. Zivjinovic. 1972.

Jewish Nobles and Geniuses in Modern Hungary. By William O. McCagg,Jr. 1972.

Mixail Soloxov in Yugoslavia: Reception and Literary Impact. By Robert F. Price. 1973.

The Historical and National Thought of Nicolae Iorga. By William O. Oldson. 1973.

Guide to Polish Libraries and Archives. By Richard C. Lewanski. 1974.

Vienna Broadcasts to Slovakia, 1938-1939: A Case Study in Subversion. By Henry Delfiner. 1974.

The 1917 Revolution in Latvia. By Andrew Ezergailis. 1974.

The Ukraine in the United Nations Organization: A Study in Soviet Foreign Policy. 1944-1950. By Konstantin Sawczuk. 1975.

The Bosnian Church: A New Interpretation. By John V. A. Fine, Jr., 1975.

Intellectual and Social Developments in the Habsburg Empire from Maria Theresa to World War I. Edited by Stanley B. Winters and Joseph Held. 1975.

Ljudevit Gaj and the Illyrian Movement. By Elinor Murray Despalatovic. 1975.

Tolerance and Movements of Religious Dissent in Eastern Europe. Edited by Bela K. Kiraly. 1975.

The Parish Republic: Hlinka's Slovak People's Party, 1939-1945. By Yeshayahu Jelinek. 1976.

The Russian Annexation of Bessarabia, 1774-1828. By George F. Jewsbury. 1976.

Modern Hungarian Historiography. By Steven Bela Vardy. 1976.

Values and Community in Multi-National Yugoslavia. By Gary K. Bertsch. 1976.

The Greek Socialist Movement and the First World War: The Road to Unity. By George B. Leon. 1976.

The Radical Left in the Hungarian Revolution of 1848. By Laszlo Deme. 1976.

Hungary between Wilson and Lenin: The Hungarian Revolution of 1918-1919 and the Big Three. By Peter Pastor. 1976.
The Crises of France's East-Central European Diplomacy, 1933-1938. By Anthony J. Komjathy. 1976.
Polish Politics and National Reform, 1775-1788. By Daniel Stone. 1976.
The Habsburg Empire in World War I. Robert A. Kann, Bela K. Kiraly, and Paula S. Fichtner, eds. 1977.
The Slovenes and Yugoslavism, 1890-1914. By Carole Rogel. 1977.
German-Hungarian Relations and the Swabian Problem. By Thomas Spira. 1977.
The Metamorphosis of a Social Class in Hungary During the Reign of Young Franz Joseph. By Peter I. Hidas. 1977.
Tax Reform in Eighteenth Century Lombardy. By Daniel M. Klang. 1977.
Tradition versus Revolution: Russia and the Balkans in 1917. By Robert H. Johnston. 1977.
Winter into Spring: The Czechoslovak Press and the Reform Movement 1963-1968. By Frank L. Kaplan. 1977.
The Catholic Church and the Soviet Government, 1939-1949. By Dennis J. Dunn. 1977.
*The Hungarian Labor Service System, 1939-1945.*By Randolph L Braham. 1977.
Consciousness and History: Nationalist Critics of Greek Society 1897-1914. By Gerasimos Augustinos. 1977.
Emigration in Polish Social and Political Thought, 1870-1914. By Benjamin P. Murdzek. 1977.
Serbian Poetry and Milutin Bojic. By Mihailo Dordevic. 1977.
The Baranya Dispute: Diplomacy in the Vortex of Ideologies, 1918-1921. By Leslie C. Tihany. 1978.
The United States in Prague, 1945-1948. By Walter Ullmann. 1978.
Rush to the Alps: The Evolution of Vacationing in Switzerland. By Paul P. Bernard. 1978.
Transportation in Eastern Europe: Empirical Findings. By Bogdan Mieczkowski. 1978.
The Polish Underground State: A Guide to the Underground, 1939-1945. By Stefan Korbonski. 1978.
The Hungarian Revolution of 1956 in Retrospect. Edited by Bela K. Kiraly and Paul Jonas. 1978.
Boleslaw Limanowski (1835-1935): A Study in Socialism and Nationalism. By Kazimiera Janina Cottam. 1978.
The Lingering Shadow of Nazism: The Austrian Independent Party Movement Since 1945. By Max E. Riedlsperger. 1978.

The Catholic Church, Dissent and Nationality in Soviet Lithuania. By V. Stanley Vardys. 1978.
The Development of Parliamentary Government in Serbia. By Alex N. Dragnich. 1978.
Divide and Conquer: German Efforts to Conclude a Separate Peace, 1914-1918. By L. L. Farrar, Jr. 1978.
The Prague Slav Congress of 1848. By Lawrence D. Orton. 1978.
The Nobility and the Making of the Hussite Revolution. By John M. Klassen. 1978.
The Cultural Limits of Revolutionary Politics: Change and Continuity in Socialist Czechoslovakia. By David W. Paul. 1979.
On the Border of War and Peace: Polish Intelligence and Diplomacy in 1937-1939 and the Origins of the Ultra Secret. By Richard A. Woytak. 1979.
Bear and Foxes: The International Relations of the East European States 1965-1969. By Ronald Haly Linden. 1979.
Czechoslovakia: The Heritage of Ages Past. Edited by Ivan Volgyes and Hans Brisch. 1979.
Prima Minister Gyula Andrassy's Influence on Habsburg Foreign Policy. By Janos Decsy. 1979.
Citizens for the Fatherland: Education, Educators, and Pedagogical Ideals in Eighteenth Century Russia. By J. L. Black. 1979.
A History of the "Proletariat": The Emergence of Marxism in the Kingdom of Poland, 1870-1887. By Norman M. Naimark. 1979.
The Slovak Autonomy Movement, 1935-1939: A Study in Unrelenting Nationalism. By Dorothea H. El Mallakh. 1979.
Diplomat in Exile: Francis Pulszky's Political Activities in England, 1849-1860. By Thomas Kabdebo. 1979.
The German Struggle Against the Yugoslav Guerrillas in World War II: German Counter-Insurgency in Yugoslavia, 1941-1943. By Paul N. Hehn. 1979.
The Emergence of the Romanian National State. By Gerald J. Bobango. 1979.
Stewards of the Land: The American Farm School and Modern Greece. By Brenda L. Marder. 1979.
Roman Dmowski: Party, Tactics, Ideology, 1895-1907. By Alvin M. Fountain, II. 1980.
International and Domestic Politics in Greece During the Crimean War. By Jon V. Kofas. 1980.
Fires on the Mountain: The Macedonian Revolutionary Movement and the Kidnapping of Ellen Stone. By Laura Beth Sherman. 1980.
The Modernization of Agriculture: Rural Transformation in Hungary, 1848-1975. Edited by Joseph Held. 1980.

Britain and the War for Yugoslavia, 1940-1943. By Mark C. Wheeler. 1980.
The Turn to the Right: The Ideological Origins and Development of Ukrainian Nationalism, 1919-1929. By Alexander J. Motyl. 1980.
The Maple Leaf and the White Eagle: Canadian-Polish Relations, 1918-1978. By Aloysius Balawyder. 1980.
Antecedents of Revolution: Alexander I and the Polish Congress Kingdom, 1815-1825. By Frank W. Thackeray. 1980.
Blood Libel at Tiszaeszlar. By Andrew Handler. 1980.
Democratic Centralism in Romania: A Study of Local Communist Politics. By Daniel N. Nelson. 1980.
The Challenge of Communist Education: A Look at the German Democratic Republic. By Margrete Siebert Klein. 1980.
The Fortifications and Defense of Constantinople. By Byron C.P. Tsangadas. 1980.
Balkan Cultural Studies. By Stavro Skendi. 1980.
Studies in Ethnicity: The East European Experience in America. Edited by Charles A. Ward, Philip Shahshko, and Donald E. Pienkos. 1980.
The Logic of "Normalization:" The Soviet Intervention in Czechoslovakia and the Czechoslovak Response. By Fred Eidlin. 1980.
Red Cross. Black Eagle: A Biography of Albania's American Schol. By Joan Fultz Kontos. 1981.
Nationalism in Contemporary Europe. By Franjo Tudjman. 1981.
Great Power Rivalry at the Turkish Straits: The Montreux Conference and Convention of 1936. By Anthony R. DeLuca. 1981.
Islam Under the Double Eagle: The Muslims of Bosnia and Hercegovina, 1878-1914. By Robert J. Donia. 1981.
Five Eleventh Century Hungarian Kings: Their Policies and Their Relations with Rome. By Z.J. Kosztolnyik. 1981.
Prelude to Appeasement: East European Central Diplomacy in the Early 1930's. By Lisanne Radice. 1981.
The Soviet Regime in Czechoslovakia. By Zdenek Krystufek. 1981.
School Strikes in Prussian Poland, 1901-1907: The Struggle Over Bilingual Education. By John J. Kulczycki. 1981.
Romantic Nationalism and Liberalism: Joachim Lelewel and the Polish National Idea. By Joan S. Skurnowicz. 1981.
The "Thaw" In Bulgarian Literature. By Atanas Slavov. 1981.
The Political Thought of Thomas G. Masaryk. By roman Szporluk. 1981.
Prussian Poland in the German Empire, 1871-1900. By Richard Blanke. 1981.
The Mazepists: Ukrainian Separatism in the Early Eighteenth Century. By Orest Subtelny. 1981.
The Battle for the Marchlands: The Russo-Polish Campaign of 1920. By Adam Zamoyski. 1981.
Milovan Djilas: A Revolutionary as a Writer. By Dennis Reinhartz. 1981.